CONTRACTOR'S GUIDE TO

QuickBooks® 2012

Karen Mitchell

Craig Savage

FREE DOWNLOAD includes:
Sample & Company files

- Turn your estimate into a bid.
- Turn your bid into a contract.
- ConstructionContractWriter.com

Craftsman Book Company
6058 Corte del Cedro / P.O. Box 6500 / Carlsbad, CA 92018

Acknowledgments

The authors wish to express their thanks to *Sarah Vernon*, *Tina Svalina* and *Laurence Jacobs* for all the work they did to get this book in your hands.

Looking for other construction reference manuals?
Craftsman has the books to fill your needs. **Call toll-free 1-800-829-8123**
or write to Craftsman Book Company, P.O. Box 6500, Carlsbad, CA 92018 for
a **FREE CATALOG** of over 100 books, including how-to manuals,
annual cost books, and estimating software.
Visit our Web site: http://www.craftsman-book.com

Library of Congress Cataloging-in-Publication Data

Mitchell, Karen, 1962-
  Contractor's guide to Quickbooks 2012 / Karen Mitchell, Craig Savage.
     p. cm.
  Includes bibliographical references.
  ISBN 978-1-57218-272-1
  1. Construction industry--Accounting--Computer programs. 2. Construction
industry--Finance--Computer programs. 3. Building--Estimates--Computer
programs. 4. QuickBooks. I. Savage, Craig, 1947- II. Title.

  HF5686.B7M4935 2012
  657'.869028553--dc23

                    2012017162

Text update edited by Tina Svalina

Cover design by John Wincek

Contents

Introduction

Why You Need This Book

With the release of the 2012 version, *QuickBooks* underwent some major changes, or as Intuit calls them, new features. These new features can help the construction office automate more tasks right inside of QuickBooks. In other words, this release will help the contractor run a more efficient office so he/she can spend more time managing projects and making money.

Some of the new 2012 features relating to the construction industry that we like are:

▌ *Lead Center*, for tracking sales leads.

▌ *Calendar*, so you can see at a glance what's due to be paid, due to be received from customers, and what you have on your to do list.

▌ *Batch Timesheets* for those having crews or field employees with similar timesheets.

▌ Modification to the *Enter Memorized Transaction* screen, which makes it easier to batch-process monthly recurring bills.

▌ *One Click Create* — the next big thing is the One Click Create button that Intuit added to QuickBooks this year. Once you get used to it, you'll wonder how you managed without it.

▌ *Improved Excel Integration* — Automatic updating of data from QuickBooks to your customized Excel reports.

We've described each of the new 2012 features listed above (and a few more) in detail later in this section. There are more added features, but the ones listed above are our favorites for contractors, and the ones we really want to bring to your attention.

Also in the 2012 New Features section is information describing the different versions of QuickBooks — including Pro, Premier Contractor

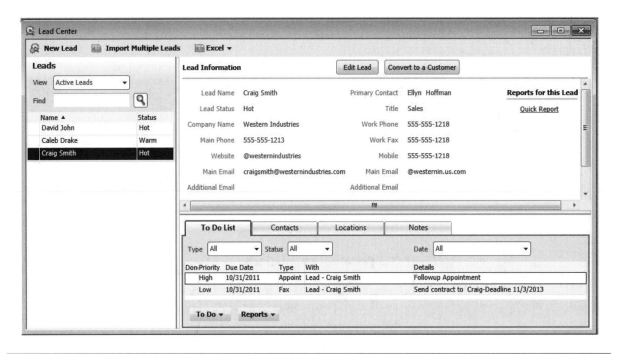

Intro-1

This is an example of a lead who called in to get more information about the business. All the information for the lead is tracked along with a nice To Do List at the bottom.

Edition, and Enterprise. This book is designed for all 2012 versions of QuickBooks, including Pro, Contractor, Accountant, and Enterprise. If you have a different version, you might want to read through that section to learn about the additional features built into that edition.

Your next question might be "Which version should I buy: Pro, Contractor or Enterprise?" The answer to that question is another question: Do you have the additional $100 per user for Premier Contractor Edition or an extra couple thousand for Enterprise? If so, get the upgrade. They're worth the additional expense. But if you're on a budget and don't need the features we describe in that section, save your money. You can always upgrade in the future. For now, buy Pro. Chances are it will take you a couple of years to outgrow it.

2012 New Features

Lead Center

The new Lead Center makes it easy to keep track of your sales leads, and track phone calls and tasks on your financial to do list. When your lead converts to a customer, you can move the contact information into the Customer Center with one click. One of its nice features is that the lead center will track active, converted, hot, warm, and cold leads.

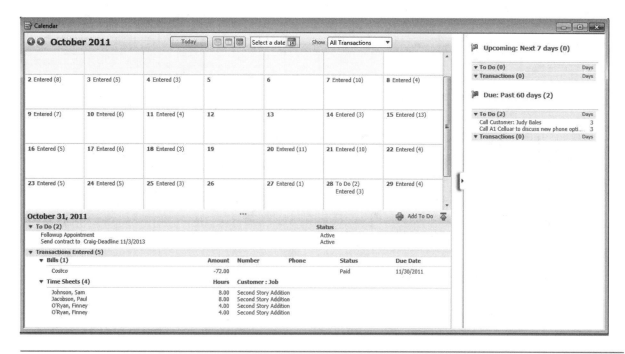

Intro-2

The calendar view helps you keep track of your bookkeeping and accounting-related items, as well as the lead tracking To Do Lists. You can sort it by specific types of transactions (at the top).

Calendar View

See your invoices, billing and other important tasks in a Calendar View.

Batch Timesheets

If you have crews that work together on projects, you'll appreciate Batch Timesheets. This feature will help you create the same timesheet for everyone on the crew, including employees *and* subs.

Enhancements to the Memorized Transactions

The ability to set up memorized transactions for recurring billing, invoices, and estimates has been available for a long time. But in this version, it's easier to review and process memorized transactions, as this new screen allows you to select more than one at a time.

Memorized transactions are handy on the 1st and the 15th of the month — when you have a number of recurring bills that need reviewing and entering. If the transaction doesn't have to be reviewed and edited before it's created, you would memorize it to automatically post the transaction; that way you don't have to remember to create it. Office rent is a good example of a fixed recurring bill that needs to be entered prior to the first day of each month. An example of a memorized transaction that would be modified would be a cell phone bill, where the amount changes every month.

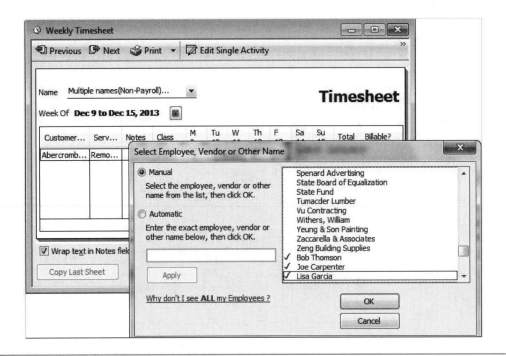

Intro-3

Shows you how to create the same timesheet for members of a crew who worked together during the week. The task(s), of course, can be changed after the individual timesheet is created.

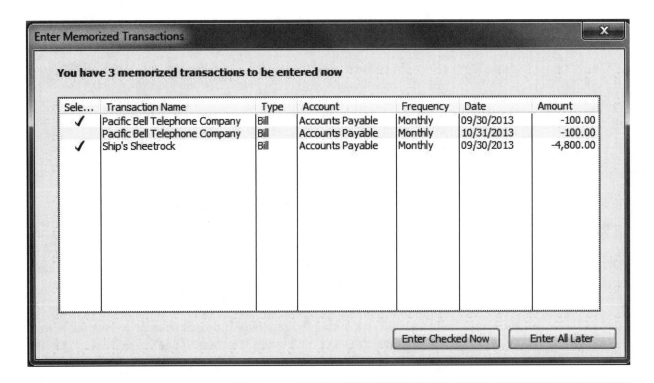

Intro-4

An example of the new screen that helps us pick more than one memorized transaction at a time.

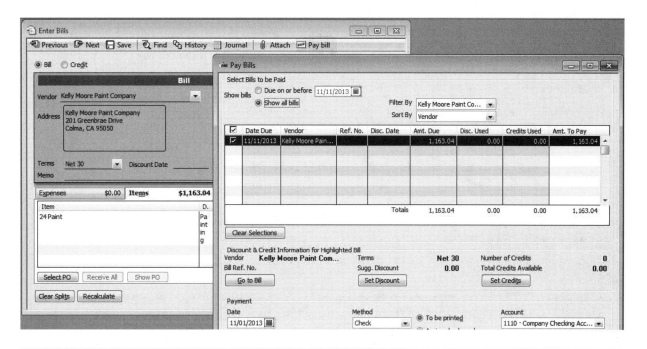

Intro-5
Here we created a bill (on the Enter Bills screen in the background) and hit the Pay bill button. In the Pay Bills screen in the foreground, the bill you just entered appears, ready for you to print or pay online via bill pay.

One Click Create

QuickBooks was one of the pioneers of the "drill down" technology — something that we now can't imagine living without. The interesting thing is that our kids think we're from another planet when we refer to the days before drill down. Believe it or not, there are accounting software programs available for purchase that *don't* have drill down ... or the ability to go from a transaction on a report back to the document, like the check or the deposit screen you originally used when entering the transaction.

You'll find that the One Click Create feature is like drill down — in the long run it could save you and your staff a lot of time. You'll soon be wondering how you managed without it.

Small construction firms usually need to process transactions quickly. They don't always have the luxury of entering a bill and waiting until the 1st or 15th to print all the checks that need to be issued for the prior 15 days. At times they need to enter a bill and turn right around and pay that bill immediately. The pay bill icon takes you directly from the bill to the pay bills screen; no more scrolling through multiple vendors and bills to find the one you want to pay.

Search Tool

This is a time-saving feature. It's now easier to find transactions as well as view the pertinent information surrounding the search.

Intro-6

In this example, we entered $1200 in the amount search. When we hit the search button all transactions with the $1200 amount will be shown.

Intro-7

This is an example of what the search screen shows us after it has completed the search for $1200.

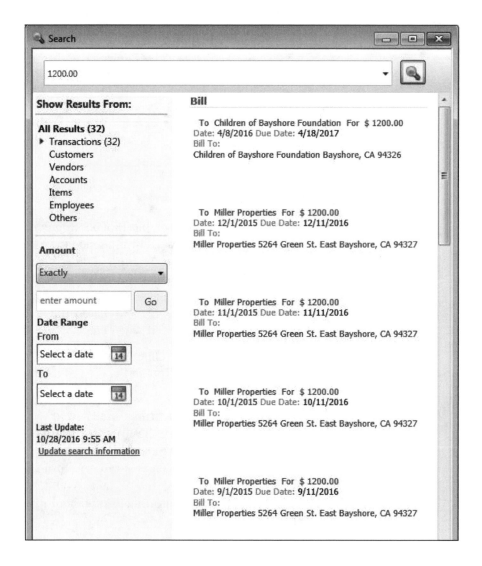

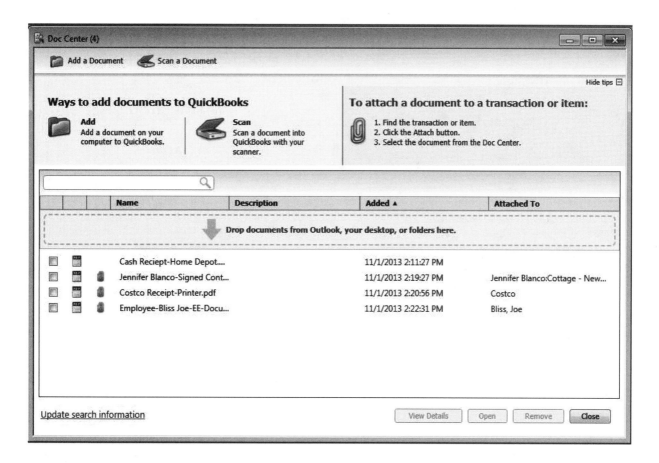

Intro-8

This screen shows you how easy it is to drag and drop items like a signed contract, Costco receipt, employee W-4 and a cash receipt from Home Depot to the vendor, customer and employee card in QuickBooks.

Document Center

This feature was included in version 2011, but for an additional fee. Now, with version 2012, you can attach original documents, such as subcontractor invoices, supplier receipts, etc. by dragging and dropping them into QuickBooks. This feature can also save you time because you can look things up faster in QuickBooks than in your filing cabinet.

1099 Wizard

This feature allows you to e-file directly through QuickBooks. The 1099 E-File Service makes it easy for small businesses to file 1099s electronically in minutes. With 1099 E-File service you can skip the 1096 (not required when you e-file). Also, with one flat fee per company, you can file an unlimited number of forms. Later in the book, we'll describe 1099s, as well as how to create them in QuickBooks.

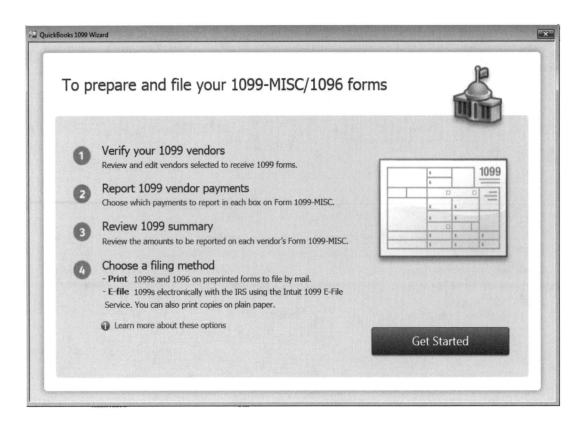

Intro-9

This new screen in version 2012 makes it easier to prepare and file your 1099 forms. The new feature is near the bottom and labeled E-file. In the past we had to print and send in the 1099s.

Excel Integration Refresh

In the 2012 version, when you export your QuickBooks reports to Excel, all you have to do is refresh the report for the new time period. The saved Excel file and its formatting will be automatically applied to each new report.

QuickBooks Pro, Premier and Enterprise Editions

At the minimum, a construction company should be using QuickBooks Pro because:

▌ Simple Start, the most basic version of QuickBooks, is very limited and doesn't have what you'll need to run your construction office.

▌ Pro includes job costing and estimating.

▌ Premier Contractor Edition costs between $100 and $200 more per user, depending on where you buy it. It adds a very useful feature that will warn you while entering bills if a subcontractor's worker's compensation and general liability insurance has expired. It also includes construction industry reports like accounts payable, sorted by job. Below you'll see an additional list of added features that are included in Premier, as well as how to use them.

▌ Enterprise Solutions allows up to 30 users to access the program at the same time — a true multiuser program. It costs a couple of thousand more but it's still less expensive than moving to vertical market or industry-specific programs like Masterbuilder or Timberline. Keep in mind that anything in Pro and Premier is also in Enterprise.

QuickBooks Premier Contractor Edition Features

If you're using QuickBooks Premier Contractor (or Accountant) Edition, you have access to a few additional features, including:

▌ Fixed asset tracking

▌ Loan manager

▌ Cash flow projector

▌ Forecasting

▌ Business planning

Fixed Asset Tracking

Fixed asset tracking allows you to record each asset you purchase in the Fixed Asset Item List located under the Lists menu. Use this list to track each item you purchase, including: property, automobiles and trucks, equipment, large tools, and computer purchases. Only use the Fixed Asset Item List for items that cost over $500, as shown in the screen in Intro-10, on the next page.

Unfortunately, the Fixed Asset Item List doesn't set up depreciation schedules or post depreciation for you. Instead, it gives you one convenient location to store information about an asset, such as date of purchase, purchase price, where you bought it, when, for how much you sold the asset, and so on. Your accountant can use the information from the fixed asset item to calculate depreciation, but you or your accountant will have to post a general journal entry to record depreciation.

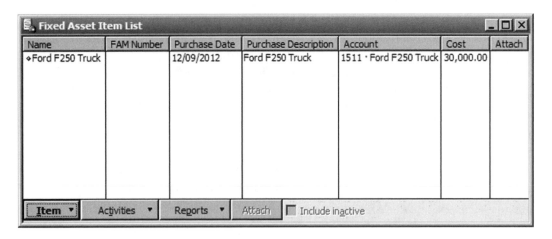

Intro-10
The Fixed Asset Item List is only used for items over $500.

Loan Manager

The Loan Manager is a payment calculator that computes the principal and interest portion of your loan payment, plus handles any fees or charges. It helps you track loans based on the information in your Long Term Liability and Other Current Liability accounts in QuickBooks. When you use the Loan Manager, you can track all of your loans in one location and be reminded of upcoming payments. Use the Loan Manager to:

▌ Add and remove loans you want to track.

▌ View payment schedules.

▌ Set up loan payments.

▌ Analyze different loan scenarios.

The Loan Manager creates payment schedules that you can view and print, allowing you to track loan-related information on a per-payment and per-total-payments basis. Plus, when you need to edit or make changes to a loan, the Loan Manager recalculates your payment information and payment schedule. Before using the Loan Manager, walk through our example below.

To set up a loan in the Loan Manager:

1. First, make sure you have a liability account set up for the loan. For example, if you took out a loan to purchase a truck, set up a loan account for the truck. See Intro-11.

   ▌ Click **Home**, then click **Chart of Accounts**, or from the **Lists** menu, choose **Chart of Accounts**.

   ▌ Pull down the **Account** menu at the bottom of the window and choose **New**.

Intro-11

Use the Add New Account window to create a liability account for a loan.

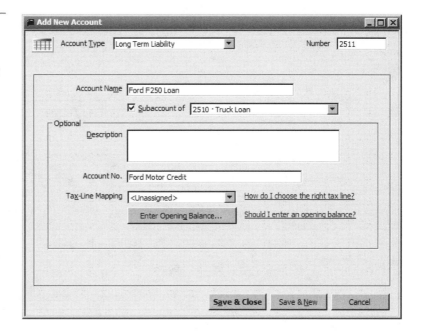

Select the account type:

(a) For short-term loans (one year or less), from the **Other Account Type** drop list, choose **Other current liability** as the account type.

(b) For long-term loans, choose **Long Term Liability**.

Click **Continue**.

Enter the name of the lender and a description of the loan.

Leave the opening balance at 0.00.

Click **Save & Close**.

2. Next, set up an asset account for the truck.

Click **Home**, then click the **Chart of Accounts** icon, or from the **Lists** menu, choose **Chart of Accounts**.

Pull down the **Account** menu at the bottom of the window and choose **New**.

Select the account type. Click **Continue**.

Create the new account similar to the example in Intro-12, on the next page.

Click **Save & Close**.

3. Now we'll set up a Fixed Asset Item for the truck. Make sure you have a vendor set up for making loan payments. For example, if you'll be paying Ford Motor Credit, get that vendor entered now. For more information on entering vendors, see Chapter 8.

Intro-12

Use the Add New Account window to create a new asset account for a truck.

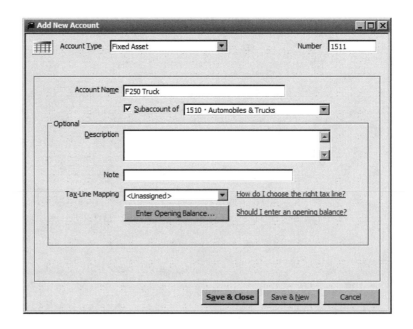

Intro-13

Use the New Item window to create a fixed asset item for a truck.

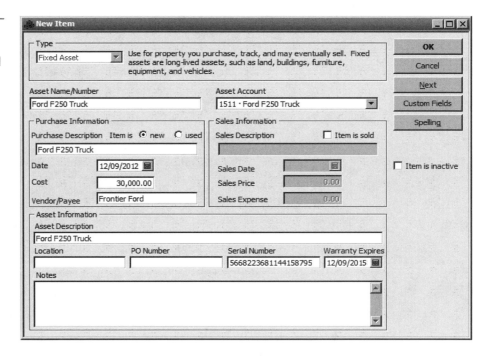

▌ From the **Lists** menu, choose **Fixed Asset Item List**.

▌ Pull down the **Item** menu at the bottom of the window and choose **New**.

▌ Create the new account similar to the example in Intro-13.

▌ Click **OK**.

Intro-14

Enter the loan amount as a negative number on the Expenses tab.

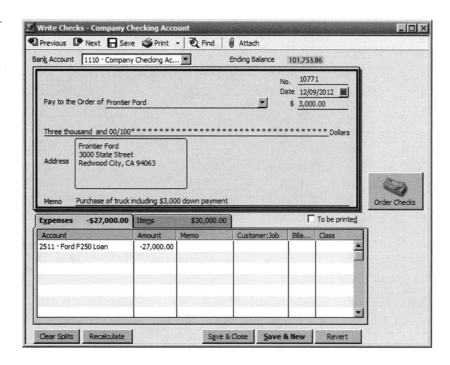

4. Next, we'll enter a transaction that records the purchase of the asset and the creation of a loan in the liability account you set up. For this example, let's say you purchased a truck for $30,000, put down $3,000, and took out a loan for $27,000.

- ▌ Click **Home**, then click the **Write Checks** icon, or from the **Banking** menu, choose **Write Checks**.

- ▌ Fill out the top portion of the check as shown in Intro-14.

- ▌ Click the **Expenses** tab.

- ▌ From the drop-down list in the **Account** column, select the liability account you created for the truck. In our example, it's 2511 Ford F250 Loan. In the **Amount** column, enter the amount of the loan as a negative number, as shown.

- ▌ Click the **Items** tab.

- ▌ From the drop-down list in the **Item** column, select the fixed asset item you created for the truck. In the **Amount** column enter the cost of the truck. See Intro-15.

- ▌ Click **Save & Close**.

5. From the **Banking** menu, select **Loan Manager**.

6. Click **Add Loan**.

7. Fill in the Enter account information for this loan section, as shown in Intro-16. Click **Next**.

Intro-15

Use the Items tab of the Write Checks window to record the cost of the truck.

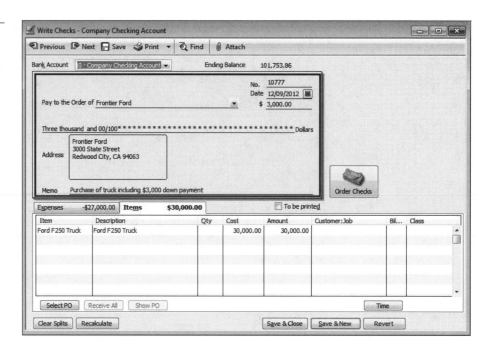

Intro-16

Enter the account information for the loan.

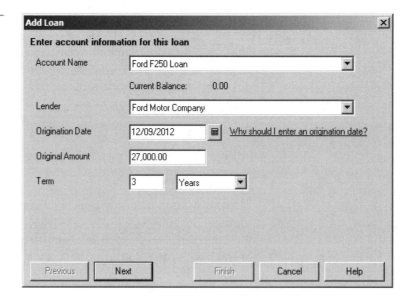

8. Fill in the Enter payment information for this loan section, as in Intro-17. Click **Next**.

9. Fill in the Enter interest information for this loan section as shown in Intro-18.

10. Click **Finish**. The loan will now appear in the Loan Manager window. See Intro-19.

Intro-17

Enter the payment information for the loan.

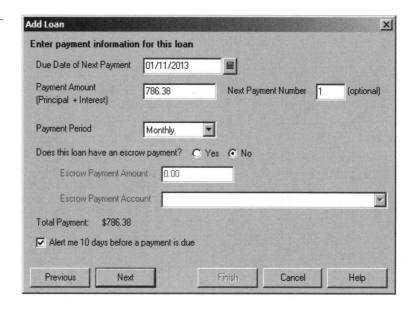

Intro-18

Enter the interest information for the loan.

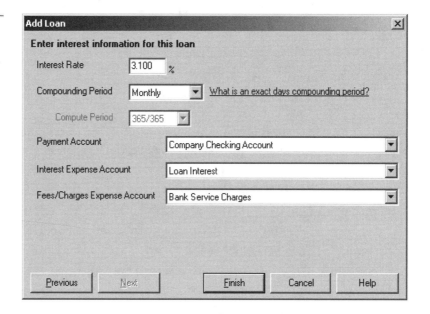

Making Loan Payments from Loan Manager

If you're using Loan Manager to handle your loans, you should pay all of your business loans from the Loan Manager.

When you're ready to make a payment, click **Set Up Payment** in the Loan Manager. From that window, the Loan Manager takes you directly to the Write Checks or Enter Bills windows, where you can edit your payments.

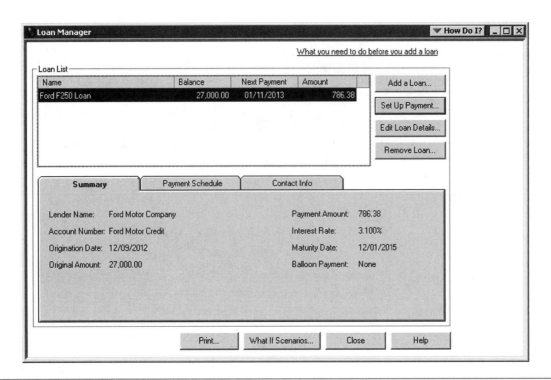

Intro-19
Track loan-related information in the Loan Manager.

Keep in mind that you won't be allowed to automatically create a loan payment if you haven't logged in the balance of the loan as a liability.

Cash Flow Projector

This report helps forecast how much cash you'll have by projecting your cash inflows, cash disbursements, and bank account balances on a week-by-week basis.

To see a list of the transactions that make up an amount, double-click the amount.

You can change the report date range, you can change the forecasting periods, and you can delay receipts for late customer payments. QuickBooks Help file will step you through these tasks.

▌ To create this report, click the **Report Center**, or from the **Reports** menu, choose **Company & Financial** and then **Cash Flow Forecast**.

Forecasting

Forecasting allows you to make predictions about future revenue and cash flow, as well as assess "what if" scenarios to help you make better business decisions.

A forecast can be created from scratch, from actual data from the previous fiscal year, or from the previous fiscal year's forecast. A forecast is uniquely identified by its fiscal year, and if desired, further identified by Customer:Job or Class.

▌ To use the forecasting feature, from the **Company** menu select **Planning & Budgeting**, then **Set Up Budgets**.

Business Planning

Using your QuickBooks data and answering simple step-by-step questions, a balance sheet, profit and loss statement, and statement of cash flows will automatically be projected for the next three years. The business plan is based on the format recommended by the U.S. Small Business Administration for loan applications or a bank line of credit.

▌ To use the Business Planning feature, from the **Company** menu, select **Planning and Budgeting**, and then **Use Business Plan Tool**.

What You Can Expect from This Book

According to a recent national survey, more construction contractors use QuickBooks than all other accounting programs combined. When set up properly, QuickBooks can handle the accounting for most small- to medium-sized (to $10 million a year) construction companies. But despite the sales hype, QuickBooks isn't easy to set up and learn. Dozens of options and preference settings may lead you down the wrong road, resulting in hours of frustration. We've spent years testing the options and preferences in QuickBooks to help you get it right the first time. Follow our examples and you'll have an effective accounting system that provides all the information any successful business needs — and in the shortest time possible.

QuickBooks doesn't replace bookkeepers or tax accountants. But it does help organize and standardize your bookkeeping system. Every report your accountant needs is readily available. This makes it easier for your accountant to prepare tax returns and you to pull reports so you can understand where you stand financially. Having an organized set of books will save you and your tax accountant a great deal of frustration, time and money during tax season.

In this book, we'll explain how to:

▌ set preference options correctly for your company

▌ set up a Chart of Accounts that matches the work you do

▌ set up, edit, and use classes

▌ set up customers and jobs

▌ set up vendors and subcontractors

▌ set up employee payroll

▌ get your current account balances into QuickBooks

▌ track transactions through QuickBooks

▌ create and use estimates

▌ set up a simple and effective job cost system

▌ create and send invoices

▌ enter vendor bills

▌ write checks

▌ process payroll

▌ get payroll tax and workers' comp expenses into job cost reports

▌ get an owner's time into job cost reports (for a sole proprietorship)

▌ run workers' comp reports

▌ create and interpret job cost reports to keep track of your business

▌ prepare financial statements

▌ set up end-of-the-month and end-of-the-year procedures

In short, we'll show you how to get everything a construction company needs out of QuickBooks. If you understand and apply the methods in this book, you should see real improvement in the effectiveness of your accounting system. And, you'll gain the personal and financial rewards that come from working not just harder, but smarter.

Why Should You Believe Us?

Both authors have been in the construction industry and used QuickBooks for many years. We've helped hundreds of contractors set up and use QuickBooks. We're confident that what we've done for others we can do for you, too.

Karen Mitchell is a partner at Online Accounting (www.onlineaccounting.com), a business that focuses on getting contractors organized using QuickBooks. Karen conducts seminars nationwide for contractors who use QuickBooks. She is a frequent speaker at many construction trade shows such as: A/E/C SYSTEMS, JLC Live!, and NAHB's PCBC (Pacific Coast Builders Conference). In addition to this book, Karen has written many other books, some of which include: *The Organized Contractor*, *Construction Forms for Contractors*, and industry-specific books for architects, engineers, interior designers and real estate investors.

Craig Savage has been a general building contractor, remodeler and custom homebuilder for over 25 years. He was an editor at *The Journal of*

Light Construction magazine for many years, director of the *JLC LIVE! Training Shows*, Vice President of Marketing & Sales at www.BobVila.com, and most recently, VP of Marketing at Building Media, Inc.

In his free time Craig is a construction management computer consultant. He started *Construction Business Computing* and *Macintosh Construction Forum* newsletters, and his articles have appeared in *Architectural & Engineering Systems, Architectural Record, Fine Homebuilding Magazine, Computer Applications Newsletter, Remodeling News, NAHB Commercial Builder, NAHB Single Family Forum, Remodeler Magazine, Mac Week, Document Imaging, Imaging World,* and *A/E/C Computer Solutions*.

Craig is a regular speaker at the A/E/C Systems, NAHB, NARI, CSI, and PCBC annual conventions. He also instructs at seminars sponsored by the University of Wisconsin College of Engineering, and the University of California Santa Barbara Extension.

Other books he has co-written for Craftsman Book Company are *Construction Forms & Contracts* and *Quicken for Contractors*. With Taunton Press he wrote *Trim Carpentry Techniques*.

What Does the Download Include?

You may have bought this book because it comes with a free downloadable QuickBooks company and sample data file. The company file includes a Chart of Accounts, items list, class list, and memorized reports that you can easily adapt to your business. Just plug in your own company data — vendors, subs, customers, etc. — and you're up and running.

However, the download doesn't include QuickBooks. You won't get much out of this book without a working copy of QuickBooks. So the first step will be buying and installing QuickBooks if you don't have it already.

Fortunately, you can get QuickBooks at most large software outlets. For the lowest price, try searching for a dealer on the Web.

How to Download

To use the download provided with this book, you'll need a computer running Windows XP or higher, and up to 160MB available on your hard drive.

If you're using a version of QuickBooks older than the 2012 edition, many of the illustrations in this book may not look exactly like what's on your screen. That's because this manual is based on QuickBooks version 2012. If you're using version 2003 - 2011, the changes will be mostly cosmetic.

Download Instructions

To download the QuickBooks data files, use your Internet browser to go to the Web page www.craftsman-book.com/quickbooks2012. Click the **download now** button and follow the instructions on the screen. By default, the files will be installed to C:\Program Files\Intuit\QuickBooks.

Get Help by Phone

If you need help downloading the file, call Craftsman Book Company (Monday through Friday from 8 a.m. to 5 p.m. Pacific time) at 760-438-7828.

If you need help with QuickBooks, call Intuit technical support (Monday through Friday from 6 a.m. to 4 p.m. Pacific time) at 888-320-7276 or call Online Accounting (Monday through Friday from 8 a.m. to 5 p.m. Mountain time) at 888-254-9252.

Removing the Installed Files

To remove any of the programs installed from the Contractor's Guide to QuickBooks Download from your hard drive:

▌ Choose **Start**, **Control Panel**, then click on **Add or Remove Programs**.

▌ Click the name of the program you want to remove, **Contractor's Guide to QuickBooks 2012**.

▌ Click **Change/Remove**.

▌ Click **Yes**.

Conclusion

Most contractors would agree that accounting is what they like least about running a construction business. When we started out, many, many years ago, we felt the same way. We had a well-founded fear of accounting and an irrational loathing of computers. But using a computer for the first time isn't much different from using a Skilsaw for the first time. Treat it with respect. You'll gain confidence with every use.

We wrote this book because so many of our friends and colleagues asked us for a simple guide to setting up a construction accounting system. We've worked hard to keep it simple and still provide all the information you need. We feel the mission has been accomplished and hope you agree.

Now it's time to take the plunge. In Chapter 1, we'll dive right in by giving you some choices on how best to start using QuickBooks for your bookkeeping and accounting.

Setting Up Your QuickBooks Company

Getting Started

Before moving forward, you should have both QuickBooks 2012 and the sample download files installed on your computer.

As explained in the Introduction, to download the QuickBooks sample data files, use your Internet browser to go to the Web page on Craftsman's website: www.craftsman-book.com/quickbooks2012. Click the **download now** button and follow the instructions on the screen. By default, the files will be installed to C:\Program Files\Intuit\QuickBooks.

QuickBooks Company Files

QuickBooks keeps all of your company records on disk in a single file. QuickBooks refers to this file as your "company" file and that's what we'll call it in this manual. For many users, the first task is setting up a company file using QuickBooks' "EasyStep Interview." We've designed a better way, as you'll soon see. And we recommend that you try it our way.

You can set up as many company data files as you want. The only requirement is that each one must have a different file name. We recommend that you use our *sample.qbw* file for practice while you experiment with QuickBooks. When you've gained enough confidence to take off the training wheels, you can start your own "real" company with real records in the Company file.

Storing all company records in a single file simplifies moving your QuickBooks company from one computer to another. A utility program built into QuickBooks makes it easy to create a backup of any company file. We'll have more to say on making backups and moving your company file later in this book.

How to Find Your Company Data File

We've created the company data file and a sample file to get you started off on the right foot. Regardless of where you've installed Intuit's QuickBooks, the *Contractor's Guide to QuickBooks* setup program will install the example files to C:\Program Files\Intuit\QuickBooks.

To search for your QuickBooks folder:

▌ Click **Start**, **Search**, then **All Files and Folders**.

▌ Enter QBW32.EXE, and click **Search**. Under "In Folder" you'll see the location of QBW32.EXE. Remember that folder. You may need to find it occasionally.

To find all the QuickBooks company data files on your hard drive:

▌ Click **Start**, **Search**, then **All Files and Folders**.

▌ Enter *.QBW, and click **Search**. Under "In Folder" you'll see the name and location of all company files on your hard drive.

Four Choices

Where you go from here depends on your preference and what accounting program you're using now. Here are the possibilities:

1. You're new to QuickBooks: We suggest you use our preformatted company.qbw file. Start at Section 1 below — Begin With Our Sample and Company Data Files.

2. You're using a prior version of QuickBooks: Begin at Section 2 — Upgrading an Old QuickBooks Company to version 2012.

3. You're using Quicken (another Intuit product): Begin at Section 3 — Converting a Quicken Company Data File to QuickBooks.

4. You've been using QuickBooks 2012 and want to set up your company data file to match our suggestions: Begin at Section 4 — Converting an Existing QuickBooks 2012 Company Data File to Our Setup.

Section 1   Begin With Our Sample and Company Data Files

We've created a sample company data file that has all the elements of a real QuickBooks construction company. We call the file *sample.qbw*. It includes:

▮ a Chart of Accounts for a sole proprietorship

▮ a list of items

▮ sample customers and jobs

▮ sample vendors

▮ a list of classes

▮ payroll items set up to track workers' compensation costs and help with the workers' comp report

▮ memorized transactions

▮ memorized reports

You can use any sample file for practice while you're learning how QuickBooks works. Of course, we think you'll find our *sample.qbw* data file the best one to use to learn QuickBooks. We've designed it specifically for the construction industry.

However, don't use sample data files for your actual company data. When you're ready to begin entering actual records, use the company file we have on the download called *company.qbw*. This file includes:

▮ a Chart of Accounts

▮ items

▮ payroll items

▮ classes

▮ memorized reports

We recommend modifying the company data file rather than creating your own company data file from scratch.

Besides saving time, *company.qbw* is structured to prevent errors and make it easier for you to enter your own company information. To begin:

▮ Start QuickBooks.

▮ From the **File** menu, choose **Open or Restore Company** or click **Open or restore an existing company** in the No Company Open window.

▮ Select **Open a company file**, as seen in Figure 1-1. Click **Next**.

▮ Select *company.qbw* (the .qbw extension may not display, depending on your computer configuration), then click **Open**.

If you don't see *sample.qbw* and *company.qbw* in the list of QuickBooks company data files, you need to doublecheck that you downloaded them correctly. For instructions, refer back to the Getting Started section at the beginning of this chapter.

Figure 1-1

The Open or Restore
Company window.

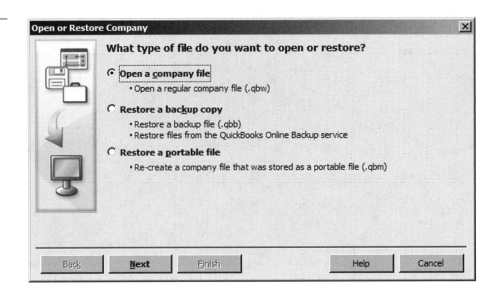

First, let's add your company information to the new file:

▌ From the **Company** menu, choose **Company Information**.

Then fill in your company information:

▌ **Company Name** — Enter your business name.

▌ **Address** — Enter the address you want QuickBooks to print on invoices and purchase orders.

▌ **Legal Name** — If you registered your business with a name different from the name in the Company box, enter it here. For example, if you're incorporated as A. C. Company but do business as Any Construction Company, enter the incorporated company name here.

▌ **Legal Address** — Enter the address you want QuickBooks to print on legal forms.

▌ **First month in your fiscal year** and **First month in your tax year** — Enter your company's first accounting month. Usually this is January.

▌ **Income Tax Form Used** — This depends on the type of ownership of your business. Use the drop-down list here to choose the tax form for the type of ownership your business is held under. For example, if you own the business with someone else and it hasn't been incorporated, select Form 1065 (Partnership). If you own the business yourself and it hasn't been incorporated, select Form 1040 (Sole Proprietor). If the business has been incorporated as a regular C corporation, select Form 1120 (Corporation) or Form 1120S for an S corporation.

Figure 1-2
The No Company Open
window.

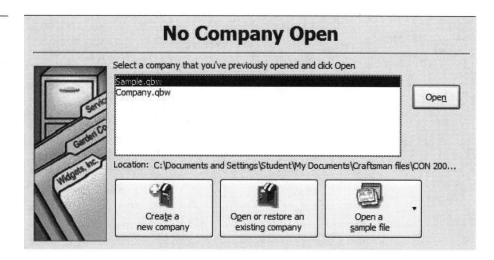

Federal Employer Identification No. — Enter your company's EIN if you'll be processing payroll.

Click **OK**.

From the **File** menu, choose **Close Company**.

It's important to note here that you've changed the company name that appears on the title bar of QuickBooks. But you haven't changed the name of your QuickBooks company data file. It's still *company.qbw*.

To change the *company.qbw* data file name:

Open the QuickBooks folder.

Right click on *company.qbw*.

From the pop-up menu, choose **Rename**.

Enter the file name you prefer over the *company.qbw* data file name. That's the new file name of your company.

To use our *sample.qbw* data file:

From the **File** menu, choose **Open or Restore Company** or click **Open or restore an existing company** in the No Company Open window. See Figure 1-2.

Select **Open a company file**, as shown in Figure 1-1.

Click **Next**.

Select *sample.qbw* and click **Open**.

Now you're ready for Chapter 2, where we set up company preferences. You can skip the remainder of this chapter.

Figure 1-3
Check box to initiate
QuickBooks update.

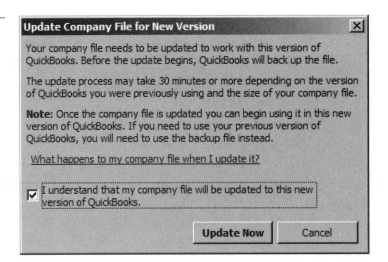

Section 2 Upgrading an Old QuickBooks Company to Version 2012

To update your QuickBooks company file:

▌ Install and start QuickBooks.

▌ In the No Company Open window, click on **Open or restore an existing company**.

▌ Select **Open a company file**. Refer to Figure 1-1.

▌ Click **Next**.

▌ Select your existing QuickBooks file and click **Open**.

▌ You'll be prompted to enter or create an Admin user name and password, as well as to select a security question. Enter the information and click **OK**.

▌ At the Update Company File for New Version window, put a check in the box to confirm you want to update the file. Click **Update Now** (Figure 1-3).

▌ You'll get a message prompting you to back up your data. Click **OK**. If QuickBooks doesn't display that message, it isn't set to open your old company file.

▌ At the Create Backup window, select **Local backup** (Figure 1-4).

▌ Click **Next**.

▌ In the Backup Options window, Figure 1-5, click **Browse**.

▌ Select a location to store the backup file. Typically, this will be a CD-RW or USB flash drive. Make your selection and click **OK**.

▌ Click **OK** in the Backup Options window.

▌ In the Save Backup window, click **Save**.

Figure 1-4

The Create Backup Copy window.

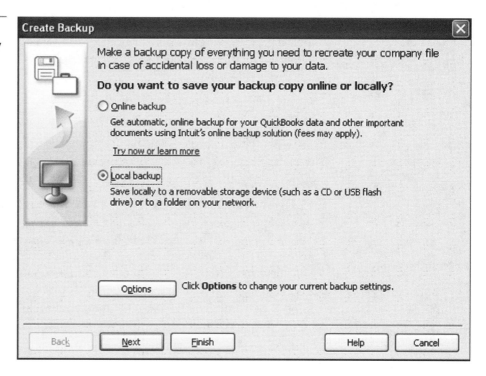

Figure 1-5

Use the Backup Options to specify the device for backup.

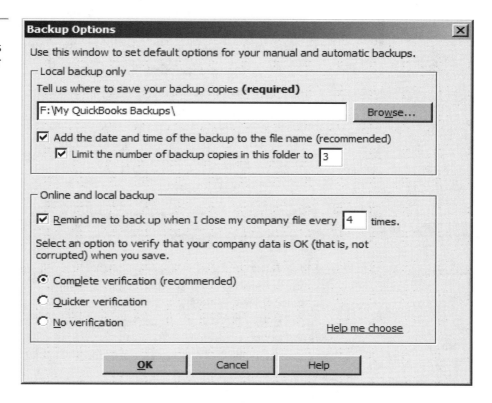

QuickBooks will display a message that it's updating your data. The updating program scans your data three times. The process may seem to get stuck at a certain percentage. If there's still activity on your hard drive, don't worry. Let the update continue.

Before the file opens, confirm that you want to update the file by clicking **Yes**.

When your company has been updated, you can work through the rest of the book to set up your company data. Chapters 2 through 9 will walk you through setting up QuickBooks using our methods.

If your company is different from what we recommend, you may want to follow what we recommend anyway. For example, in Chapter 3 you may find that your Chart of Accounts is different from our sample Chart of Accounts. Compare your Chart of Accounts to ours to find the differences. Add new accounts where needed and consider making inactive any accounts that aren't on our recommended list. You can inactivate accounts, items, payroll items, classes, customers and jobs, vendors, and employees. Anything marked inactive isn't deleted. It just doesn't show up on the list.

To make an account, item, payroll item, class, customer and job, vendor, or employee inactive:

▌ Open the appropriate list (i.e. Lists menu, or Customer, Vendor, or Employee Center).

▌ Select the name of the item in the appropriate list.

▌ Right click the item and select **Make Inactive**.

To see everything on the list, including anything inactive:

▌ Click **Include Inactive** at the bottom of the List window.

▌ For customers, vendors and employees, click the appropriate center. In the drop-down **View** field, select **All.**

Now you can skip the rest of this chapter and begin by setting up your QuickBooks preferences in Chapter 2.

Section 3 Converting a Quicken Company Data File to QuickBooks

Since Intuit is the developer of both Quicken and QuickBooks, it would seem logical that you should easily be able to "upgrade" from Quicken to QuickBooks; however, it simply isn't very practical to do so. Although QuickBooks has a built-in conversion tool for Quicken, when your data is moved over, it tends to end up in the wrong place. In addition, during the conversion process it creates new accounts, classes, customers, jobs and classes, which can make a mess of your new QuickBooks file.

In order to move successfully from Quicken to QuickBooks:

1. Keep Quicken installed on your computer, as well as your Quicken data file, in case you need to look up transactions prior to your QuickBooks start date.

2. Pick a date to start using QuickBooks. It's best to start at the beginning of a calendar or fiscal year, but you could also start at the beginning of a quarter.

3. Start using QuickBooks as instructed in Section 1 — Begin With Our Sample and Company Data Files.

Section 4 · Converting an Existing QuickBooks 2012 Company Data File to Our Setup

To convert to our setup, you'll want to work through these chapters following our suggestions:

▍ Chapter 2 Preferences — Set up your preferences the way we suggest in Chapter 2.

▍ Chapter 3 Chart of Accounts — Compare your Chart of Accounts to ours and add, change, or inactivate accounts as needed.

▍ Chapter 4 Items — Add, change, or inactivate items as needed.

▍ Chapter 5 Payroll Items — Add, change, or inactivate payroll items as needed.

▍ Chapter 6 Classes — Add, change, or inactivate classes as needed.

▍ Chapter 7 Customers — Add, change, or inactivate customers as needed.

▍ Chapter 8 Vendors — Add, change, or inactivate vendors as needed.

▍ Chapter 9 Employees — Add, change, or inactivate employees as needed.

During this process, if you find particular items that you want to keep but don't want to appear on any list, you can inactivate them.

To make an account, item, payroll item, class, customer and job, vendor, or employee inactive:

▍ Open the appropriate list (i.e. Lists menu, or Customer, Vendor, or Employee Center).

▍ Select the name of the item in the appropriate list.

▍ Right click the item and select **Make Inactive**.

To see everything on the list, including anything inactive:

▍ Click **Include Inactive** at the bottom of the List window.

▍ For customers, vendors and employees, click the appropriate center. In the drop-down **View** field, select **All.**

Now the item won't show up in any list. However, it's not deleted, so you can activate it again later if you wish.

Go through Chapters 10 through 16 to make sure you understand how to enter transactions correctly into QuickBooks. In Chapters 17 and 18 you'll see how QuickBooks will make it easier for you to get the reports you need for your business.

Preferences are used to customize QuickBooks. For instance, you can turn payroll on or off, change the accounting basis for your reports, or set an interest rate for statement finance charges. There are 23 separate windows you can use to set your preferences, with several options in each window.

In this chapter we'll cover the preferences that are specific to the needs of a construction business. Any preferences not discussed aren't critical; you can set them as you like or use the defaults. We recommend you use the preferences as they default, except as noted. In order to work with these options, you have to open a company file.

Each preference has two tabs — *My Preferences* and *Company Preferences*, as shown in Figure 2-1. The My Preferences tab is specific to your login name and your specific needs in QuickBooks. In a multi-user environment, you can customize QuickBooks to look and act differently for each user by customizing preferences in each My Preferences tab. The Company Preferences are universal. If you change these preferences, then the preference changes company-wide, not just for an individual user.

To set your preferences, go to the **Edit** menu, select **Preferences**, and then select, one by one, the preferences shown on the following pages.

The screen shots taken in this chapter are based on 2012 QuickBooks Premier Accountant's Edition. If you're using a Premier version of QuickBooks — including the Contractor's, Accountant's, Professional Services or Manufacturing/Wholesale version — you should see the same image. If you're using QuickBooks 2012 Pro or an earlier version of QuickBooks, you may not have as many options available to you as with Premier. That doesn't mean your version isn't as good; it means those extra preferences aren't available to you. Pro works fine for most construction companies, so don't worry that you may be missing features. This book and the concepts we teach in this book all work with Pro. Unless we explicitly mention that a feature is only available in Enterprise or a Premier edition, you can assume you can get the same thing shown using Pro.

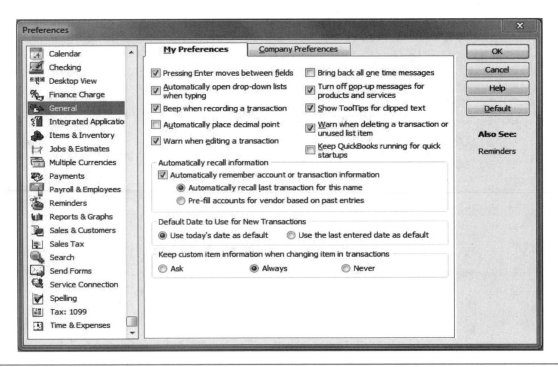

Figure 2-1
Use the My Preferences tab window to set the recommended settings for General Preferences.

General Preferences

QuickBooks defaults to the General Preferences window when you choose the Preferences command for the first time.

In the General Preferences window you can set defaults to move easily from one part of QuickBooks to another, change the way the QuickBooks windows look on your computer, and change several other items. The settings are self-explanatory so set them to suit your business.

▌ Click the options as you wish.

▌ Click the **Accounting** icon to move to the next set of Preferences.

If you changed the settings in the General Preferences window, QuickBooks will ask if you want to save the changes. You'll be asked this question whenever you change a Preferences window and don't click **OK** to leave the window.

▌ Click **Yes** in the Save Changes window.

Accounting Preferences

Click the **Accounting** icon. Click the Company Preferences tab (Figure 2-2). Here's a list of the Accounting Preferences options and what they do:

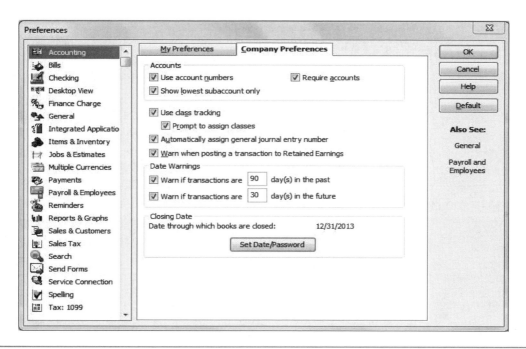

Figure 2-2
Use the Company Preferences tab window to set the recommended settings for Accounting Preferences.

Use account numbers — Lets you use numbers for accounts in your Chart of Accounts. In Chapter 3 we'll explain why we strongly suggest using account numbers to identify the accounts in your Chart of Accounts. For an example of what a Chart of Accounts looks like, see our sample Chart of Accounts in Chapter 3.

Show lowest subaccount only — Displays the subaccount rather than the header accounts when you view the allocation account on a transaction. This helps the data entry operator see the proper account when viewing transactions.

Require accounts — Warns and forces you to allocate each transaction to an account.

Use class tracking — Lets you classify transactions into Labor, Materials, Subcontractors, Equipment Rental, and Other. This type of subtotaling is important when your tax preparer fills in the Cost of Goods section of your tax return. You'll probably also want to know exactly how much you've spent on these categories for each job.

Prompt to assign classes — We strongly suggest that you put a ✓ in the box. It will remind you to allocate each transaction to a class: Labor, Materials, Subcontractors, Equipment Rental, Other Job Related Costs. See Chapter 6 — Classes for more information.

Automatically assign general journal entry number — Put a ✓ in the box. It's better to allow the system to automatically assign a number than to keep track of the number manually.

Warn when posting a transaction to Retained Earnings — We suggest this option be selected. It will protect your books from getting out of balance. The Retained Earnings account balance is the total sum of money that has been made or lost since the beginning of the business. Each year QuickBooks automatically closes out your income and expenses and the difference gets posted into the Retained Earnings account. For example, let's say your first year in business ended with a net profit of $1,000. Your second year in business ended with a net loss of $500. The balance in Retained Earnings should be $500. Posting a transaction to Retained Earnings would cause your books to get out of balance and your tax preparer to spend hours fixing the error and costing you money.

Date Warnings — Check the date warnings box to be prompted if a transaction is being entered with a date more than 30 days into the future or more than 90 days in the past. The timeframes can be adjusted to whatever you wish.

Closing Date — Date through which books are closed. As soon as you submit your books to your CPA or tax preparer, you should immediately return to this screen and enter your year-end date. For example, if you've submitted paperwork or financials to your tax preparer through 12/31/13, click **Set Date/Password** and enter that date. Then enter a password in **Closing Date Password** and confirm password. Entering a date and password won't prevent data entry — it'll only warn the user that the books are closed. The user will have to enter the correct password in order to post/record a transaction in a closed year.

▌ Click the options in the **Accounting Preferences** window as you wish.

▌ Click the **Bills** icon to move to the next set of Preferences.

▌ Click **Yes** in the Save Changes window.

Bills Preferences

Click the **Company Preferences** tab.

If you want QuickBooks to remind you about bills to be paid, use Bills Preferences. Initially, QuickBooks uses 10 days as the lead time for paying bills and putting a message in the Reminder List. See Figure 2-3 for the Bills Preferences options.

Bills are due — Typically, this is 30 days. Enter a different number of days if you wish.

Warn about duplicate bill numbers from same vendor — Select this if you want to be notified if you try to enter the same bill twice. This is a nice feature if you get lots of bills from certain vendors. It will help you avoid overpaying a vendor, or paying twice for the same bill.

Figure 2-3

Use the Company Preferences tab window to set the recommended settings for Bills Preferences.

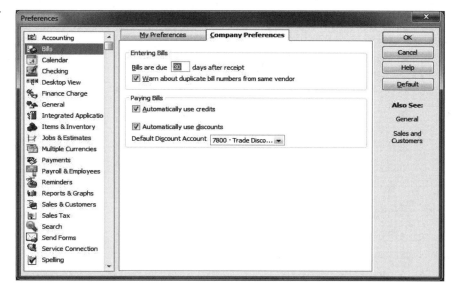

Automatically use discounts and credits — Select this if any of your vendors let you take a discount if you pay early (or within 10 days). Enter a default account number to record all the discounts you receive. We used account number 7800 Trade Discount.

▌ Click the **Checking** icon to move to the next set of Preferences.

▌ Click **Yes** in the Save Changes window.

Checking Preferences

The My Preferences tab of the Checking Preferences window will help you automatically link bank accounts to specific functions or tasks. For example, suppose you have payroll and general checking accounts, and a savings account. If you usually pay payroll from the payroll account, write checks from the general account and make deposits into the savings account, you can use the Checking — My Preferences tab to link the appropriate bank accounts whenever you perform one of these actions. Having the correct bank account appear automatically should cut down on data entry errors. However, keep in mind that the My Preferences tab in this window lets you set preferences for a particular person or computer. If you sign on with a different name, you'll need to set the preferences again for that sign-on name. You can see the setup we used in Figure 2-4.

The Company Preferences tab of the Checking Preferences window lets you set up universal preferences for printing and processing checks.

Figure 2-4

Use the My Preferences tab of Checking Preferences to set preferences for a certain person or computer.

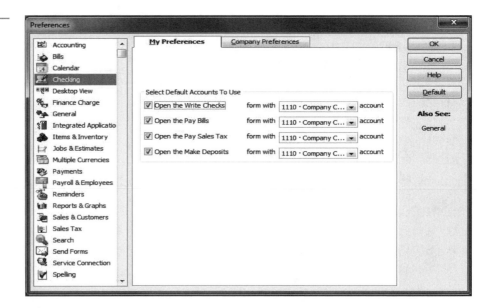

Figure 2-5

Use the Company Preferences tab of Checking Preferences to set general preferences for printing and processing checks.

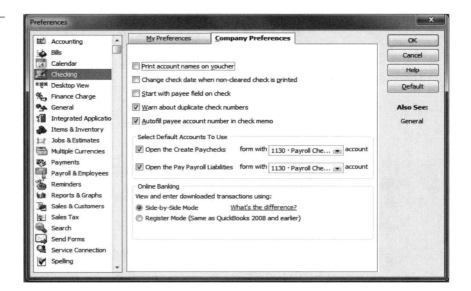

Here's what the options shown in Figure 2-5 do:

Print account names on voucher — If you use checks with voucher attachments, the payee, date, account name, memo, amount, and total amount will appear on the voucher. If you don't select this, QuickBooks omits the account name(s) but prints the rest of the information.

Change check date when check is printed — Shows the date the check was printed, not the date it was created in QuickBooks. Check this if you enter your checks on a different day than you print or send them out.

Figure 2-6

Use the Company Preferences tab window to set the recommended settings for Finance Charge Preferences.

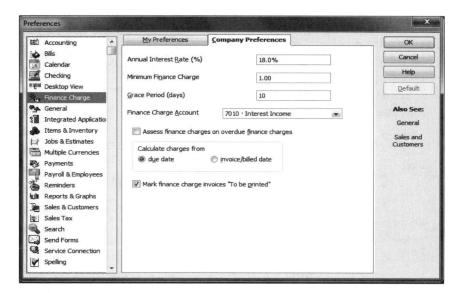

Start with payee field on check — Lets you skip check number and date fields and enter information in the payee field. QuickBooks will fill in the date and next check number automatically. Select this option if you're current with entering your data and stick to a consistent check number sequence.

Warn about duplicate check numbers — It's a good idea to select this to reduce the chance of duplicating a check entry.

Autofill payee account number in check memo — If you select this box, the vendor account will print on the memo field on the check.

Select Default Accounts To Use — Enter the correct default accounts you use for payroll here. If you have more than 20 employees, it's a good idea to use a separate payroll checking account. It takes too long to reconcile a general checking account if you process payroll each week and print more than 20 checks for each payroll.

▌ Click the options and enter accounts as you wish in the **My Preferences** and **Company Preferences** windows.

▌ Click the **Finance Charge** icon to move to the next set of Preferences.

▌ Click **Yes** in the Save Changes window.

Finance Charge Preferences

Now you're ready to set the Finance Charge Preferences. See Figure 2-6.

It's up to you whether or not to charge your customers a fee for late payments. Many companies use the finance charge as a threat to keep payments timely, but in practice few of them actually collect the charges. If

Figure 2-7

Use the New Account window to create an account that will track your finance charges.

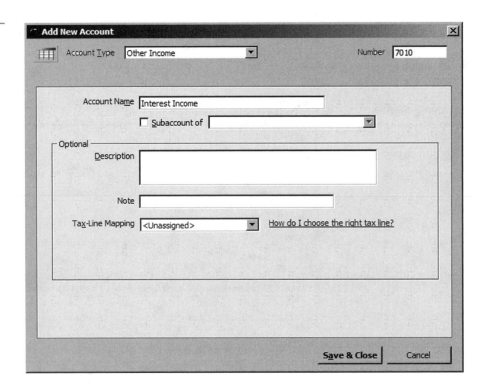

you decide to charge for late payments, we suggest you explain the charges very clearly in all your contract documents so your customers aren't surprised when they're hit with these "extras."

Finance Charge Preferences let you set the percentage and minimum finance charge you want to add to overdue invoices, and the grace period. In Figure 2-6 it's set at 10 days. When you enter an amount in Minimum Finance Charge, the amount is applied regardless of the amount overdue.

Here's another example of a grace period. If your terms are net 30 and you want to start charging interest after a 30-day grace period, enter 30. Then if you send out an invoice dated January 1, QuickBooks waits until January 31 to assess finance charges on any unpaid amount.

If you use finance charges, you must enter the account you use to track them. If you don't have this account in your Chart of Accounts, you need to create it now.

▌ At **Finance Charge Account**, pull down the menu and choose **Add New** (at the top of the list). This will bring up the New Account window. Figure 2-7 shows how we entered account 7010 Interest Income (You don't need to add this account if you started with the Company file from the Download).

▌ In **Account Type**, choose **Other Income** from the pull-down list.

▌ In **Number**, we entered **7010**. That's Interest Income from the Chart of Accounts (see Chapter 3).

Figure 2-8

Use the Company Preferences tab window to set the recommended settings for Items & Inventory Preferences.

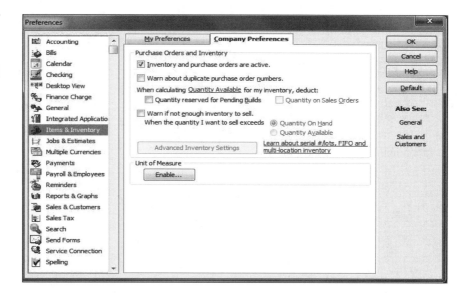

▌ In **Account Name**, we entered **Interest Income**.

▌ Click **Save & Close**.

Unless you want to play hardball, don't select Assess finance charges on overdue finance charges. See Figure 2-6.

▌ Click the **Items & Inventory** icon to move to the next set of Preferences.

▌ Click **Yes** in the Save Changes window.

Items & Inventory Preferences

If your business is inventory-based, you can select your preferences for inventory and purchase orders in the Items & Inventory Preferences window. See Figure 2-8 for the Items and Inventory options.

Inventory and purchase orders are active — Select this if you plan to use purchase orders to track which materials are on order, when you ordered them, who you ordered them from, or if you plan to use purchase orders to track committed costs (see Chapter 14).

Warn about duplicate purchase order numbers — Select this if you want to be warned when you create a duplicate purchase order.

▌ Click on the **Jobs & Estimates** icon to move to the next set of Preferences.

▌ Click **Yes** in the Save Changes window.

Figure 2-9

Use the Company Preferences tab window to set the recommended settings for the Jobs & Estimates Preferences.

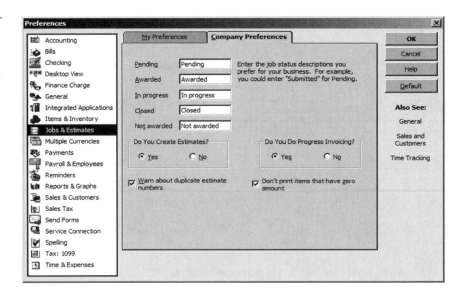

Jobs & Estimates Preferences

Whenever you click Customer Center, you get a list of your customers, their jobs, and one of five possible descriptions for the status of each job. The default descriptions are Pending, Awarded, In progress, Closed, and Not awarded. If you want to use other descriptions for job status, enter them on the Jobs and Estimates Preferences screen. To change a description, just enter the new description. See Figure 2-9.

▌ Set remaining options as you prefer. If you will be billing customers based on a percent complete by phase of construction, answer **Yes** to the question **Do You Do Progress Invoicing?** For more information on this, see Chapter 13.

▌ Click the **Payroll & Employees** icon to move to the next set of Preferences.

▌ If you get the Save Changes window, click **Yes**.

Payroll & Employees Preferences

Payroll and Employee Preferences are extremely important. The way you set these preferences determines how QuickBooks will associate costs, such as payroll taxes and wages, to job cost reports. See Figure 2-10 for the settings we recommend.

Full payroll — Uses the QuickBooks payroll module to allocate gross wages and payroll taxes to jobs. Select this even if you use a payroll service. For a more detailed discussion, see Chapter 15.

Figure 2-10

Use the Company Preferences tab window to set the recommended settings for Payroll & Employees Preferences.

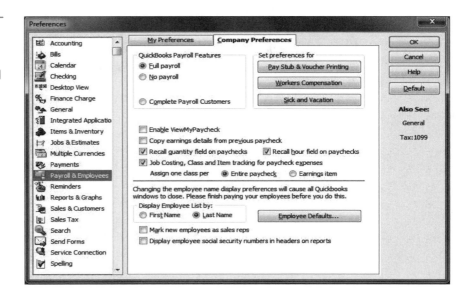

Figure 2-11

Use the Employee Defaults window to set the defaults you'll use for each new employee you enter into QuickBooks.

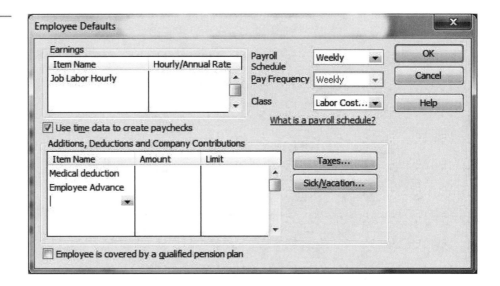

Job Costing, Class and Item tracking for paycheck expenses — Make sure you select this preference. It will automatically disburse employer payroll taxes to the job, item (job phase), and class (labor).

Assign one class per — Since we'll use one class (labor) for all transactions on a timecard, we'll select **Entire paycheck** to assign the labor class to the entire timecard. This will save you time when you enter timecards and process payroll.

You can also set the options you want to use when entering employee information by clicking the **Employee Defaults** button. Let's do that now to display the window shown in Figure 2-11.

▌ Click **Employee Defaults**.

The defaults you set here will appear on the New Employee, Payroll Info Tab window each time you enter a new employee.

▌ Change the **Employee Defaults** as you wish.

▌ Click **OK** to save the template.

If you are using QuickBooks Enhanced Payroll service, you will have access to a feature that helps you prepare your workers' compensation report. Although it doesn't print the report for you, or allocate workers' comp costs to jobs, it will give you the information you'll need to fill out the report. The reason QuickBooks doesn't prepare your workers' comp report for you is because there is a vast array of different insurance companies you can purchase insurance from and each one has a different report type. To use the feature, click **Set Preferences** in the Workers' Compensation box.

Some changes you make to Payroll & Employees Preferences may cause QuickBooks to advise you of the effects of the changes you've made. Select **OK** to activate these warnings.

▌ Click the **Reminders** icon to move to the next set of Preferences.

▌ Click **Yes** in the Save Changes window.

Reminders Preferences

QuickBooks has an extensive set of task reminders. It can remind you to print checks, payroll checks, invoices, or to pay bills and deposit money. These can be handy functions, especially if you have several people working on your accounting system. Or they can be annoyances if you already have a schedule and live by it. QuickBooks lets you "have it your way" by turning these Reminder Preferences on or off.

The Reminders Preferences screen gives you three options for each task — Show Summary, Show List, or Don't Remind Me. For some of the tasks you can set the number of days before you're warned. To follow our example, set your Reminders Preferences to match Figure 2-12 for now.

▌ Click the **Reports & Graphs** icon to move to the next set of Preferences.

▌ Click **Yes** in the Save Changes window.

Figure 2-12

Use the Company Preferences tab window to set the recommended settings for Reminders Preferences.

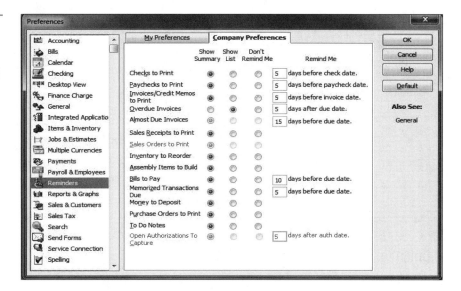

Reports & Graphs Preferences

If you select Accrual in the Summary Reports Basis section of the Company Preferences tab, QuickBooks will include unpaid vendor bills and customer invoices when figuring income and expenses, Accounts Payable, and Accounts Receivable, even though you haven't received the money. If you select Cash, only the vendor bills and customer invoices that have been paid will show up on reports.

Generally, it's a good idea to run your business on an accrual basis so you can see how much money you've earned and committed to spend over a given time period. The cash basis shows only how much money you received in a month and how much money you paid out. The accrual basis will give you a better picture of monthly income versus expenses.

For now, select the options as shown in Figures 2-13 and 2-14. You can do any fine-tuning later when you have more experience using reports.

▌ Click the **Sales & Customers** icon to move to the next set of Preferences.

▌ Click **Yes** in the Save Changes window.

Sales & Customers Preferences

Many options on Sales & Customers Preferences aren't important to the construction industry, so we don't describe them here.

▌ Click the **Company Preferences** tab.

▌ Select options as shown in Figure 2-15.

Figure 2-13

This Company Preferences tab window shows the recommended settings for Reports & Graphs.

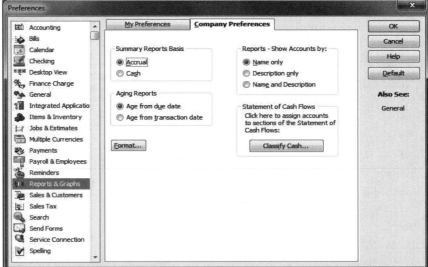

Figure 2-14

Use the My Preferences tab window to set your own preferences for Reports & Graphs.

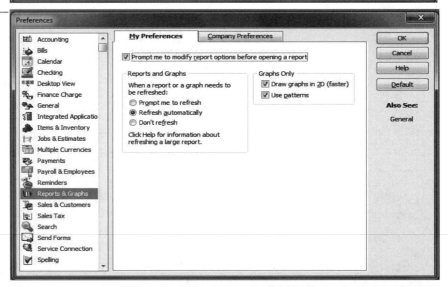

Figure 2-15

Use the Company Preferences tab window to set the recommended settings for the Sales & Customers Preferences.

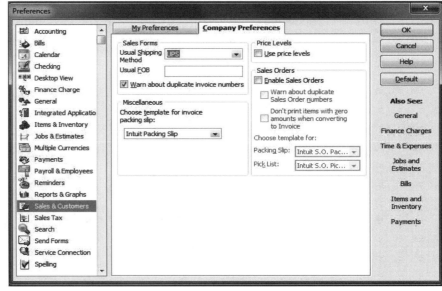

Figure 2-16

Use the Company Preferences tab window of Sales Tax Preferences to specify your company preferences for sales tax.

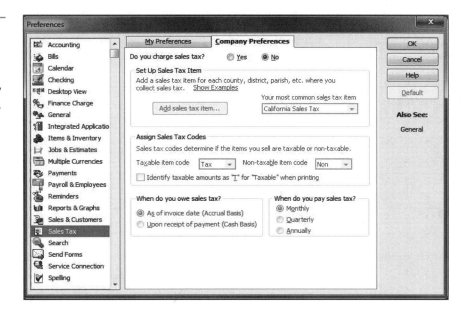

Select **Warn about duplicate invoice numbers** if you want to track invoices by number and want to avoid issuing two invoices with the same number.

▍ Click the **Sales Tax** icon to move to the next set of Preferences.

▍ Click **Yes** in the Save Changes window.

Sales Tax Preferences

These Preferences are self-explanatory and will depend on the requirements in your state. See Figure 2-16.

▍ Select options as you wish.

▍ Click the **Send Forms** icon to move to the next set of Preferences.

▍ Click **Yes** in the Save Changes window.

Send Forms Preferences

If you choose to send forms, such as a customer invoice, via email, you can set the Send Forms preferences to automatically attach a cover message. See Figure 2-17.

▍ Select options as you wish.

▍ Click the **Service Connection** icon to move to the next set of Preferences.

▍ Click **Yes** in the Save Changes window.

Figure 2-17

Use the Company Preferences tab window of Send Forms Preferences to set your company preferences for sending forms.

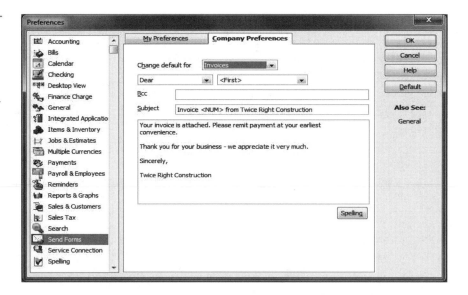

Figure 2-18

Service Connection Preferences determine how you connect to Internet applications.

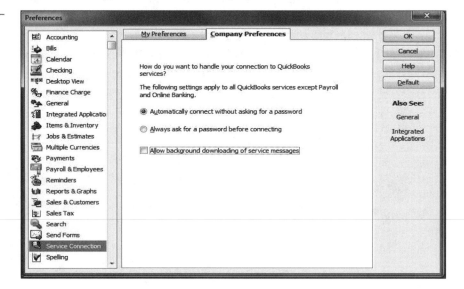

Service Connection Preferences

Service Connection Preferences lets you choose how you want to handle connections to QuickBooks services. If you're just getting started with QuickBooks, you're probably not using any of these services. In this case, select the settings as shown in Figure 2-18.

▌ Select the options you want.

▌ Click the **Spelling** icon to move to the next set of Preferences.

▌ Click **Yes** in the Save Changes window.

Figure 2-19

Use the My Preferences tab window of the Spelling Preferences to get QuickBooks to check the spelling on your forms.

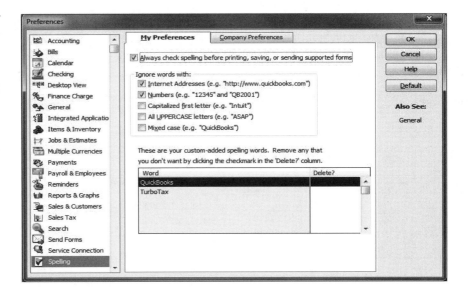

Spelling Preferences

With the Spelling Preferences you can send invoices to customers without the worry that you've misspelled something. See Figure 2-19.

We recommend that you select **Always check spelling before printing, saving, or sending supported forms.** Then QuickBooks will find any misspelled words so you can fix them before your customer finds them and begins to wonder about you.

▌ Select options as you wish.

▌ Click the **Tax:1099** icon to move to the next set of Preferences.

▌ Click **Yes** in the Save Changes window.

Tax: 1099 Preferences

1099s are forms that your business files with the IRS to report the total amount paid to each vendor or subcontractor in a calendar year. You must file a 1099 for each vendor or subcontractor who has provided over $600 of labor during the year. If you work with vendors or subcontractors to whom you send 1099 forms, you can set up QuickBooks to track all 1099-related payments. At the end of the year, QuickBooks can print your 1099 forms. You're not required to send 1099 forms to material suppliers, or to vendors from whom you purchase materials.

Figure 2-20

Use the Company Preferences tab window to specify your company preferences for 1099 tax categories.

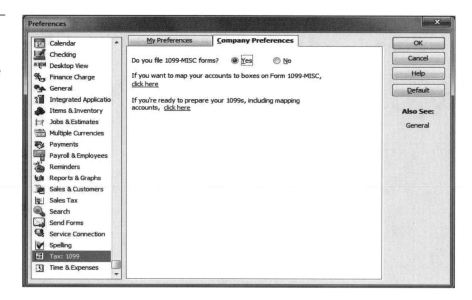

It's easier to complete this section if you've already set up your Chart of Accounts. So, you may want to do that first and then come back here. If you're ready now, proceed and see Figure 2-20.

▌ First answer the **Do you file 1099-MISC forms?** question.

▌ Hit the click here button below **If you want to map your accounts to boxes on Form 1099-MISC, click here.** See Figure 2-20.

▌ You should now be at a screen similar to Figure 2-21. The first thing you need to do is change the selection from **Show 1099 Accounts** to **Show all accounts** (as shown).

▌ Change the pull down box under **Apply payments to this 1099 box** to the one shown in Figure 2-21 and 2-22.

▌ When you are finished, select the **Save & Close** button.

▌ Click the **Time & Expenses** icon to move to the next set of Preferences.

▌ Click **Yes** in the Save Changes window.

Time & Expenses Preferences

It's very easy to track time spent on a job using the time tracking function in QuickBooks . This is one of the most important functions QuickBooks can perform for you. Accurate time tracking lets you compare your actual labor to your estimated labor. In other words, it's a link in the "feed-back" loop from estimate to job cost and back to estimate.

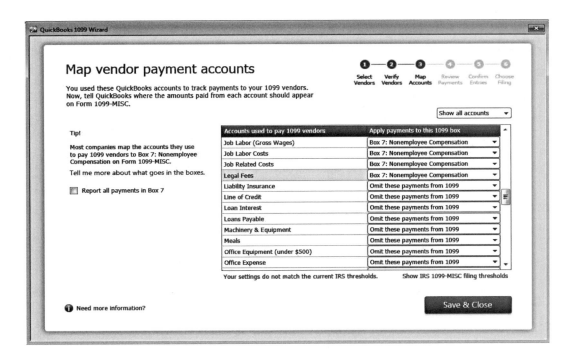

Figure 2-21

In the **Apply payments to this 1099 box** select as shown.

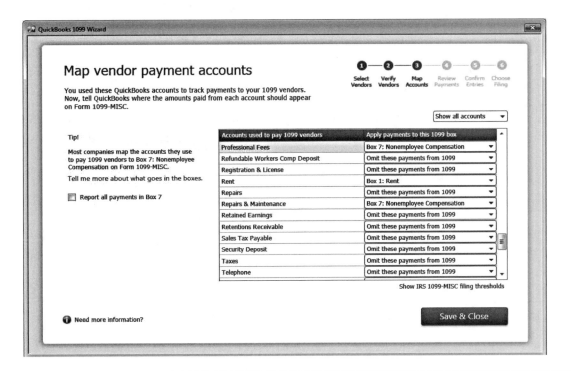

Figure 2-22

Select all accounts that you might allocate a subcontractor or outside consultant expense to, so a 1099 can be created at year end.

Figure 2-23

Use the Company Preferences tab window to set your Time & Expenses Preferences.

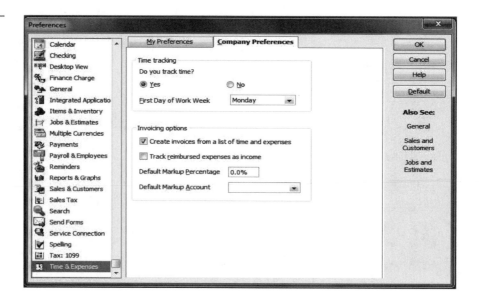

In **First Day of the Work Week** select the day your printed timecards start. In our example, we start our work week on Monday and end the week on Sunday. If you start your week on Thursday and end on Wednesday, select Thursday. If you pay your employees biweekly or on the 1st and 15th, select the day you've been using on your timecards. When QuickBooks processes payroll, it will know to take the dates that make up the pay period, not the full week entered. See Figure 2-23.

▌ Select options as you wish.

▌ Click **OK**.

We recommend that you don't select **Track reimbursed expenses as income**. Then you'll get reports showing customer invoices as construction income and vendor bills as job costs. If you do select it, QuickBooks records income and expense on time and materials jobs by shifting amounts into, and out of, the same account.

Now you should have your QuickBooks company file set up and your preferences customized. The next step is to create or change your Chart of Accounts. In the next chapter we'll explain what a Chart of Accounts is and how to add, delete, or edit accounts.

Chapter 3

Chart of Accounts

The Chart of Accounts is the backbone of your accounting system. That's why it's so important to understand how it works. Think of the Chart of Accounts as a file cabinet with a file for each type of accounting information you want to track. For example, if you need to know how much money you spend on postage, you'll set up a file (an account in the Chart of Accounts) for Postage Expense.

The Chart of Accounts

Although QuickBooks doesn't require the use of account numbers in the Chart of Accounts, we recommend numbering your accounts. Here's the standard numbering scheme for the Chart of Accounts:

1000 - 1999 Assets
2000 - 2999 Liabilities
3000 - 3999 Capital
4000 - 4999 Income or Revenue
5000 - 5999 Job Costs
6000 - 6999 Overhead Costs
7000 - 7999 Other Income
8000 - 8999 Other Expense

Now let's look at each type of account in the Chart of Accounts.

Assets

Assets are things your company owns. They're usually divided into two groups — current assets and fixed assets. Current assets are generally numbered from 1000 - 1499. These are assets that you can easily turn into cash, such as checking accounts, savings accounts, money market and CD accounts, Accounts Receivable, and inventory. For example, use account

[handwritten margin note: any purchase over $500 = fixed asset]

number 1100 for your company checking account because a checking account is a current asset.

Fixed assets are usually numbered from 1500 - 1999. These are items you would have to sell to generate cash. Automobiles, equipment, and land are examples of fixed assets. For example, you bought a new table saw for $1,100. Since the cost was over the minimum amount considered a fixed asset ($500), the saw will be recorded as an asset, not an expense.

Liabilities

Liabilities are debts your company owes. For example, you borrow $20,000 and when the loan is deposited into the checking account, the deposit is recorded in a liability account such as Bank Loans, not an income account such as Construction Revenue.

Capital

Your capital account structure depends on whether the company's ownership is set up as a sole proprietor, partnership or corporation.

If your company ownership is that of a *sole proprietor or single-member LLC*, you need an Owner's Investment account and an Owner's Drawing account. Use the Owner's Investment account to keep track of the total amount of money the owner invested since starting the business, plus or minus the net profit or loss each year since then. Use the Owner's Drawing account for money the owner takes out of the business for personal use, such as checks to the grocery store, dry cleaners, ATM transactions and transfers on checks written to the owner's personal checking or savings. It's important to keep in mind that the owner of a sole proprietorship doesn't get a regular "employee" paycheck with money deducted for payroll taxes. Instead, the owner pays quarterly estimated taxes, which should always be allocated to the Owner's Drawing account.

If your company is a *general partnership, limited liability partnership (LLP), or limited liability company (LLC) filing as a partnership* you need to set up Capital and Drawing accounts for each partner.

If your company is an *S-corporation, C-corporation,* or an *LLC filing as a corporation*, it has a Common Stock and sometimes a Preferred Stock account. They represent the total sum of stock the company has issued.

Income (Revenue)

Income, or revenue, is derived from the everyday work of your business, such as remodeling income or construction revenue. Other types of income, such as rents from buildings you own, belong in a separate Other Income account numbered between 7000 - 7999.

Job Costs

Job Costs (also called Cost of Goods Sold) are all the costs of building your product. If you're a home builder, job costs are whatever it costs you to build a home, including the direct labor, materials, subcontractors, equipment rental, and other job-related costs. If you design homes, job costs include all the costs associated with designing a home, such as design labor, drafting materials, supplies, and engineering costs. If you do both designing and building, you'll have both sets of costs. It's important to note here that the *sample.qbw* and *company.qbw* data files on the Download included with this book are set up to have just *one* total Job Cost. We use classes to break down that total into labor, materials, subcontractors, equipment rental, and any other costs related to a particular job.

Overhead Costs

Overhead Costs are fixed costs you have even if you run out of work. Rent, telephone, insurance, and utilities are overhead costs.

Other Income

Other Income is income you earn outside the normal way you do business, including interest income, and gain on the sale of an asset, insurance settlement, or stock sale.

Other Expense

Other Expense is an expense that's outside of your normal business, such as a loss on the sale of an asset or stockbroker fees.

How to Use the Sample Chart of Accounts

If you haven't already done so, take a look at the Chart of Accounts in the *sample.qbw* file on the Download you got with this book. It has example transactions, a few jobs, vendors, customers, items, classes, memorized reports, memorized transactions, and a Chart of Accounts. You can use the sample company to test a new idea and get acquainted with QuickBooks.

If you're ready for the real thing, you can use the Chart of Accounts in the *company.qbw* file from the Download for a jump start. This is a general Chart of Accounts for a sole proprietor building contractor. See the Chart of Accounts listings on the next pages for examples specific to a sole proprietor or partnership, and a corporation.

Chart of Accounts
Sole Proprietor or Partnership

Account	Type
1110 · Company Checking Account	Bank
1111 · Adjustment Register	Bank
1120 · Company Savings Account	Bank
1130 · Payroll Checking Account	Bank
1140 · Petty Cash Account	Bank
1210 · Accounts Receivable	Accounts Receivable
1300 · Inventory Asset	Other Current Asset
1310 · Employee Advances	Other Current Asset
1320 · Retentions Receivable	Other Current Asset
1330 · Security Deposit	Other Current Asset
1340 · Vendor Deposits	Other Current Asset
*1390 · Undeposited Funds	Other Current Asset
1400 · Refundable Workers' Comp Deposit	Other Current Asset
1510 · Automobiles & Trucks	Fixed Asset
1520 · Computer & Office Equipment	Fixed Asset
1530 · Machinery & Equipment	Fixed Asset
1540 · Accumulated Depreciation	Fixed Asset
2010 · Accounts Payable	Accounts Payable
2050 · MasterCard Payable	Credit Card
2060 · Visa Card Payable	Credit Card
2100 · Payroll Liabilities	Other Current Liability
2200 · Customer Deposits	Other Current Liability
2201 · Sales Tax Payable	Other Current Liability
2240 · Workers' Comp Payable	Other Current Liability
2300 · Loans Payable	Other Current Liability
2310 · Line of Credit	Other Current Liability
2410 · Construction Loan	Other Current Liability
2510 · Truck Loan	Long Term Liability
3000 · Opening Balance Equity	Equity
**3100 · Owner's Equity	Equity
3110 · Owner's Capital	Equity
3130 · Owner's Draws	Equity
3910 · Retained Earnings	Equity
3999 · Owner's Time to Jobs	Equity
4110 · Construction Income	Income
4810 · Vendor Refunds	Income
4910 · Workers' Comp Dividend	Income
5110 · Job Related Costs	Cost of Goods Sold
5200 · Job Labor Costs	Cost of Goods Sold
5210 · Job Labor (Gross Wages)	Cost of Goods Sold
5220 · Officer's Direct Labor	Cost of Goods Sold
5230 · Workers' Comp Costs	Cost of Goods Sold
5240 · Direct Payroll Taxes	Cost of Goods Sold
5250 · Direct Employee Benefits	Cost of Goods Sold
6020 · Advertising	Expense

add when add employees

6040 · Amortization Expense	Expense
6050 · Bad Debt	Expense
6060 · Bank Service Charges	Expense
6070 · Bid Deposit	Expense
6075 · Bond Expense	Expense
6090 · Business License & Fees	Expense
6100 · Car/Truck Expense	Expense
6101 · Gas & Oil	Expense
6103 · Repairs & Maintenance	Expense
6105 · Registration & License	Expense
6107 · Insurance-Auto	Expense
6130 · Cleaning/Janitorial	Expense
6135 · Computer Supplies/Equipment	Expense
6140 · Contributions	Expense
6150 · Depreciation Expense	Expense
6160 · Dues and Subscriptions	Expense
6180 · Insurance	Expense
6181 · Disability Insurance	Expense
6182 · Liability Insurance	Expense
6185 · Workers' Comp	Expense
6200 · Interest Expense	Expense
6201 · Finance Charge	Expense
6202 · Loan Interest	Expense
6203 · Credit Card Interest	Expense
6300 · Office Expense	Expense
6330 · Office Supplies	Expense
6350 · Office Equipment (under $500)	Expense
6500 · Payroll Expenses (office)	Expense
6501 · Payroll (office staff)	Expense
6502 · Payroll Tax Expense	Expense
6503 · Officer's Wages	Expense
6504 · Designer's Wages	Expense
6508 · Vac/Holiday/Sick Pay	Expense
6509 · Employee Bonus	Expense
6510 · Employee Benefits	Expense
6570 · Professional Fees	Expense
6571 · Accounting	Expense
6572 · Legal Fees	Expense
6573 · Computer Consultants	Expense
6610 · Postage and Delivery	Expense
6650 · Rent	Expense
6670 · Repairs	Expense
6671 · Building Repairs	Expense
6672 · Computer Repairs	Expense
6673 · Equipment Repairs	Expense
6800 · Telephone	Expense
6820 · Taxes	Expense
6830 · Training & Conferences	Expense
6900 · Travel & Entertainment	Expense
6901 · Entertaining Clients	Expense

6902 · Meals	Expense
6903 · Air Fare	Expense
6904 · Hotels/Lodging	Expense
6920 · Tools & Machinery (under $500)	Expense
6970 · Utilities	Expense
7010 · Interest Income	Other Income
7030 · Other Income	Other Income
7800 · Trade Discounts	Other Income
8010 · Other Expenses	Other Expense
*2 · Purchase Orders	Non-Posting
*4 · Estimates	Non-Posting

*QuickBooks sets up these accounts for you automatically. The account number for undeposited funds may not be the same number you listed.

** If your business is a partnership between Partner 1 and Partner 2, this section would look like this:

3100 · Partner 1 Equity	
3110 · Partner 1 Investments	Equity
3120 · Partner 1 Drawing Account	Equity
3200 · Partner 2 Equity	Equity
3210 · Partner 2 Investments	Equity
3220 · Partner 2 Drawing Account	Equity

Chart of Accounts
Corporation

Account	Type
1110 · Company Checking Account	Bank
1111 · Adjustment Register	Bank
1120 · Company Savings Account	Bank
1130 · Payroll Checking Account	Bank
1140 · Petty Cash Account	Bank
1210 · Accounts Receivable	Accounts Receivable
1300 · Inventory Asset	Other Current Asset
1310 · Employee Advances	Other Current Asset
1320 · Retentions Receivable	Other Current Asset
1330 · Security Deposit	Other Current Asset
1340 · Vendor Deposits	Other Current Asset
*1390 · Undeposited Funds	Other Current Asset
1400 · Refundable Workers' Comp Deposit	Other Current Asset
1510 · Automobiles & Trucks	Fixed Asset
1520 · Computer & Office Equipment	Fixed Asset

1530 · Machinery & Equipment	Fixed Asset
1540 · Accumulated Depreciation	Fixed Asset
2010 · Accounts Payable	Accounts Payable
2050 · MasterCard Payable	Credit Card
2060 · Visa Card Payable	Credit Card
2100 · Payroll Liabilities	Other Current Liability
2200 · Customer Deposits	Other Current Liability
2201 · Sales Tax Payable	Other Current Liability
2240 · Workers' Comp Payable	Other Current Liability
2300 · Loans Payable	Other Current Liability
2310 · Line of Credit	Other Current Liability
2410 · Construction Loan	Other Current Liability
2510 · Truck Loan	Long Term Liability
3000 · Opening Balance Equity	Equity
3100 · Common Stock	Equity
3200 · Shareholder Distribution	Equity
3910 · Retained Earnings	Equity
4110 · Construction Income	Income
4810 · Vendor Refunds	Income
4910 · Workers' Comp Dividend	Income
5110 · Job Related Costs	Cost of Goods Sold
5200 · Job Labor Costs	Cost of Goods Sold
5210 · Job Labor (Gross Wages)	Cost of Goods Sold
5220 · Officer's Direct Labor	Cost of Goods Sold
5230 · Workers' Comp Costs	Cost of Goods Sold
5240 · Direct Payroll Taxes	Cost of Goods Sold
5250 · Direct Employee Benefits	Cost of Goods Sold
6020 · Advertising	Expense
6040 · Amortization Expense	Expense
6050 · Bad Debt	Expense
6060 · Bank Service Charges	Expense
6070 · Bid Deposit	Expense
6075 · Bond Expense	Expense
6090 · Business License & Fees	Expense
6100 · Car/Truck Expense	Expense
6101 · Gas & Oil	Expense
6103 · Repairs & Maintenance	Expense
6105 · Registration & License	Expense
6107 · Insurance-Auto	Expense
6130 · Cleaning/Janitorial	Expense
6135 · Computer Supplies/Equipment	Expense
6140 · Contributions	Expense
6150 · Depreciation Expense	Expense
6160 · Dues and Subscriptions	Expense
6180 · Insurance	Expense
6181 · Disability Insurance	Expense
6182 · Liability Insurance	Expense
6185 · Workers' Comp	Expense
6200 · Interest Expense	Expense
6201 · Finance Charge	Expense

6202 · Loan Interest	Expense
6203 · Credit Card Interest	Expense
6300 · Office Expense	Expense
6330 · Office Supplies	Expense
6350 · Office Equipment (under $500)	Expense
6500 · Payroll Expenses (office)	Expense
6501 · Payroll (office staff)	Expense
6502 · Payroll Tax Expense	Expense
6503 · Officer's Wages	Expense
6504 · Designer's Wages	Expense
6508 · Vac/Holiday/Sick Pay	Expense
6509 · Employee Bonus	Expense
6510 · Employee Benefits	Expense
6570 · Professional Fees	Expense
6571 · Accounting	Expense
6572 · Legal Fees	Expense
6573 · Computer Consultants	Expense
6610 · Postage and Delivery	Expense
6650 · Rent	Expense
6670 · Repairs	Expense
6671 · Building Repairs	Expense
6672 · Computer Repairs	Expense
6673 · Equipment Repairs	Expense
6800 · Telephone	Expense
6820 · Taxes	Expense
6830 · Training & Conferences	Expense
6900 · Travel & Entertainment	Expense
6901 · Entertaining Clients	Expense
6902 · Meals	Expense
6903 · Air Fare	Expense
6904 · Hotels/Lodging	Expense
6920 · Tools & Machinery (under $500)	Expense
6970 · Utilities	Expense
7010 · Interest Income	Other Income
7030 · Other Income	Other Income
7800 · Trade Discounts	Other Income
8010 · Other Expenses	Other Expense
*2 · Purchase Orders	Non-Posting
*4 · Estimates	Non-Posting

*QuickBooks sets up these accounts for you automatically. The account number for undeposited funds may not be the same number you listed.

Figure 3-1

You can change the type, number, name, description, note, tax-related information, or opening balance for any existing account in the Edit Account window.

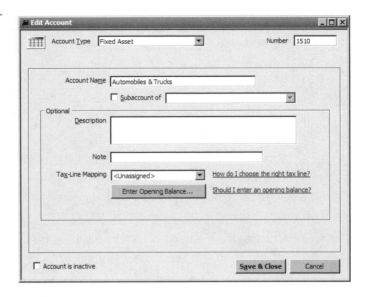

Take a little time now to compare the account list on the last five pages to your existing Chart of Accounts. You'll probably need to make changes for your business. For example, if you currently use expense accounts that you don't find listed in our Chart of Accounts, you'll need to add those accounts. But we'll add a word of caution here. Keep in mind that items such as payroll items and material items are linked to 5110 Job Related Costs and 4110 Construction Income accounts in the Chart of Accounts. You don't want to change these two account numbers or names.

Change, Add to, and Print Your Chart of Accounts

To change an existing account:

▌ Click **Home**, then click the **Chart of Accounts** icon, or from the **Lists** menu, choose **Chart of Accounts**.

▌ Click once to highlight the account you want to edit. Pull down the **Account** menu at the bottom of the window and choose **Edit Account**.

Figure 3-1 shows an example of the screen you'll see.

▌ Change the information for the account and click **Save & Close**. For information on Opening Balances see Chapter 10.

After changing an account, make sure all transactions are correctly assigned. To do that:

▌ Click **Home**, then click the **Chart of Accounts** icon, or from the **Lists** menu, choose **Chart of Accounts** and select the account you changed.

▌ At the bottom of the Chart of Accounts window, pull down the **Activities** menu and choose **Use Register**.

Figure 3-2

Use the New Account window to create a new account in your Chart of Accounts.

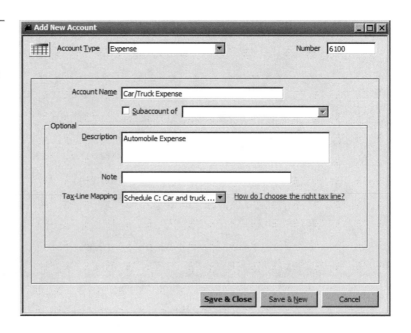

Now check the register and make sure everything listed really should be assigned to the account. If a transaction belongs in another account, double click on the transaction in the register and reassign it to the correct account.

To add a new account to your Chart of Accounts:

▌ Click **Home**, then click **Chart of Accounts**, or from the **Lists** menu, choose **Chart of Accounts**.

▌ Pull down the **Account** menu at the bottom of the window and choose **New**.

▌ Select the account type. Click **Continue**.

▌ Add the information for the account and click **Save & Close**.

Figure 3-2 shows an example of how to enter a new account for car/truck expenses to your Chart of Accounts.

To get more detail about a specific account, you can break it down by subaccounts. Figure 3-3 shows an example of a new subaccount window for subaccount 6101 Gas & Oil.

▌ Add the information for the subaccount and click **Save & Close**.

After you've finished changing your Chart of Accounts, you can print a new list and keep it handy for future reference. To do that:

▌ From the pull-down **Reports** menu in the Chart of Accounts window, choose **Account Listing**.

▌ Click **OK** to display the report.

▌ Click **Print**.

Figure 3-3

You can create subaccounts to get a more detailed breakdown of an account.

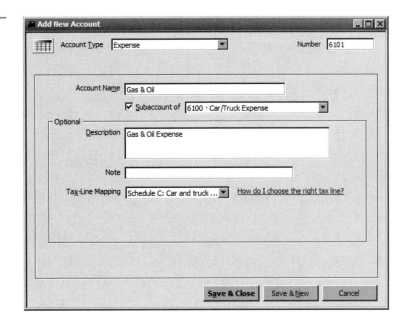

In this chapter we explained your Chart of Accounts. In the next chapter, Items, we'll show you how to set up items that match your job phases or divisions. Then we'll show you how to link each item to an account.

Chapter 4

Items

Although QuickBooks uses the name *Items*, think of them as job phases — like the 50 CSI divisions, HomeTech's 25 Remodeling phases, the 31 phases in the *sample.qbw* company file, or job phases you've defined for your own business. They're like containers where you store information.

Using QuickBooks Items, you can break any job into measurable, trackable units. For example, you can track wall framing costs to find out if you're over your estimate. It's important to do that *before* it's too late to correct any problems.

The *sample.qbw* file you received with this book uses items for estimating, invoicing, and job costing. Although we've put an Items List on *company.qbw*, our set of items probably won't match yours exactly. But you can easily add, delete, and edit the items to suit your job costing needs.

One important thing to understand about items is that they link to the Chart of Accounts. When you set up a job cost item, link it to both a job related cost account, like 5110 Job Related Costs, and an income account, like 4110 Construction Income.

To compile a project report (Job Profitability, Job Estimates vs Actuals, and Job Costs, for example), you need to use items. In the *sample.qbw* data, we've created several items. You can study this list to see how we use the items in estimates and invoices shown in this book. Then you can set up items to best suit your own business. To see the Items List in *sample.qbw*:

▌ Open *sample.qbw*.

▌ Click **Home**, then click **Items & Services**, or from the **Lists** menu, choose **Item List**.

The project reports built into QuickBooks use items to break job cost reports into smaller units — called job phases. Job phases should be the phases you actually use to estimate a job. That way you can get reports comparing your estimated costs to your actual job costs. You'll find that these reports are invaluable for running a profitable business.

Figure 4-1
The Item List window shows information about each item created in QuickBooks.

Entering Items for a Non-Inventory-Based Business

If you don't track inventory, you can use service inventory items to divide jobs into phases of construction. For example, if you use a specific list such as the 50 CSI divisions to make estimates, you can create that list in QuickBooks using service items.

Let's see how the company on *sample.qbw*, Twice Right Construction, did it. Twice Right computerized their estimating and job costing using QuickBooks items. Figure 4-1 shows some of their QuickBooks items.

To create a new service item:

▌ Click **Home**, then click **Items & Services**, or from the **Lists** menu, choose **Item List**. In the Item List window, pull down the **Item** menu and choose **New**. See our example in Figure 4-2.

Figure 4-2

Use the New Item window to create a new service item.

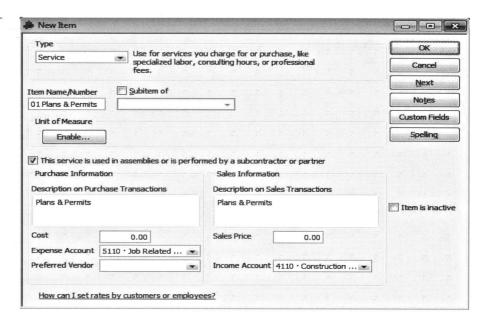

- For **Type**, select **Service**. A "service" type will allow you to post labor, materials, subcontractor costs, etc. to it.

- Make sure you select the box in front of **This service is used in assemblies or is performed by a subcontractor or partner**. *This is important.* Selecting this box, and specifying the correct Expense Account and Income Account, makes it easy to keep your accounting accurate. Notice that the cost of the item is linked to the account you're using for Job Related Costs (5110 in our example). The price you're going to charge the customer will be linked to your Construction Income account (4110 in our example).

- Click **OK** to create the new item.

You can use subitems to do more in-depth job cost analysis. To set up a subitem, select an item and then create its subitems. For example, first set up an item 02 Site Work, then set up a subitem called 02.10 Demo.

To create a subitem:

- Click **Home**, then click **Items & Services**, or from the **Lists** menu, choose **Item List**. In the Item List window, pull down the **Item** menu and choose **New**.

- For **Type**, select **Service**. A "service" type will allow you to post labor, materials, subcontractor costs, etc. to it.

- Select **This service is used in assemblies or is performed by a subcontractor or partner**. This will allow us to track estimated costs and actual costs for this item.

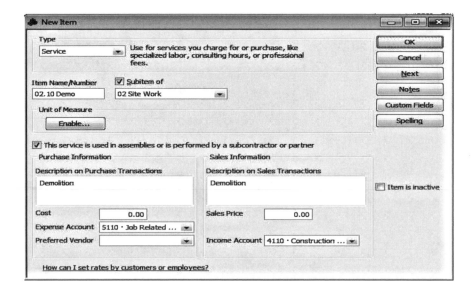

Figure 4-3
You can create subitems to get a more detailed breakdown of an item.

▌ Click **Subitem of** then select the existing item this will be a subitem of. In our example, shown in Figure 4-3, we create the subitem 02.10 Demo of the item 02 Site Work.

▌ Fill in all other fields the same as you would for any item.

▌ Click **OK** to create the subitem.

Entering Items for an Inventory-Based Business

Most general contractors and remodeling contractors don't have, or track, inventory (and in fact we discourage them from doing so). But if you're an electrical, mechanical, roofing subcontractor, or a specialty contractor you'll probably have a use for tracking inventory.

You can set up inventory items to track the materials you stock so you'll know when it's time to reorder them. You can keep track of how many parts are in stock after a sale, how many you've ordered, the cost of the goods you've sold, and the value of your inventory. You'll use purchase orders to track the materials you've bought, and invoices to record sales of materials. Just remember to use the same inventory part item on both invoices and purchase orders.

To create a new inventory item:

▌ Click **Home**, then click **Items & Services**, or from the **Lists** menu, choose **Item List**. In the Item List window, pull down the **Item** menu and choose **New**.

Figure 4-4

Use the New Item window to create a new inventory item.

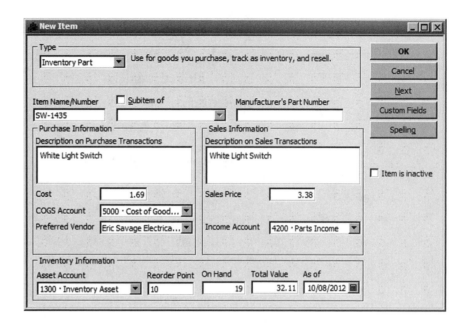

■ For **Type**, select **Inventory Part**. See our example in Figure 4-4. If Inventory Part doesn't show up in your pull-down list under **Type**, then you'll need to change your Purchases & Vendors Preferences. To do that, from the **Edit** menu, choose **Preferences**, click **Items & Inventory**, click the **Company Preferences** tab, and select **Inventory and purchase orders are active**. Click **OK**.

■ In the New Item window, in **Item Name/Number**, enter a short reference to uniquely identify the inventory item.

■ In **Description on Purchase Transactions**, enter any description you like (but remember the description is automatically placed on a purchase order). For example, some people use the vendor's part number and description here to help the vendor identify what you're buying.

■ In **Cost**, enter the cost of the item.

■ In **COGS Account**, enter the appropriate Cost of Goods Sold account.

■ In **Preferred Vendor**, enter the vendor you usually order the material from.

■ In **Description on Sales Transactions** enter a description. This description prefills on your invoices automatically.

■ In **Sales Price**, enter the amount you charge a customer for the item.

■ In **Income Account**, select the appropriate account. You may need to create a new account.

▐ In **Inventory Information**, enter the amounts for **Reorder Point** and **On Hand**. If this is a new item in your inventory, leave **On Hand** and **Total Value** at zero. If this item is already in your inventory, you'll have to fill in these fields to get the inventory up to current levels.

▐ Click **OK** to create the new item.

Creating a Group of Items

You can group items together and refer to them as one unit. For example, you could make a "Plans & Permits" group item by grouping the items for plans, building permits and city license fee. Each item in the Plans & Permits group item has its own cost and selling price. When you choose an item for your estimate or invoice, you simply have to enter a quantity to get the total price for the Plans & Permits group item.

Suppose you want to use two formats for estimates: one that's an expanded detail view for your own job costing, and another that's a condensed version in a summary format that you can print out for a customer. This is especially useful if you've created a large number of subitems for each of your primary items. The condensed format might be appropriate if you're estimating the job on a fixed contract price and don't want to give the customer too much detail.

To create a new group item:

▐ Click **Home**, then click **Items & Services**, or from the **Lists** menu, choose **Item List**. In the Item List window, pull down the **Item** menu and choose **New Item**. See our example in Figure 4-5.

▐ In **Type**, select **Group**. In **Group Name/Number**, enter a name for the new group. In **Description**, enter a short description of the group you're creating.

▐ Select **Print items in group** if you want all the items printed when you print the group item on an invoice. This will list each item in the group individually on the invoice. If you don't select this, only the group item name will appear on the invoice.

▐ Click in the column titled **Item**. Click the down arrow that appears and select the first item you want to include in the group. If you don't enter a quantity for the item, a value of 1 will be assumed.

▐ Add other items as you wish.

▐ Click **OK** to create the group item.

Figure 4-5
Use grouped items to make estimating and invoicing quick and efficient.

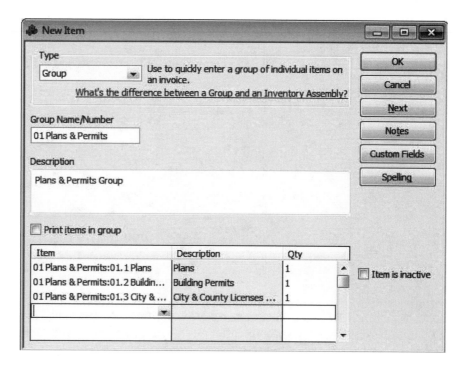

After you've created a group item, you can edit it if you need to. Any item can be in more than one group. To edit a group item:

▌ Click **Home**, then click **Items & Services**, or from the **Lists** menu, choose **Item List**.

▌ In the Item List window, double click the group item you want to edit and make changes in the Edit Item window.

▌ Click **OK**.

Entering Non-Job-Related Items

In the Item List in the *sample.qbw* data file, you'll notice that near the end of the list we have several items that aren't job related. These are items that you may or may not use, such as Deposit, Beginning Balance (Beg Bal), Subtotal and Markup. Use the Deposit item if you accept job deposits from customers *and* you subtract the deposits from the invoice. For more information on job deposits, and using subtotal items, see Chapter 13. Figure 4-6 shows how we created the Deposit item.

Figure 4-6

Set up the Deposit item as a template for customer deposits.

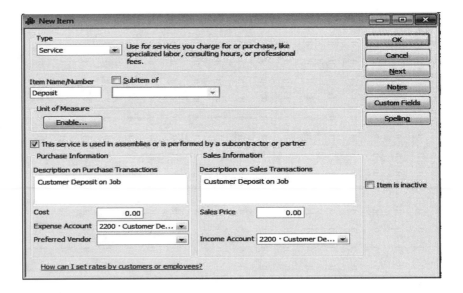

Use the Beg Bal item when entering your outstanding invoices — both Accounts Receivable and Accounts Payable. Figure 4-7 shows how we created the Beg Bal item.

Use the Subtotal item for invoicing customers on a time and materials basis.

▍ Click **Home**, then click **Items & Services**, or from **Lists** menu, select **Item List**.

▍ In the Item List Window, click on the **Item** pull-down menu and select **New**.

▍ In **Type**, select **Subtotal**, see Figure 4-8.

▍ In **Item Name/Number**, type Subtotal.

▍ In **Description**, enter Subtotal.

▍ Click **OK** to create the Subtotal Item.

The Markup item is used for invoicing customers on a time and materials basis when you want to include a separate line item for Markup.

▍ Click **Home**, then click **Items & Services**, or from **Lists** menu, select **Item List.**

▍ In the Item List Window, click the **Item** pull-down menu and select **New.**

▍ In **Type**, select **Other Charge**, see Figure 4-9.

▍ In **Item Name/Number**, type Markup.

▍ In **Description**, enter Markup.

▍ Click **OK** to create the Markup Item.

After you finish setting up the items you need, you're ready to go on to Chapter 5 to set up payroll items.

Figure 4-7
Use the Beginning Balance item to enter outstanding invoices for Accounts Receivable and Accounts Payable.

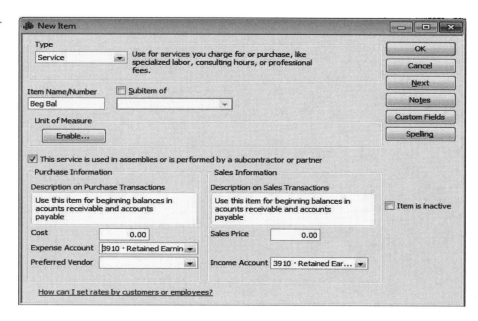

Figure 4-8
The Subtotal item is used on a time and materials invoice, as in Chapter 13.

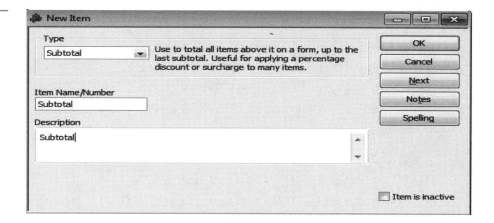

Figure 4-9
Create a Markup item if you will be creating a time and materials invoice, as in Chapter 13.

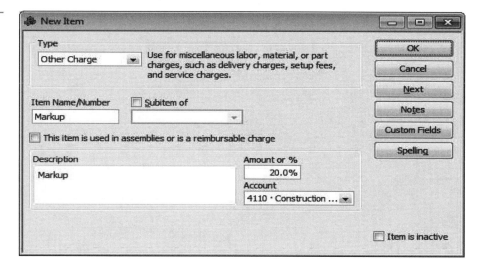

Chapter 5

Payroll Items

In QuickBooks, you must set up payroll items to track wages, employer and employee payroll taxes, employee and employer paid benefits, and any deductions from an employee's check. In this chapter, we'll show you how to set up the payroll items you need. In Chapter 15 (Payroll), we'll show you how to actually use the payroll items to process your payroll.

Throughout the chapter, we'll show you how to link each payroll item to the correct account in your Chart of Accounts to make sure your financial reports will be accurate. The accounts used in our examples are from the Chart of Accounts in the data file *sample.qbw* on the Download. If your Chart of Accounts is different, be sure to link the payroll item to the correct account. Toward the end of this chapter you'll learn how to allocate the owner's time to jobs. If your construction company has an owner(s) who works on jobs but doesn't get paid on payroll, it's important for job costing that his time is allocated to jobs. If not, those jobs will appear more profitable.

Your Payroll Items List

Figure 5-1 shows you the payroll item list from the sample file we included with this book. That list is a good example of what you want your payroll item list to look like when you're done customizing. In the rest of this chapter, we'll be giving you step-by-step instructions on how to set up payroll items for job labor, office wages, officer's salary (for S and C Corporations), workers' compensation, and owner's time to jobs (for Sole Proprietorships and Partnerships).

If you started using QuickBooks by using the Company file that came with this book, you can skip this section. That file already has this payroll item set up for you. But if you didn't, you'll need to follow the directions in this section to set up a new payroll item to track job-related wages correctly. Adding this payroll item for job labor will allocate hourly wages you pay to field employees to the "Job-Related Labor" section of your Chart of Accounts.

To add a new item for Job Labor:

▌ From the **Lists** menu, choose **Payroll Item List**.

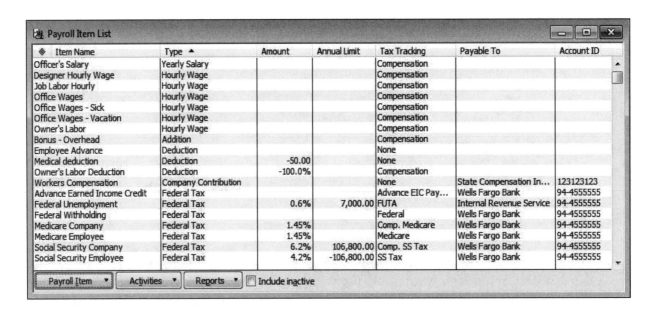

Figure 5-1
This Payroll Item List displays information about the payroll items created in QuickBooks.

▌ In the Payroll Item List window, pull down the **Payroll Item** menu and choose **New**.

▌ In the Select Setup Method window, choose **Custom Setup**.

▌ Click **Next**.

▌ In the Payroll item type window, select **Wage** (**Hourly Wages, Annual Salary, Commission, Bonus**), as shown in Figure 5-2.

▌ Click **Next**.

▌ In the Wages window, select **Hourly Wages**, as shown in Figure 5-3.

▌ Click **Next**.

▌ In the next Wages window, select **Regular Pay**, as shown in Figure 5-4.

▌ Click **Next**.

▌ In the Name used in paychecks and payroll reports window, enter Job Labor Hourly, as shown in Figure 5-5.

▌ Click **Next**. If you type a name that's already a payroll item, a Warning box will appear requesting you use a different name.

▌ In the Expense account window, enter the account number for tracking this expense. It's 5210 - Job Labor (Gross Wages) in our example, shown in Figure 5-6. Be sure you select the proper account from your Chart of Accounts here.

▌ Click **Finish**.

Figure 5-2

You need to create an hourly wage payroll item for each workers' comp classification.

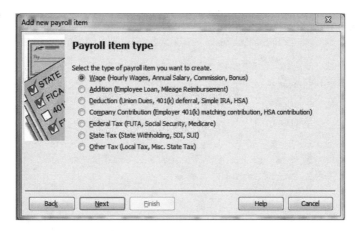

Figure 5-3

In this example, we've specified hourly wage for the workers' comp payroll item we're entering.

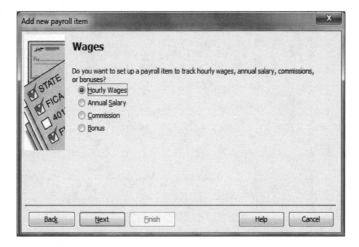

Figure 5-4

Select regular pay for each workers' comp payroll item.

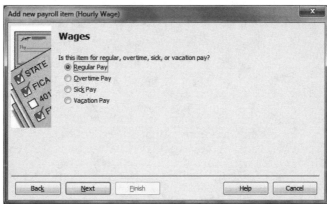

Adding and Linking Payroll Items

We suggest you add new payroll items because the default items don't default to the correct account in the Chart of Accounts. We want to make sure field labor is correctly allocated to job costs and office labor is correctly allocated to an overhead expense.

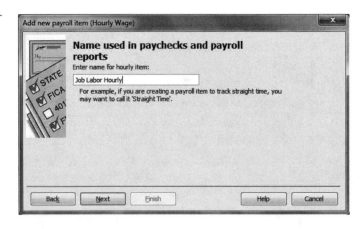

Figure 5-5

It's important to accurately classify each payroll item by name.

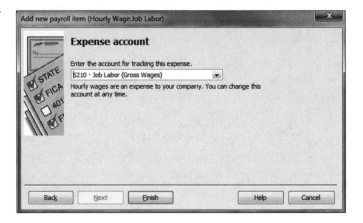

Figure 5-6

In this example, 5210 - Job Labor (Gross Wages) is the correct expense account.

Adding New Payroll Items for Office and Officer's Wages

You should enter a new wages payroll item for overhead or office and officer's wages because you'll want to capture the costs associated with your office and officer's wages payroll. To add a new item for Office Labor:

▌ From the **Lists** menu, choose **Payroll Item List**.

▌ In the Payroll Item List window, pull down the **Payroll Item** menu and choose **New**.

▌ In the Select Setup Method window, choose **Custom Setup**.

▌ Click **Next**.

▌ In the Payroll item type window, select **Wage** (**Hourly Wages, Annual Salary, Commission, Bonus**), as shown in Figure 5-7.

▌ Click **Next**.

▌ In the Wages window, select the appropriate option, keeping in mind that you have to set up a separate payroll item for hourly office and salaried officer's wages, as shown in Figure 5-8.

Figure 5-7

Select a Wage item type for the Office Labor payroll item type.

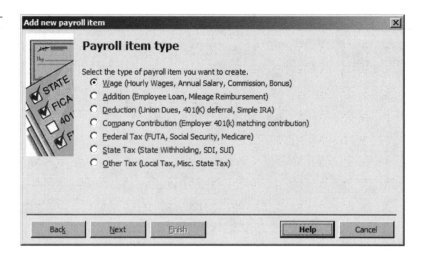

Figure 5-8

Select Hourly Wages for the Office Labor payroll item.

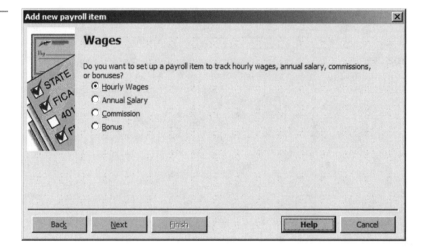

▌ Click **Next**.

▌ In the next Wages window, select **Regular Pay**, as shown in Figure 5-9.

▌ Click **Next**.

▌ In the Name used in paychecks and payroll reports window, enter the name of the office or officer labor item. In our example shown in Figure 5-10, it's Office Wages.

▌ Click **Next**. If you type a name that's already a payroll item, a Warning box will appear requesting you use a different name.

▌ In the Expense account window, enter the account number for tracking this expense. It's 6501 - Payroll (office staff) in our example, shown in Figure 5-11. Be sure you select the proper expense account from your Chart of Accounts. The Expense Account you select here links the payroll item to your Chart of Accounts.

▌ Click **Finish**.

Figure 5-9

Select Regular Pay for the Office Labor payroll item.

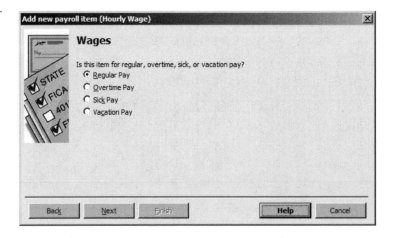

Figure 5-10

Enter the name of the Office Labor payroll item here.

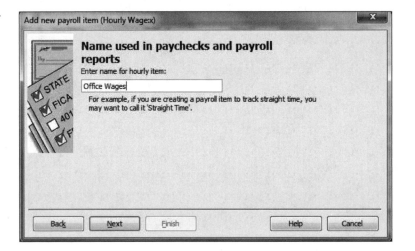

Figure 5-11

In this example, 6501 - Payroll (office staff) is the correct expense account for the Office Labor payroll item.

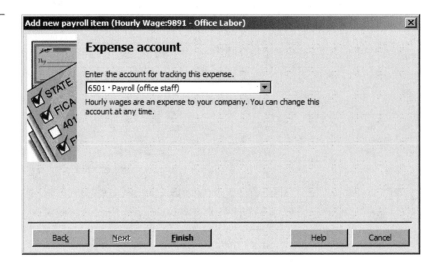

Figure 5-12

Select a Wage item type for the owner/partner payroll item.

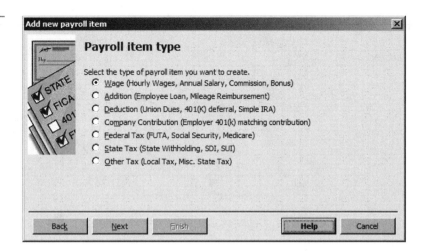

Including Sole Proprietor and Partners' Time Costs in Job Costs

If your company is organized as a sole proprietorship or a partnership, you'll be taking draws instead of issuing payroll checks for yourself or your partner. Because of this, QuickBooks reports won't show any costs for your or your partner's time.

To get these costs into any job cost report, you have to transfer owner or partner time (in dollars) using an hourly wage payroll item and a deduction payroll item. In Chapter 15, Payroll, we'll show you how to actually use the hourly wage item to enter owner or partner time on a timesheet, process payroll, and then deduct the payroll back out of your accounting using the deduction payroll item.

In this section, we'll just show you how to set up the two payroll items you need — Owner's Labor and Owner's Labor Deduction.

Setting Up an Hourly Wage Payroll Item for an Owner or Partner

▌ From the **Lists** menu, choose **Payroll Item List**.

▌ In the Payroll Item List window, pull down the **Payroll Item** menu and choose **New**.

▌ In the Select Setup Method window, choose **Custom Setup**.

▌ Click **Next**.

▌ In the Payroll item type window, select **Wage** (**Hourly Wages, Annual Salary, Commission, Bonus**) as shown in Figure 5-12.

▌ Click **Next**.

Figure 5-13

Select Hourly Wages for the owner/partner payroll item.

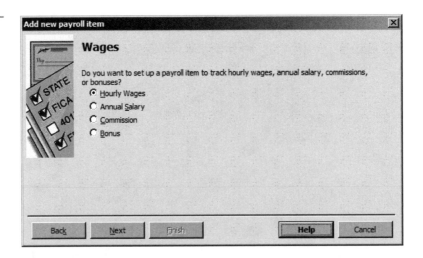

Figure 5-14

Select Regular Pay for the owner/partner payroll item.

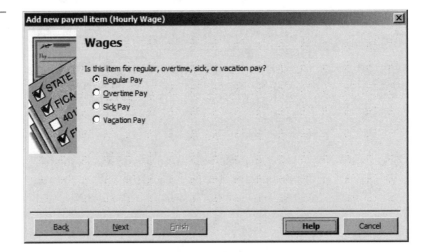

▌ In the Wages window, select **Hourly Wages** as shown in Figure 5-13.

▌ Click **Next**.

▌ In the next Wages window, select **Regular Pay**, as shown in Figure 5-14.

▌ Click **Next**.

▌ In the Name used in paychecks and payroll reports window, enter the name of the overhead labor item. In our example in Figure 5-15, it's Owner's Labor.

▌ Click **Next**.

▌ In the Expense account window, enter the account number for tracking this expense. It's 3999 - Owner's Time to Jobs, in the example in Figure 5-16. Be sure you select the proper expense account from your Chart of Accounts. The Expense Account you select here links the payroll item to your Chart of Accounts.

▌ Click **Finish**.

Figure 5-15

Enter the name of the owner/partner payroll item here.

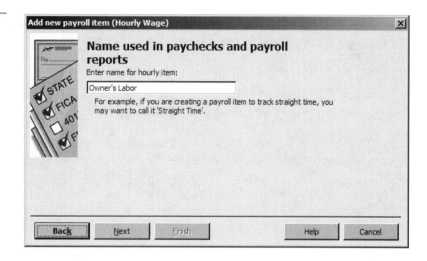

Figure 5-16

It's important to enter the appropriate expense account number to maintain correct accounting records. In this example, 3999 - Owner's Time to Jobs is the correct account.

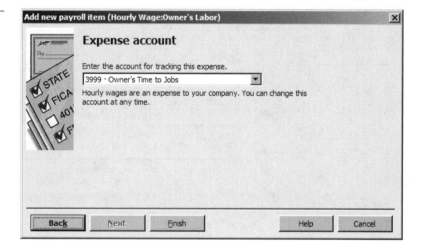

Setting Up a Deduction Payroll Item for an Owner or Partner

When you set up this deduction item, you'll be able to reverse wages and payroll taxes from the owner's check.

- From the **Lists** menu, choose **Payroll Item List**.

- In the Payroll Item List window, pull down the **Payroll Item** menu and choose **New**.

- In the Select Setup Method window, choose **Custom Setup.**

- Click **Next**.

- In the Payroll item type window, select **Deduction (Union Dues, 401(K) deferral, Simple IRA)**, as shown in Figure 5-17.

- Click **Next**.

Figure 5-17

You also need to set up a Deduction payroll item type when you set up an owner/partner payroll item.

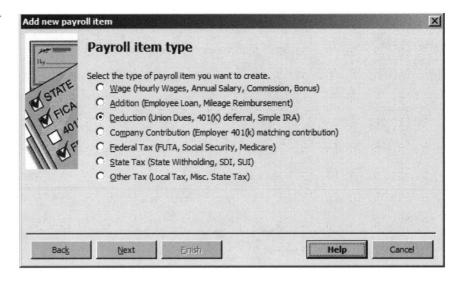

Figure 5-18

Enter the Owner's Labor Deduction in the name field.

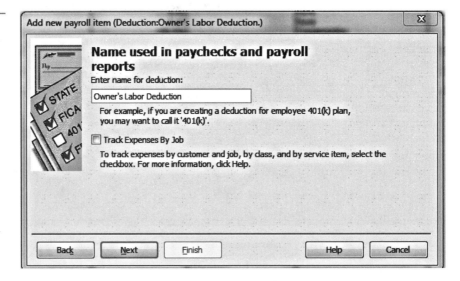

▌ In the Name used in paychecks and payroll reports window, enter the name of the deduction item. In our example shown in Figure 5-18, it's Owner's Labor Deduction.

▌ Click **Next**.

▌ In the Agency for employee-paid liability window, leave the first box blank. In the second box, in this case, you wouldn't use a number, just a description of how you're using this payroll item. In our example, we've entered Deduct Owner's Labor, as shown in Figure 5-19.

▌ In Liability account, enter 3999 - Owner's Time to Jobs.

▌ Click **Next**.

Figure 5-19

Leave the Name field blank, enter a short description in the Number field, and in the Liability Account field enter account number 3999 - Owner's Time to Jobs.

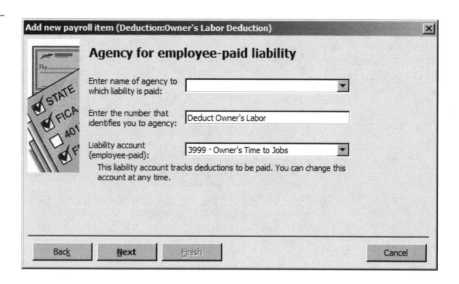

Figure 5-20

Select Compensation from the tax classification list for the Owner's Labor deduction payroll item.

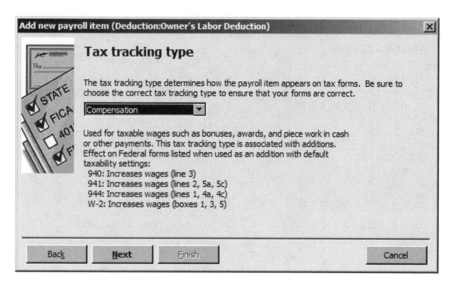

▌ In the Tax tracking type window, select **Compensation** from the pull-down list, as shown in Figure 5-20. This is important!

▌ Click **Next**.

▌ In the Taxes window, because this deduction isn't associated with any taxes, don't select anything, just click **Next**. QuickBooks will give you the Payroll Item Taxability warning box. Ignore the warning and click **Yes**. See Figure 5-21.

Figure 5-21

Leave the tax boxes blank because there's no tax associated with the Owner's Labor deduction.

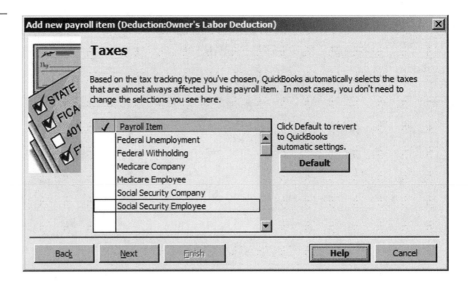

Figure 5-22

Select Neither when you set up the deduction payroll item for owner/partner labor.

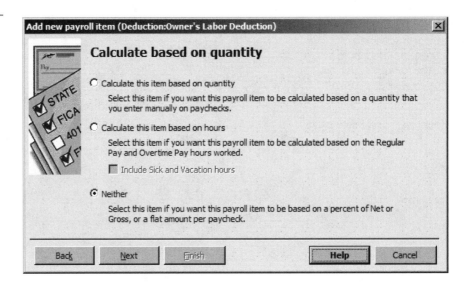

▌ In the Calculate based on quantity window, select **Neither**. See Figure 5-22.

▌ Click **Next**.

▌ In the Default rate and limit window, enter 100% to automatically deduct 100% of the owner's time. See Figure 5-23.

▌ Uncheck the annual limit box.

▌ Click **Finish**.

Figure 5-23

Use a default rate of 100% to automatically deduct the owner's time.

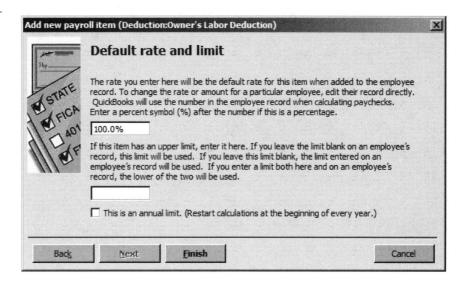

Keep in mind that this chapter just showed you how to set up payroll items. Later in the book, in Chapter 15, we'll show you how to use the payroll items set up here to process a payroll.

After setting up payroll items, you're ready to move on to setting up classes.

Chapter 6

Classes

Classes are one of the "containers" that QuickBooks gives you to earmark transactions and retrieve them later in useful reports. Classes, in fact, are accessible from almost every transaction in QuickBooks. So, when you fill in timecards, you can pick a class to "aim" the time to. Or if you're filling in an invoice, you can pick a class to toss the line item cost into.

Using Classes to Track Cost Categories

We recommend using classes to track Labor, Materials, Subcontractors, Equipment Rentals, and Other.

Your tax preparer can use class reports to get information to prepare your tax return. It doesn't matter whether you're a sole proprietor, partnership, or corporation, your tax return has a section for Cost of Goods Sold. In a construction company, that's a job-related cost. The Cost of Goods Sold section on the tax return asks for a summary of your job costs by Labor, Materials, Subcontractors, Equipment Rental, and Other. If you break out your classes into these categories, you can easily produce the reports your tax preparer will need.

We've included a memorized report named "Job Cost Class Report" in the *sample.qbw* file. This report shows total Revenue, Labor, Materials, Subcontractors, and Other subtotaled for the year. Figure 6-1 shows part of a report on the class "Material Costs — Job Related." In Chapter 17 (Reports), we'll show you how to access this report.

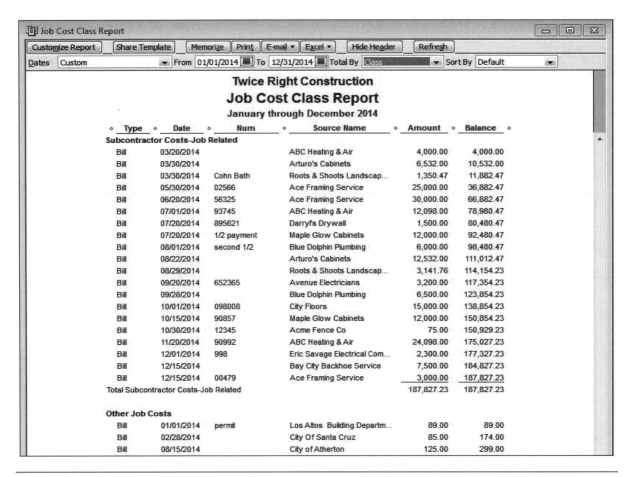

Figure 6-1
Part of a memorized Job Cost Class Report on the class Material Costs — Job Related.

How to Create a Class

Before we tell you how to create a class, you need to make sure the Class Tracking Preference is turned on. To do this:

▌ From the **Edit** menu, choose **Preferences** and click the **Accounting** icon.

▌ On the Company Preferences tab, select **Use class tracking**.

▌ Click **OK**.

Now to create a class:

▌ From the **Lists** menu, choose **Class List**. See Figure 6-2.

▌ In the Class List window, pull down the **Class** menu and choose **New**.

▌ Enter a name for the new class.

Figure 6-2

You can use the Class List provided in the company.qbw file as a model for your business.

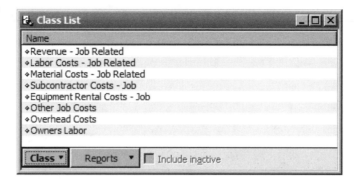

Figure 6-3

You can create subclasses to get a more detailed breakdown of a class.

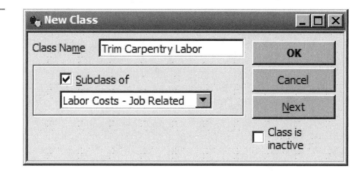

If you want more detailed information — a breakdown on labor, perhaps — you can define this new class as a subclass of another class. For instance, you might want to track a specific type of labor, such as trim carpentry, to see if it's coming in as estimated. Just tell your trim carpenters to accurately record the time they spend doing casing and base, and enter the time in a subclass you set up to track that task. Then you can pull up a report that calculates the total amount of time/money spent doing casing and base. If you divide the total amount of casing and base installed by the cost of doing it, you'll get a unit cost for placing casing and base. The next time you bid casing and base, you'll have a better unit cost and should be able to make more money on that phase of your business.

To create a subclass as shown in Figure 6-3:

▍ Click the box in front of **Subclass of** and enter the appropriate class name.

You'll also notice Class is inactive in the New Class window (see Figure 6-2). If you don't want a class to appear in the Class List, you can check this field to keep it from appearing in the list. To make the class active again, click Include inactive in the Class List window. Inactive classes are marked with a small "x" icon beside the class name. Click this icon to activate the class again.

▍ Click **OK** to create the new class as a subclass.

After you finish setting up the classes you want to use, move on to the next chapter where we'll show you how to set up customers and jobs.

Chapter 7

Customers and Jobs

QuickBooks tracks jobs by customer — but it's important to understand that a customer can have more than one job. You can set up a main job, then track changes by setting up additional jobs using a change order number. Or you may do more than one job for a customer and want to keep them separate. Then you can assign the jobs different names, such as Rachel Olsen: Bathroom Addition and Rachel Olsen: Guest Cottage. First set up the customer, then add the job or jobs.

How to Set Up a Customer

QuickBooks keeps your customer information in the Customer Center. See Figure 7-1.

Use the Customer Center to keep track of a customer's billing and shipping address, and business, home, and fax telephone numbers. The billing address might be the existing residence and the shipping address might be the address of the new residence if you're building a new home for the client.

To enter a customer:

▌ Click the **Customer Center** icon on the menu bar, or from the **Customers** menu, choose **Customer Center**.

▌ In the Customer Center window, click **New Customer & Job**, then **New Customer**.

▌ Enter the customer name. See Figure 7-2. Enter the last name first if you'd like to sort your list alphabetically by last name. Fill in the rest of the fields in the **Address Info** tab.

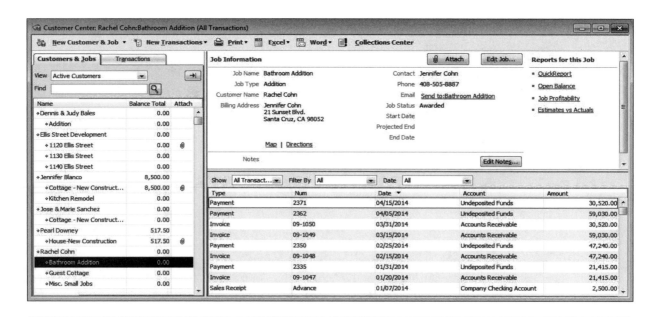

Figure 7-1

The Customer Center window displays all your existing customers and their associated jobs.

Figure 7-2

Use the Address Info tab to make additions or changes to a customer's name, contact, phone, or address.

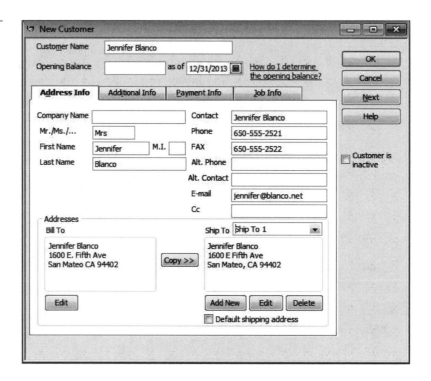

Figure 7-3

The Additional Info tab lets you track more details about a customer. You can even create custom fields specific to your needs here.

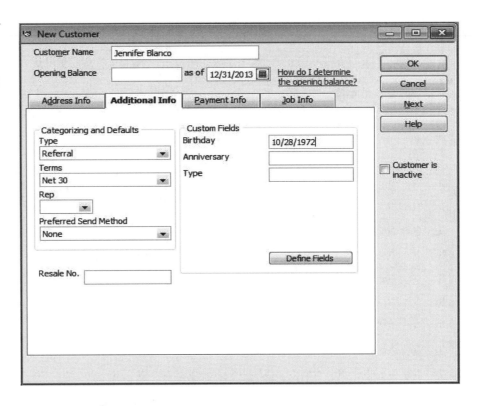

The Additional Info Tab

In the Additional Info tab window, you'll find drop-down lists for Customer Type, Terms, and Rep. You can use Customer Type as a "container" to track customers based on something that's meaningful to you. For example, you could record how the customer got your company's name — newspaper ad, referral, Chamber of Commerce, etc. See Figure 7-3.

▌ In **Type**, select the method your customer used to get your name (used to track marketing efforts). In our example, we used **Referral**.

▌ In **Terms**, select the terms of credit you wish to offer the customer and what you want printed on the invoice.

▌ In **Rep**, you can assign a salesperson to the customer and track sales by representative. If you don't have salespersons, enter the project manager's initials to track who is responsible for the job. The rep's initials can be printed on invoices.

You can also create and use custom fields in this window. You can track information about a customer, such as their birthday or anniversary, so you can do some "target" marketing with a birthday card or gift. You might also use this section to record the type of client. Some contractors track whether a client is "from Hell" or "from Heaven." Naturally, you'd charge those categorized as "from Hell" more for your efforts.

Figure 7-4
Use the Set up Custom Fields for Names window to enter a label for a custom field and specify if it will be used for customers, vendors, or employees.

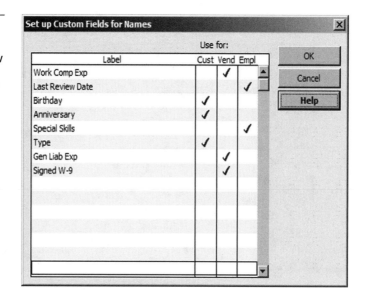

To create a custom field:

▌ In the Custom Fields area, click **Define Fields**.

▌ In the Set up Custom Fields for Names window, under **Label**, enter the field names you want to create. See Figure 7-4.

▌ Click to place a checkmark in the column where you'll be using this field (Customers & Jobs, Vendors, Employees).

▌ Click **OK** to create the new fields.

The Payment Info Tab

You can enter customer payment information in the Payment Info tab window. See Figure 7-5. If you require your customers to pay by credit card (very rare in construction), you can enter the customer's credit card in formation on this screen. If you enter your customer's credit card number and expiration date in QuickBooks, you should immediately set up password protection and make sure that only a trusted few have access to viewing customer payment information.

▌ Click the **Payment Info** tab of the New Customer window to fill in more information about a customer.

▌ In **Account No.**, enter the account number or the PO number your customer requested you put on each invoice you send to them.

Figure 7-5

Enter customer payment information in the Payment Info tab window.

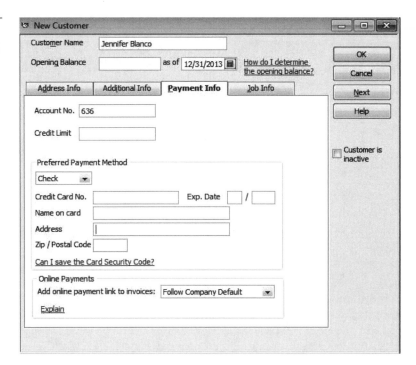

- Skip the Job Info tab when you're entering information for a new customer. We'll cover it in the next section.

- Click **OK** to enter the new customer.

Adding a Job for a Customer

Whether you do one or more jobs for a customer, it's a good idea to set up each job separately. For example, if Twice Right remodels a kitchen for Jennifer Blanco, and then later builds her a guest cottage, both the kitchen and the guest cottage are separate jobs, but they should both be attached to the same customer — Jennifer Blanco. To add a job for a customer:

- In the Customer Center window, right click the customer's name and choose **Add Job**.

- Enter a job name in the box next to **Job Name** on the New Job window. In our example, we entered Cottage — New Construction.

- Change information on the **Address Info** and **Additional Info** tabs if necessary.

- Click the **Job Info** tab, shown in Figure 7-6.

Figure 7-6

Use the Job Info tab to record all the pertinent information for a particular job.

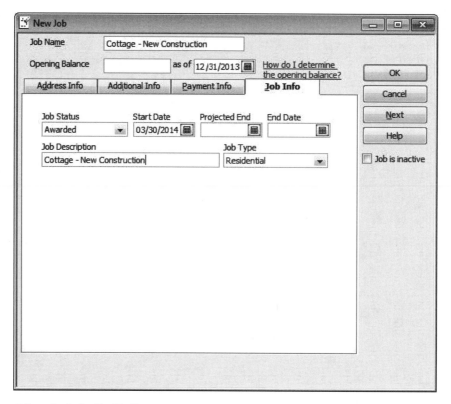

The Job Info Tab

You can enter Job Status, Start Date, Projected End, End Date, Job Description, and Job Type on the Job Info tab.

The Job Status box lets you track the status of your jobs. Pending, Awarded, In progress, Closed, Not awarded, and None are your choices. You can do a report on jobs Pending, or jobs Not awarded. A report on Not awarded vs. all your jobs will tell you the ratio of jobs you're getting to the jobs you're bidding. Use this information when you create your marketing budget. Figure 7-6 shows a Job Info tab window.

▌ From the pull-down Job Status list, choose the status of the job.

▌ In **Start Date**, enter the start date for the job.

▌ In **Projected End**, enter the projected end date for the job.

▌ In **End Date**, enter the actual date the job ended. (You'll need to come back later and fill this in.)

▌ In **Job Description**, enter the description for the job. You would fill this in if you use job numbers instead of names in the Job Name field.

The Job Type box in the Job Info tab window has a drop-down list from which you can choose a job type. For example, you could set up a job type such as Residential, Commercial, or Remodel, with subtypes for Contract

Figure 7-7

You specify a name for a new job type in the New Job Type window.

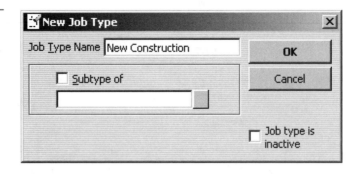

Figure 7-8

Use subtypes to get a detailed breakdown of a job type.

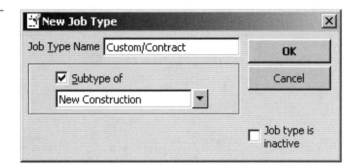

or Speculation. Then, whenever you get a new job, you can choose which job type the job falls under. Later (at year's end, for example) you can sort jobs by type to make a report that evaluates profitability by job type. Information like this can help you decide whether or not to continue to do one type of work. If your commercial jobs aren't as profitable as your residential work, you might decide to stop bidding commercial jobs.

Setting Up a New Job Type

To set up a new job type:

▌ From the drop down **Job Type** list in the Job Info tab window, choose **Add New**.

▌ In the New Job Type window, in **Job Type Name**, enter the new job type name. See Figure 7-7.

▌ If you want the new job type to be a subtype of another job type, click **Subtype of** and enter the appropriate job type. See Figure 7-8.

▌ Click **OK** to enter the new job type and return to the New Job window.

▌ Click **OK** in the New Job window to add the job for the customer.

▌ Click the **X** in the upper right of this window to close the Customer Center.

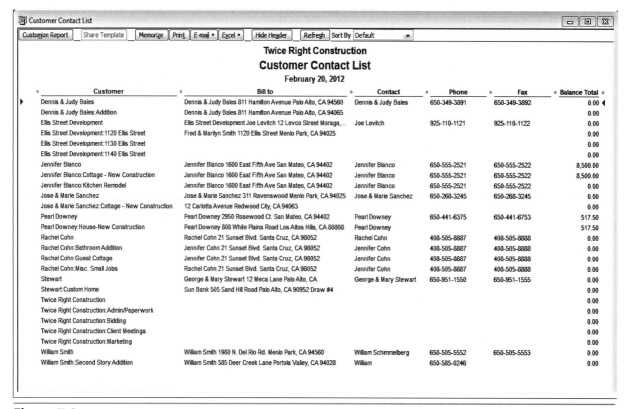

Figure 7-9
You can create and export a Customer Contact List report.

Exporting or Printing Your Customer List

You can export your Customer:Job list to a program such as Excel, ACT, or any other program that can import delimited text. You can also print out reports for your field personnel.

To run a customer report:

❚ From the **Reports** menu, choose **Customers & Receivables**, then **Customer Contact List.**

❚ In the Modify Report window, select the columns you want to display on your report.

❚ Click **OK**.

To export a customer list:

❚ Create a Contact List report as outlined above.

❚ In the Customer Contact List report window, click **Export** (Figure 7-9).

❚ Select **Create New Worksheet**.

❚ Select the export options you wish to use and click **Export**.

Now that you've finished entering your customers and jobs, let's move on to Chapter 8 to set up your vendors and subcontractors.

Vendors and Subcontractors

In QuickBooks, there's no difference between a subcontractor and a vendor. Whether they supply you with materials, services, or both, you set up vendors and subs the same way. But how you set them up will determine how you can create your reports on them. It's important to closely follow our instructions for setting up vendors, especially when setting up 1099 vendors.

Setting Up 1099 Vendors

You're required to annually report, on IRS Form 1099, the total paid to each vendor that supplied over $600 of labor. If you send 1099-MISC forms to any vendors or subcontractors, you can set up QuickBooks to track all 1099-related payments. Then at the end of the year, QuickBooks can print your 1099-MISC forms.

To set up QuickBooks to track 1099s, you need to set the Tax:1099 preference. If you haven't previously linked your 1099 accounts, refer back to pages 51-52 of the Preferences chapter to learn how to do it.

To create a new 1099 vendor:

▌ Click the **Vendor Center** icon on the menu bar, or from the **Vendors** menu, choose **Vendor Center**. See Figure 8-1.

▌ In the Vendor Center window, click **New Vendor**. Figures 8-2 and 8-3 show New Vendor windows for Eric Savage Electrical Company.

▌ In **Vendor Name**, enter the name as you want it to appear in the QuickBooks vendor list.

▌ In **Company Name**, enter the vendor name. This name won't appear on the 1099 form if you also fill in **First Name**, **M.I.**, and **Last Name**.

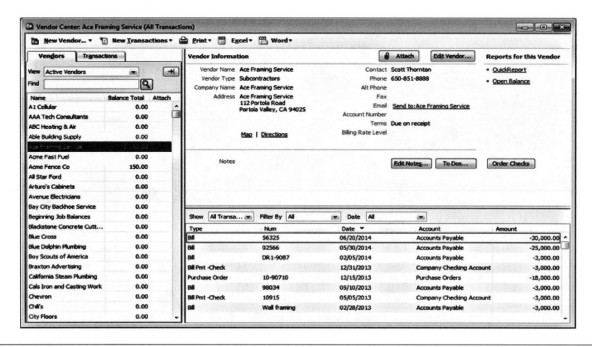

Figure 8-1

The Vendor Center window displays each vendor you have entered into QuickBooks and the amount you owe each vendor.

Figure 8-2

Use the Address Info tab to add or change a vendor's name, contact, phone, or address.

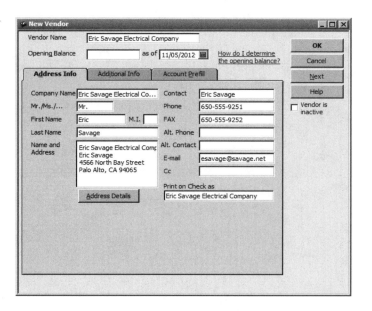

If the vendor is a sole proprietor, you have to print the person's name, not the company name, on the 1099. Because of this, you'll need to enter the person's legal name in the First Name, M.I., and Last Name fields. If the vendor's ownership is classified as a partnership, don't fill in the First

Figure 8-3

Use the Additional Info tab to track more details about a vendor. You can also create custom fields specific to your needs here.

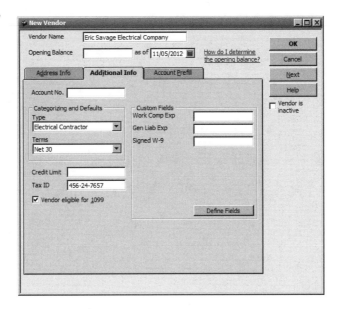

Name, M.I., or Last Name fields (you can enter a contact name in the contact field). Enter the legal partnership name in the Company Name field. If the vendor is incorporated you don't have to send them a 1099.

If part of the address in the Address field includes a name on line 2 or below, be sure the name is identical to the Company Name field or the First Name, M.I., and Last Name fields. Otherwise, it will print as part of the address on the 1099 form.

▌ Be sure you enter the company's two-letter state abbreviation and zip code. Click the **Address Details** button to enter this information.

▌ Click **OK.**

▌ Click the **Additional Info** tab. See Figure 8-3.

▌ Fill in **Tax ID**. If the vendor is a sole proprietor, enter the vendor's Social Security Number or EIN (employer identification number).

▌ Select **Vendor eligible for 1099**.

▌ Fill in **Account No.** if you wish. If you have an account number with a vendor, you can enter it here and it'll automatically be printed in the Memo field on each check to the vendor.

You can set up custom fields on the Additional Info tab. You may want to add custom fields to track workers' comp and general liability insurance expiration dates, and one to indicate if you've received a signed W-9 from the vendor. See Figure 8-3.

Figure 8-4

Use the Set up Custom Fields for Names window to enter a label for a custom field and specify if the custom field will be used for customers, vendors, or employees.

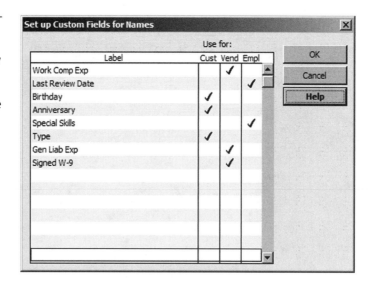

To create a custom field:

▌ In the Custom Fields area of the Additional Info tab window, click **Define Fields**.

▌ In the Set up Custom Fields for Names window, under **Label**, enter the field names you'd like to create. See Figure 8-4.

▌ In the columns to the right, check the boxes to select whether the label is used for customers, vendors, or employees.

▌ Click **OK** to create the new labels.

If you're using QuickBooks Premier Contractor Edition, there's no need to create custom expiration dates. There are already two fields on the Additional Info tab: Work Comp Expires and Gen Liability Expires. Simply enter the expiration dates and, when entering transactions, you'll be notified if the insurance expiration dates have passed. See Figure 8-5.

The Account Prefill tab is only used for vendors whose costs are non-job related (overhead costs), such as a computer consultant or a marketing firm. See Figure 8-6.

Now you're ready to save all information about the vendor:

▌ Click **OK**.

Setting Up a Non-1099 Vendor

Non-1099 vendors are set up the same as 1099 vendors with these two exceptions: First, you don't have to enter a tax ID number. Second, you don't select Vendor eligible for 1099 in the Additional Info tab.

Figure 8-5

QuickBooks Premier Contractor Edition has built-in fields for Work Comp and General Liability expiration dates.

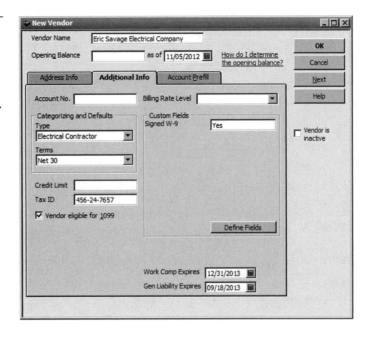

Figure 8-6

Use the Account Prefill tab only for non-1099 vendors.

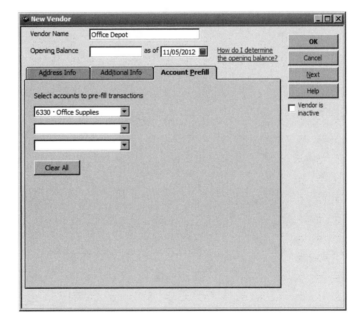

You can opt to "prefill" expense accounts when entering transactions. This adds speed and accuracy to your data entry.

Click the Account Prefill tab (Figure 8-6). Here, you can choose up to three expense accounts per vendor, that will automatically appear when you enter vendor bills and write checks.

Now that you've finished setting up your vendors, let's set up your employees. If you don't have employees, skip Chapter 9 and move on to Chapter 10 where we will cover Opening Balances.

Employees

There are two instances when you'll want to set up employees in QuickBooks:

▌ if your company has employees and you process your own payroll

▌ if you want to track employee time by job, and your payroll is processed by an outside service

Setting Up Your Employee List

The Employee Center includes a listing of every employee record you enter into QuickBooks. Each employee's record contains all the information you need to calculate payroll, whether the employee is on monthly salary or getting a weekly paycheck based on hours worked.

The Payroll module in QuickBooks is very flexible. You can use it to figure out all common payroll items such as federal taxes, FUTA, Social Security, Medicare, state unemployment insurance, and state disability. Naturally, you can track, calculate, and print W2s, 1099s, and Forms 940 and 941. You can also track sick time and vacation pay and create your own custom additions and deductions.

It's easy to add, edit, or delete employees from the Employee Center. To add employees, use the employee template you set up in the Payroll and Employees preference in the Employee Defaults window. The template contains the information common to all employees, so you only have to enter individual employee information to set up a new employee. If an employee goes out on disability or maternity leave, you can designate him/her as "Inactive."

To set up an employee:

▌ Click the **Employee Center** icon in the menu bar, or from the **Employees** menu, choose **Employee Center**. See Figure 9-1.

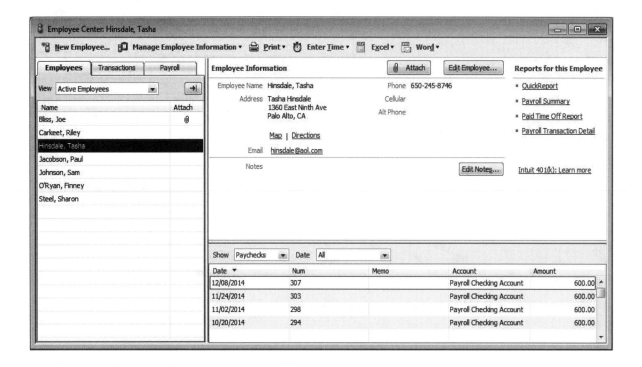

Figure 9-1
The Employee Center window displays the Social Security number and the name of every employee you've entered into QuickBooks.

▌ In the Employee Center window, click **New Employee**. The figures in this chapter show how we entered new employee Joe Bliss. You can use this as an example for entering your employees.

Using the Personal Tab

▌ Fill in **Mr./Ms.**, **First Name**, **M.I.**, and **Last Name**. See Figure 9-2.

▌ In **Print on Checks as**, enter the name as you want it to appear on the employee's paycheck and W2.

▌ In **SS No.**, be sure you enter the employee's Social Security number correctly. It's used on quarterly reports and W2s.

▌ The **Gender** and **Date of Birth** fields are for reference only. You use them to store employee information.

Using the Address and Contact Tab

▌ Be sure you enter the employee's address, city, two-letter state abbreviation and zip code.

▌ **Phone**, **Cellular**, **Alt. Phone**, **Fax**, **E-mail** and **Pager** fields are also for reference only. Use them to store employee information.

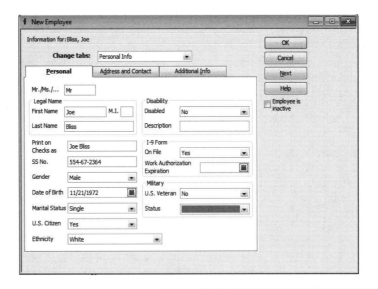

Figure 9-2
Use the Personal tab to add or change an employee's name, Social Security number, etc.

Using the Additional Info Tab

Use **Custom Fields** to create new fields to collect additional data for all your employee records. QuickBooks treats the information you enter in a custom field the same way it treats information entered into any other field. If you export a list that contains data in custom fields, QuickBooks exports that data along with the other data from the list. Then you can sort the exported field and use it to create reports that QuickBooks doesn't provide.

Here are examples of some employee custom fields you may want to create:

▌ last review date

▌ productivity numbers

▌ goals

▌ special skills

To create a custom field:

▌ In the New Employee window, click the **Additional Info** tab. See Figure 9-3.

▌ In the Custom Fields area, click **Define Fields**. See Figure 9-3. NOTE: You won't see the Billing Rate Level box if you're not using QuickBooks Premier or Enterprise.

▌ In the Set up Custom Fields for Names window, under **Label**, enter the field names you want to create. See Figure 9-4.

▌ Click in the column under Empl (Employee) to place a checkmark.

▌ Click **OK** to create the new fields.

Figure 9-3
Use the Additional Info tab to track more details about an employee. Create custom fields you need here.

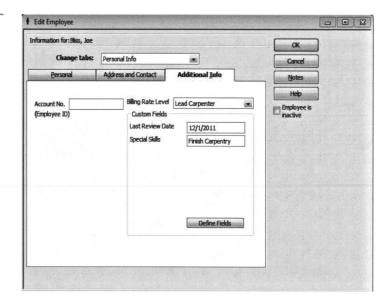

Figure 9-4
Use the Set up Custom Fields for Names window to enter a label for a custom field and specify if it will be used for customers, vendors, or employees.

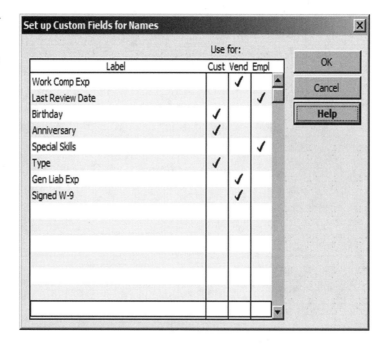

Using the Payroll Info Tab

Use the Payroll Info tab window to set up information for each employee:

- earnings
- additions, deductions, and company contributions
- pay period

Figure 9-5

Use the Payroll Info tab to record earning information, pay period frequency, additions, deductions, company contributions, and tax-related information.

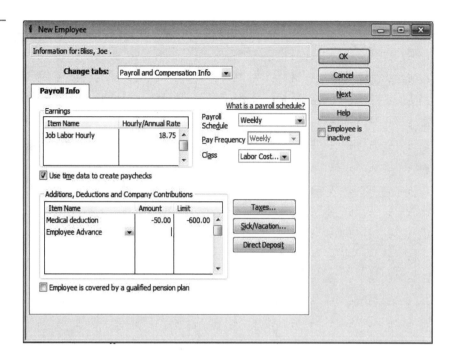

- class
- taxes
- sick/vacation
- direct deposit

To get to the Payroll Info tab window:

- In the New Employee window, from the **Change tabs** drop-down list, select **Payroll and Compensation Info**. See Figure 9-5.

- Under **Earnings**, select all payroll items from the drop-down list that apply to the employee. (See Chapter 5 if you haven't set up payroll items.)

- Select an **Hourly/Annual Rate** for the employee. Realize that the payroll item determines where the payroll expense is posted, and the hourly/annual rates are the actual base wage being used in calculating the payroll as well as the job costing. For **Hourly**, enter in the hourly rate. For **Annual Rate**, enter annual salary.

- Select the **Use time data to create paychecks** box if you plan on using the QuickBooks timecard to enter the employee's time. If you select this button, the timecard information entered will flow into the paycheck for this employee.

- Under Additions, Deductions, and Company Contributions, select all payroll items that apply to the employee.

- Select the appropriate **Pay Frequency** for the employee.

Figure 9-6

Use the Federal, State and Other tabs to specify tax information for each employee.

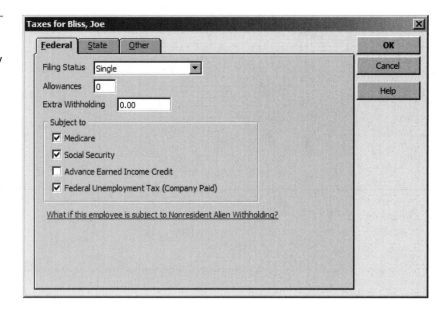

Figure 9-7

For eligible employees, use the Sick & Vacation window to track available hours and accrual information.

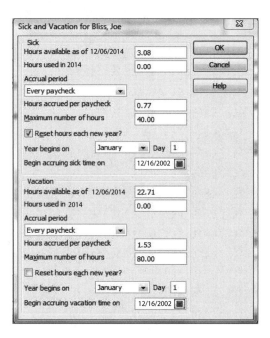

▌ Click **Taxes** and make sure you select all the appropriate boxes. See the example in Figure 9-6. Click **OK**.

▌ Click **Sick/Vacation** if the employee is eligible for sick or vacation pay. See the example in Figure 9-7. Click **OK**.

▌ If you've subscribed to QuickBook's payroll service, click **Direct Deposit** to set up direct deposit of the employee's pay if appropriate, as seen in Figure 9-5. Click **OK**.

Figure 9-8

Set up payroll information to record job costs for a sole proprietor or partner.

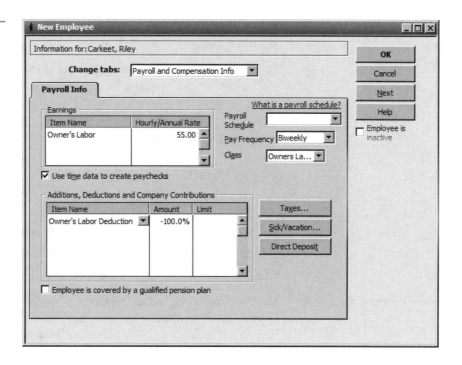

Now you're ready to save all information about the employee:

▌ In the New Employee window, click **OK**.

Setting up a Sole Proprietor/Partner (Employee) Card

In Chapter 5 we discussed how to include a sole proprietor or partner's time in job cost reports. In this section, we'll walk you through setting up the employee card for the sole proprietor or partner. Keep in mind that a sole proprietor or partner (non-incorporated business) doesn't get paid through payroll; instead, they take money out of the business in the form of a withdrawal. You'll set up an employee card if the owner works on jobs and wants to track the costs. In Chapter 15 we'll walk you through processing a zero payroll check to the owner (in order to job cost the owner's time to a job).

To set up a sole proprietor/partner employee card:

▌ In the **Employee Center** window, click **New Employee**. Refer back to Figure 9-1.

▌ Enter the Employee information on the Personal, Address and Contact, and Additional Info tabs. Refer to Figures 9-2 and 9-3.

▌ In **Change tabs**, select **Payroll and Compensation Info**. See Figure 9-8.

▌ In the **Earnings** box, select **Owner's Labor** (if you don't see it in the list refer back to Chapter 5, Payroll Items).

▌ In **Hourly/Annual** rate, enter the amount you would pay someone else with the same qualifications to do the work the owner performs on the job. The rate should be per hour including labor burden. Labor burden is the cost of payroll taxes, workers' comp and employee benefits. Do not enter in the amount the owner withdraws; instead you should enter the amount you would have to pay someone else to do that job. Later, when you're analyzing your job costs reports, you'll want to know which jobs are profitable, including all the time the owner put into the job.

▌ In **Class**, select **Owner's Labor**. If it doesn't appear in your list, you should add it now. See Chapter 6 for more information about classes.

▌ Check the box next to **Use time data to create paychecks**.

▌ Under Additions, Deductions and Company Contributions, enter **Owner's Labor Deduction** (if it doesn't appear in your list, see Chapter 5 to learn how to enter it). In **Amount**, enter 100%. It will automatically appear as negative 100% (–100%). You'll learn more about why this is important in Chapter 15.

▌ Click **OK** to save the employee information.

Now that you've finished setting up customers, jobs, vendors, and employees, it's time to tell QuickBooks what your opening balance is for each of your accounts. Chapter 10, Opening Balances, will show you how to enter those balances.

Chapter 10

Opening Balances

Getting your computerized accounting system into balance can be a trying experience. If you're already using a computerized accounting system, make sure your balances are accurate before transferring them over to QuickBooks.

Keep in mind when you begin using QuickBooks that you don't have to start with opening balances and can always go back and change your beginning balances.

Entering Opening Balances in QuickBooks

A journal entry is used to get your beginning balances into QuickBooks. If you don't know what your beginning balances are, your accountant or tax preparer can help you arrive at those numbers.

▎ From the **Company** menu, choose **Make General Journal Entries** to get the General Journal entry window.

▎ Enter **Asset**, **Liability**, and **Capital** account balances. Keep in mind that Assets usually have debit balances (except accumulated depreciation), while Liabilities and Capital have credit balances. See Figure 10-1.

> **Note:** If you're starting to use QuickBooks at the beginning of your fiscal year, you enter only Asset, Liability, and Capital account balances. Don't enter beginning income, cost of goods sold, or expense account balances.

Figure 10-1

This is an example journal entry to get beginning balances into QuickBooks.

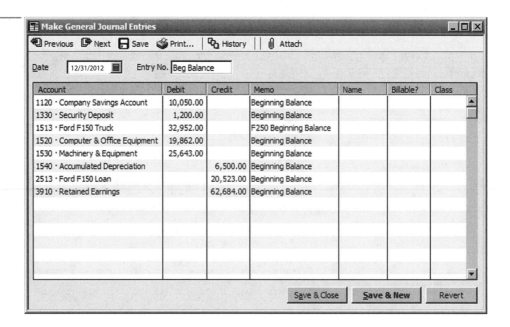

When you finish, print a Balance Sheet to make sure everything balances. To print a Balance Sheet:

▌ Click **Home**, then click **Chart of Accounts**, or from the **Lists** menu, choose **Chart of Accounts**.

▌ In the Chart of Accounts window, pull down the **Reports** menu, choose **Report on All Accounts**, then **Balance Sheet**, and then **Standard**. The date of the report should be the date you started using QuickBooks.

> **Note:** Don't enter Accounts Receivable or Accounts Payable balances. They'll come in automatically when you enter the outstanding invoices (receivables) and outstanding bills (payables).

Entering Invoices for Accounts Receivable

Accounts Receivable is money your customers owe you. If you've been using another accounting system, you should be able to print out a report with each customer's name, date of each outstanding invoice, invoice number, and the amount due.

Figure 10-2

Use the Create Invoices window to enter each outstanding invoice to make sure your Accounts Receivable balance is correct.

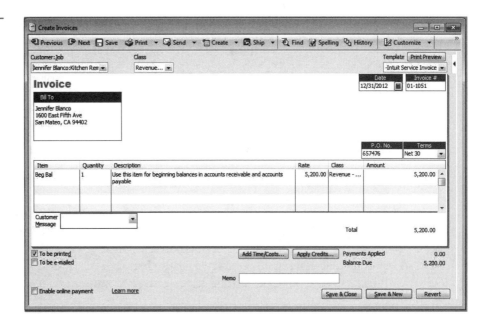

Enter each outstanding Accounts Receivable invoice as an Intuit Service Invoice with the date of the original invoice, *not* the date you enter the invoice. You won't be sending out these invoices — they're simply a way to enter your Accounts Receivable balances. In Figure 10-2, we've entered a beginning balance for Jennifer Blanco.

To enter an outstanding customer invoice:

▌ Click **Home**, then click **Create Invoices**, or from the **Customers** menu, choose **Create Invoices**.

▌ In **Template**, select **Intuit Service Invoice** from the drop-down list.

▌ In **Customer:Job**, select the customer's name and job. If you entered an estimate for this job, you'll see the Available Estimates dialog box. Click **Cancel** to close the dialog box.

▌ In **Date**, enter the original date of the invoice, not the current date.

▌ In **Invoice #**, enter the original invoice number.

▌ In **P.O. No.**, enter the purchase order number for the invoice or job if the customer gave you one.

▌ In **Terms**, select the appropriate terms for the invoice from the drop-down list.

▌ Click in the **Item** column.

▌ From the pull-down Item list, select **Beg Bal**.

▌ In **Rate**, enter the amount of the invoice.

▌ Click **Save & Close**.

Entering Bills for Accounts Payable

Accounts Payable is money you owe to vendors (and subcontractors). If you've been using another accounting system, you should be able to print out a report with the vendor's name, date of each outstanding bill, bill number, and the amount due and transfer the information to QuickBooks. Enter each outstanding Accounts Payable bill with the date of the original bill, *not* the date you enter the bill. In Figure 10-3, we've entered an outstanding bill from Eric Savage Electrical Company.

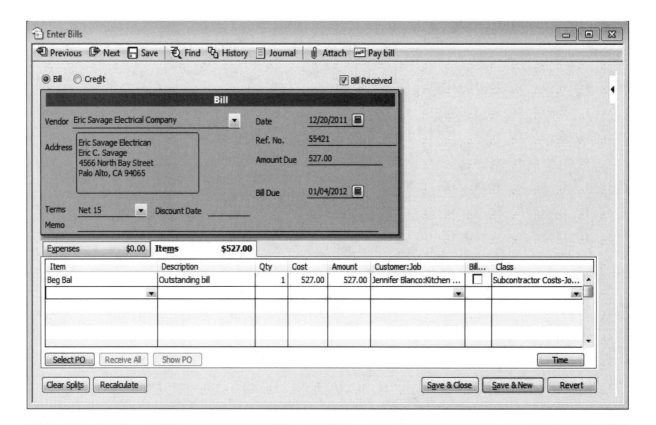

Figure 10-3

Use the Enter Bills window to enter each outstanding bill to make sure your Accounts Payable balance is correct.

To enter vendor outstanding bills:

▌ Click **Home**, then click the **Enter Bills** icon, or from the **Vendors** menu, choose **Enter Bills**.

▌ In **Vendor**, from the pull-down list, select the vendor's name.

▌ In **Date**, enter the date of the bill, *not* the current date.

▌ In **Ref. No.**, enter the vendor's invoice/bill number.

▌ In **Amount Due**, enter the full amount of the bill (including tax, shipping, etc.).

▌ In **Terms**, select the appropriate terms for the bill from the drop-down list.

▌ Click the **Items** tab.

▌ Click in the **Item** column.

▌ From the Item pull-down list, select **Beg Bal.** Enter **Qty**, **Cost**, **Customer:Job**, and **Class**.

▌ If the amount is going to be billed to your customer, check the box in the Billable column.

▌ Click **Save & Close**.

Beginning Job Balances

This section covers how to enter beginning job balances by item (job phase) for jobs that are still in progress. If you don't enter beginning job balances, job costs reports won't be accurate for jobs that have costs prior to the start of using QuickBooks.

To enter beginning job balances:

1. Click **Home**, then click **Enter Bills**. Or, from the Vendors menu, choose **Enter Bills**.

2. In the **Vendor** field, enter **Beginning Job Balances**. Press the **Tab** key. You'll be prompted to add a new vendor. Click **Quick Add**.

3. At **Date**, enter the date one day prior to starting to use QuickBooks. In our example, we started using QuickBooks on 1/1/12, so we enter beginning job balances with the date 12/31/11.

4. In **Ref No**, enter **Beg Bal Job** and the job name or number.

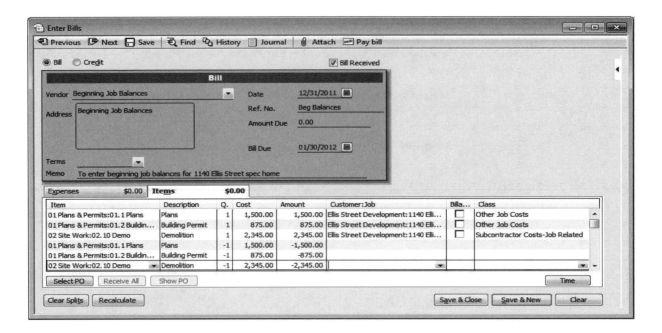

Figure 10-4

Enter each item twice - once to bring in the job balances and again, with a negative quantity, to clear the balances from your accounting.

5. In **Memo**, enter something similar to the example in Figure 10-4.

6. Click the **Items** tab.

7. Enter the balances by item for this job. Include the Customer:Job and Class information.

8. Make sure the **Billable?** field is not checked.

9. Enter the balances by item, again, just as you did above only this time enter the quantity as a negative amount. Leave Customer:Job and Class blank. This will clear out accounting, but leave the job information intact.

10. Make sure the **Amount Due** on the bill is 0. Click **Save & Close**.

11. Use this same method for all your jobs that had balances prior to the date you started to use QuickBooks.

Now you've set up opening balances in QuickBooks and you should be ready to enter new transactions in your company's data file. Remember though, you can always go back and make changes to the file if you find that something is out of balance.

Chapter 11

Organizing Work Flow

Even with the latest computer hardware and all the power of QuickBooks, you still may not have all the data you need. Why? Because to get the most from your system, you need to have an organized flow of information from the field, through the office, to your computer system. For QuickBooks to do its job you'll need to study — and possibly change — how work flows at your business.

For example, QuickBooks has a flexible and powerful payroll capability. It's especially useful for allocating the cost of labor to multiple jobs. But unless you get that payroll information into your computer system, you won't be any better off than before you started using QuickBooks.

Whether you work alone or have office help, office and paperwork flow should follow a strict process. If you don't have one consistent written method for organizing paperwork, you may find yourself wasting many valuable hours shuffling papers rather than generating income for your business.

The best way to get a new routine organized is to get everyone involved. For example, before you start using a new payroll timecard or a new process for turning in paperwork, plan a lunch meeting with all your field workers. During lunch give them something new that will help them stay organized, such as a binder with their new timecards in it, or a clipboard to keep receipts together until they get back to the office. Treating them to lunch and providing free organizing materials may help motivate them to follow your new procedures.

In our opinion, the more informed you keep the people actually doing the work, the more effective they can be. Usually job cost information needs to make a complete circle so the people creating it get feedback on how they're doing. We recommend showing your project managers a job cost report once a week. If they understand how you're using the data they provide, they'll be more likely to make sure you get it.

The Job Estimates vs. Actuals Detail is a good report to give your project manager on a weekly basis. It shows a job, broken out by phase, with its estimate, actual, and variance figures. These numbers will help the project manager see where his job is running over, or under, the estimates — while he can still do something about it. Another useful report for project managers is the Vendor Contact List Report. This report includes company name, contact name, phone number, and fax number.

Setting Up Your Office Files

One of the hardest jobs in a construction office is keeping the files current. You need an effective filing system to keep things from piling up. Here's the system we recommend.

For your financial files, let QuickBooks be your guide. Organize your file drawers the same way QuickBooks organizes its lists — by vendors, employees, and so on. It makes good sense to take advantage of the correlation between the QuickBooks lists and your paper files. Intuit spent many hours and dollars figuring out the most efficient system for filing with a computerized system. Put their expertise to work for you, and use this same system for your paper files.

Customers and Jobs Files

You'll need a file drawer, or a section of a file drawer, for customers, with separate folders for each job. For example, Rachel Olsen originally contacted us about remodeling her kitchen, and at Twice Right we have one folder labeled "Olsen, Rachel — Kitchen Remodel." Then when she decided to build a guest cottage, we started another file labeled "Olsen, Rachel — Guest Cottage." We filed all correspondence to and from Rachel in one of those folders.

Your customer folder should contain:

- any correspondence to or from the customer about the job
- the original project contract
- copies of the billings. If the billings are bulky, use a separate customer job file for billing information
- any change orders you issue

Your customer folder should *not* contain:

- vendor invoices for the job
- any documents that don't relate to the job

Figures 11-1 and 11-2 are flow charts showing recommended job and customer transaction procedures.

Figure 11-1

This flow chart shows how a job is processed. To see your jobs in QuickBooks, click the Customer Center icon.

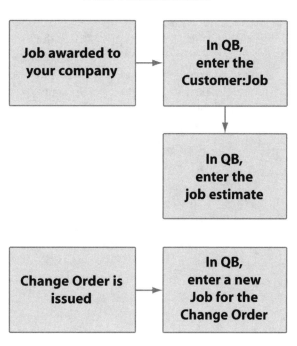

Job Transaction

Figure 11-2

This flow chart shows how things you enter in QuickBooks affect a customer.

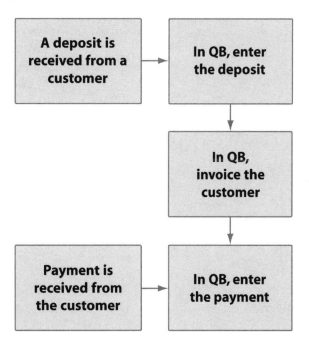

Customer Transaction

Vendor Files

You'll need a file drawer, or a section of a file drawer, for vendors. But it's really not necessary to give all vendors their own files. If you only get a few bills a year from a vendor, you may want to file that vendor's invoices in a Miscellaneous Vendors file. When the Miscellaneous Vendors file gets too big, break it down into two files, such as Miscellaneous Vendors A-L and Miscellaneous Vendors M-Z. File all bills in the vendor files whether they're job related or not.

You'll want to set up an individual file for some vendors. For example, at Twice Right Construction we have a charge account with Truitt & White Lumber Company. Because we get several invoices a month from Truitt & White, Truitt & White has its own file.

The chart in Figure 11-3 shows the workflow of vendor transactions.

Figure 11-3
This flow chart follows the path of a vendor bill from the time it's received until the bill is paid.

Vendor Transaction

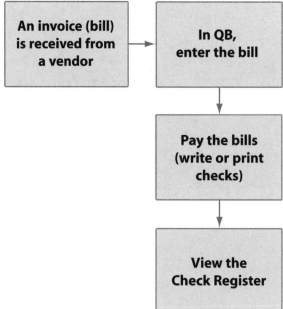

Employee Files

You'll also want to keep a file drawer, or a section of a file drawer, for employees. Since this information is confidential, be sure to keep these files in a locked file cabinet.

Your employee folder should contain:

▌ a completed employment application

▌ a completed I-9

▌ the employee's resume, if you have one

▌ employee review documents

▌ benefits documents

Organizing Your Payroll

One way to make sure you report labor accurately, on a per job basis, is to use items that describe the phases of labor. See Chapter 4 if you need more information on these items. You can print these items on the back of time-cards so employees can use them when filling out timecards. Show your employees how using the items helps the business determine true job costs and helps raise profits (and wages). They'll be more likely to fill them out carefully if they understand their importance.

Once the timecards are filled out, it's a simple matter of entering the items into a timesheet in QuickBooks. If you make the items on the back of the time-card match the names of the items in QuickBooks, then entering the timesheet in QuickBooks will simply be a matter of selecting the matching numbers. For example, suppose Joe Bliss has completed 40 hours of carpentry work in a week. His paper timecard would look something like Figure 11-4. In QuickBooks, the timecard would look like Figure 11-5. The "13" item in the Task # column of the timecard matches the "13 Windows" item in the Service Item column on the Timesheet.

If you use computers at your job sites, you can fill in electronic time-cards or summary sheets and e-mail them as attachments to the home office.

Keeping Office Paperwork Current

The most important thing is getting the field paperwork into the office. Start by working with your field people on how, and when, you want them to turn paperwork into the office. Don't get discouraged. When starting out, you'll probably get all the packing slips, invoices, and receipts turned in torn and

Date:	4/7/2013									
Employee:	Joe Bliss									
Pay period ending:	4/7/2013									
Customer/Job	Task #	Description	Mon	Tue	Wed	Thur	Fri	Sat	Sun	Total
Blanco/Kitchen	13	Windows	8	8	8					24
Blanco/Kitchen	21	Cabinets				8	8			16
Daily totals:			8	8	8	8	8			40

Figure 11-4

A typical paper timecard computed for a week.

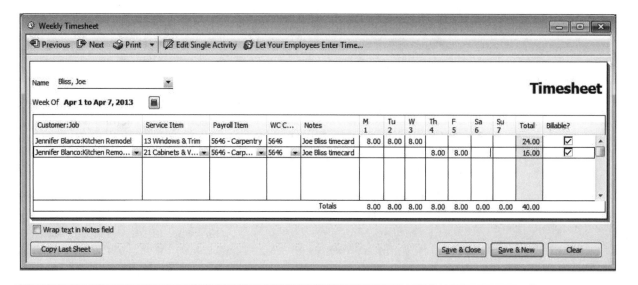

Figure 11-5

A QuickBooks timesheet looks similar to a paper timecard. Notice how the job and item entered match the job and item on the paper timecard.

crumpled, or not turned in at all, with excuses for why they were lost. But with encouragement, your field people will get the hang of it and start turning in their paperwork on a regular basis.

You'll need a place in the office, such as a basket or box, to use as an inbox for all field and office paperwork that comes into the office. Make sure the field staff can see and reach this inbox easily when they come in to drop off their paperwork.

Sort the paperwork that finds its way to the office. Put payroll timecards in a "To be approved" file. Put vendor invoices in a file for coding and approval.

Enter approved timecards and vendor invoices in QuickBooks. Then move them to the "To be paid 1 - 15th" file or the "To be paid 16th - EOM" file. After you pay an invoice or timecard, file it in the vendor file or employee file.

Another handy job-costing tip is to ask your materials suppliers and subcontractors to bill you by job. Most suppliers won't have any trouble issuing a separate invoice (or at least a separate line item) with a specific job name. Usually you can specify that no materials can be purchased without a job name being assigned to the invoice. As a check, you can also ask your field personnel to save shipping slips and bills of lading and to write the job name on them.

Change Orders

Whether change orders are issued in the office or the field, a procedure is needed to handle them consistently and smoothly. It's important to inform the office as soon as possible when there's a change order. Change orders can have a major impact on the profitability of a job. The sooner you get them into your system and begin job costing, the sooner you'll know the impact of the changes.

In the first eleven chapters of this book, we concentrated on showing you how to set up QuickBooks for a construction business. In the next chapter, we'll show you how to enter an estimate in QuickBooks.

Chapter 12

Estimating

In this chapter we'll show you how to bring outside summary estimate totals into QuickBooks. We realize that estimating is an individual thing. If your style of estimating is working for you, keep using it. Or if you already use, and are happy with, a sophisticated estimating program that returns useful information that QuickBooks doesn't track, stick with it. You can use a spreadsheet program, or Craftsman's *National Estimator*, or any of the other estimating programs on the market. As long as your estimating program can create a summary by phase report, you can use it to generate an estimate to hand-enter into QuickBooks.

You can enter the summary information into QuickBooks and track it against your actual costs. Then you can generate a report called Job Estimates vs. Actuals Detail. This report is the most useful report you can get for running your jobs on a day-to-day basis.

QuickBooks has no labor and material cost database. If you use 100 or fewer different items, you may be perfectly happy to enter those 100 items into the QuickBooks Item list. When your costs change, you can go back to the Item list and change your selling prices. But if you handle a wide variety of work and want to be ready to estimate almost anything, or if you use many unique items grouped together in a couple of dozen phases to make your estimates, you'll be asking too much from QuickBooks.

In this chapter, we'll just show you how to enter a summary estimate into QuickBooks.

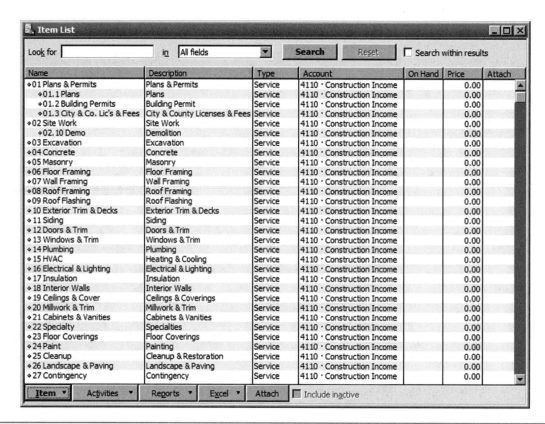

Figure 12-1
The Item List in *sample.qbw*.

Using a Summary Estimate You Make Outside of QuickBooks

Before you transfer a summary estimate, it's a good idea to set up an item in QuickBooks for each phase you use in your estimating program. See Chapter 4 for information on how to set up items. For example, suppose you decide to use our job phases partially shown in Figure 12-1. Then in QuickBooks, you should set up these items. If you used our *company.qbw* data file to set up your own company data file, these items are already set up for you.

You can also create subitems to get more detail on the phases. For example, you could set up an item for the Plans and Permits phase with subitems for plans, building permits, and city license. Subcontractors may need an entirely different list of items — one that divides their work into appropriate categories.

Once you've entered the items (or modified existing items), you can manually transfer the information from each phase in a summary estimate to a matching QuickBooks item. Let's walk through entering an estimate in QuickBooks.

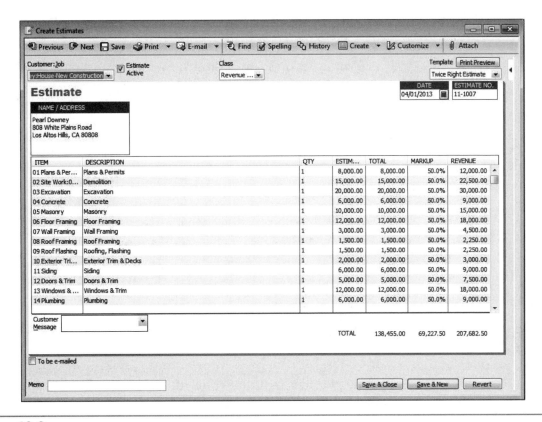

Figure 12-2
Use the Create Estimates window to quickly and easily create a new estimate for a customer.

To create a new estimate in QuickBooks using summary figures from an outside estimating program:

▌ Click **Home**, then click the **Estimates** icon, or from the **Customers** menu, choose **Create Estimates**.

▌ From the drop-down **Customer:Job** list, select the customer. In our example shown in Figure 12-2, we selected Pearl Downey:House — New Construction.

▌ From the pulldown class list, select Revenue - Job Related.

▌ Enter **Date** and **Estimate No.**

▌ To enter each line item for the estimate, click in the **Item** column, and select the item that matches the item in the outside summary estimate from the pull-down list. The description of the item will fill in automatically if you entered it when you created the item.

▌ In **Qty** and **Estimates**, enter the figures for the item from the outside summary estimate. Amount will be calculated for you by multiplying Qty by Estimate. The estimate form in Figure 12-2 has been customized to show columns for Qty, Estimate, Total, Markup, and

Revenue. We'll walk you through customizing an estimate form in the next section.

▮ In **Markup**, enter a number to add a lump sum markup. To add a percentage, enter the number and a percentage sign (say 50%). QuickBooks will calculate the appropriate markup, add it to the Total, and show the result in Revenue.

▮ Click **Save & Close** to create the estimate.

Customizing an Estimate Form

You can change the way an estimate looks both on paper and on your computer screen. To do this:

▮ Click **Home**, then click the **Estimates** icon, or from the **Customers** menu, choose **Create Estimates**.

▮ Click **Customize**.

▮ Click **Customize Data Layout**.

▮ Click **Basic Customization**.

▮ Click **Manage Templates**. Select an estimate template and click **Copy**.

▮ In **Template Name**, enter a name for your customized estimate. Click **OK**.

▮ In the Basic Customization window, you can add your company logo or any picture to your estimate by checking the box next to **Use Logo**. Click **Layout Designer** to change the columns and fields on your estimate. Click **OK**.

Take a look at each of the four tabs in the Additional Customization window. You can make changes to the form, both in what appears on the screen and what is printed. You can change headers, add or remove columns, create page footers, and set printer parameters. See Figure 12-3.

▮ When you're done, click **OK**.

Memorizing an Estimate

It's a good idea to memorize an estimate that has line items you use frequently. For example, you could create an estimate for a kitchen remodel, and memorize it as Basic, Medium, or High-end Kitchen. Then the next time you have a kitchen remodel job to estimate, simply open the memorized estimate that's most like your new job and make changes to the items that are different.

Figure 12-3

The Additional Customization window allows you to customize the estimate to fit your company's needs.

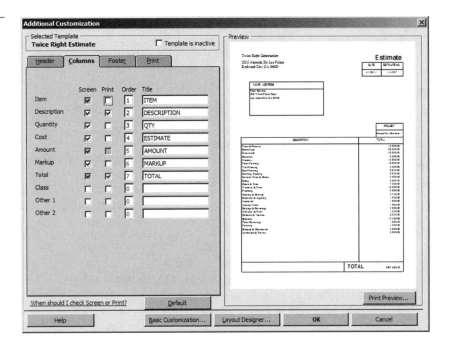

Figure 12-4

Memorize estimates that contain line items you use frequently. Be sure to give the memorized estimate a distinctive name, such as Kitchen Remodel, so it's easy to find when you need it.

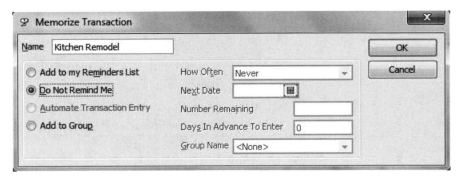

Once you memorize an estimate, you can use it as a template — like a cookie cutter to stamp out more estimates with the same items, but with different customer or job names. This can save you many hours of estimating time. There's no need to start from scratch every time you estimate a job.

To memorize an estimate:

▌ With the estimate you want to memorize on your screen, from the **Edit** menu, choose **Memorize Estimate**. When memorizing an estimate, you'll see an information window stating that QuickBooks clears out the Customer:Job field. Click **OK**.

▌ In the Memorize Transaction window, enter a name for the estimate. In our example shown in Figure 12-4, we entered *Kitchen Remodel*.

▌ Click **Do Not Remind Me** because there's no need to be reminded regularly of a memorized estimate.

▌ Click **OK** to memorize the estimate.

▌ Click the **X** in the upper right of the window to close the Estimate screen.

To use a memorized estimate:

▌ From the **Lists** menu, choose **Memorized Transaction List**.

▌ In the Memorized Transaction List window, select the memorized estimate you want to use.

▌ Click **Enter Transaction**.

Now you'll see a Create Estimates window with nothing in Customer:Job and Name/Address.

▌ From the pull-down Customer:Job list, select the customer. Or select **Add New** to add a new customer. For more information on adding customers, see Chapter 7, Customers.

Of course, you'll probably never have two identical estimates for two customers. Usually, you'll have to change the quantities and costs, and add or delete lines.

To add (or delete) a line to an estimate:

▌ Click in the **Item** column.

▌ From the **Edit** menu, choose **Insert Line** (or **Delete Line**) and make the necessary changes.

▌ Click **Save & Close** and you've got a new version of an old estimate. Note that the memorized estimate hasn't changed at all. You can still use it for another estimate.

QuickBooks lets you enter multiple estimates for one job. The advantage of having multiple estimates is that you can easily track the changes to the original estimate and proposed contract amount. Then, as the scope of work changes, you can compare the original estimate to the existing estimate and review it with the customer.

To enter a revised estimate, you should first create an estimate as described in the beginning of this chapter. Then, with the original estimate on your screen:

▌ From the **Edit** menu, select **Duplicate Estimate**.

▌ When the estimate is duplicated, make sure you change the **ESTIMATE NO.** field to reflect the revision number. For example, if your original estimate number was 01-1001, your revised estimate should be entered as 01-1001R1. If you have another revision, you should duplicate the latest estimate (01-1001R1 in our example) and enter R2 (or 01-1001R2) in the **ESTIMATE NO.** field.

▌ Click **Save & Close** to create the revised estimate.

Estimates and Progress Billing

After you create an estimate, you can easily create an invoice based on the estimate, using a progress billing invoice. For information on how to create a progress invoice, see Chapter 13. Before you create the invoice, you can see a summary of what you've billed to date, the current charges, and what will be billed later — all by phase of construction (or the items you've set up). So your final invoice is sure to cover everything in the job you haven't billed previously. You can make changes in the estimate any time you want.

From an estimate, you can:

1. Bill 100% — everything that remains to be billed.

2. Bill certain items only. You select which phases you want to bill.

3. Designate a percentage to be billed on any item you select.

If you handle larger, complex jobs that require multiple payments, progress billing may be a godsend. But progress billing only works on estimates, not invoices. To do progress billing you have to start with an estimate.

That's about all there is to know about bringing summary estimates into QuickBooks.

Getting Detailed Estimates

There are ways you can use QuickBooks to produce detailed estimates. One way involves creating a separate Items list in QuickBooks — a somewhat complex task that requires more knowledge of QuickBooks than we cover in this book. We wrote this book to take you step-by-step through a *simple* way to set up your bookkeeping in QuickBooks.

A far better option is Craftsman's *Job Cost Wizard*. Using this software, you can make estimates using Craftsman's estimating program, *National Estimator*, and import them directly into QuickBooks. From there, you can track job costs for each item or category in an estimate, compare actual with estimated costs for each part of any job, and create and send invoices.

Both programs, *National Estimator* and *Job Cost Wizard*, are included free when you order either the printed book or the download of any of Craftsman's estimating databases. All downloads are available for well under $50; books in the $70 to $80 range. Go to www.craftsman-book.com or call 800-829-8123.

Chapter 13

Receivables

In this chapter, and the next, we'll show you how to use QuickBooks on an accrual basis. The accrual basis of accounting means that you track how much money is owed to you (Accounts Receivable) and how much money you owe (Accounts Payable).

The accrual method has both benefits and drawbacks. Some of its benefits are:

▮ you can easily find out how much money you billed to customers vs. how much it cost you to earn that income

▮ you can easily find out how profitable your business was during a particular time period

▮ your job cost reports will include all costs and invoices to date

The major drawback to the accrual method is that it takes time to enter the transactions (bills and invoices). You have to enter every transaction as you receive or generate it. This requires vigilance to keep up to date. If you're a small contractor with little or no help, or no time to do bookkeeping, you're probably operating your business on a cash basis. If so, you can skip to Chapter 15, or keep reading to prepare for the time when you might switch to the accrual method.

Now on to the subject of this chapter — managing your receivables using the accrual system of accounting. Of course, you won't have any receivables if you don't send out bills, and contractors don't like to send out bills. However, with QuickBooks it's so simple there's no excuse for having a backlog of invoices that you need to send out. When you've completed a job, or at designated stages during the job, you'll want to prepare invoices to submit to your customer for payment.

In this chapter we'll show you:

▮ four different ways to invoice a customer

▮ how to handle change orders

- how to handle retainage
- how to record customer payments
- how to enter a deposit
- how to record job deposits (customer advances)

Four Ways to Invoice a Customer

The way an invoice is prepared depends on the contract terms. The main types of contracts are:

- set price (usually a small and simple verbal contract)
- time and materials or cost plus
- fixed price (usually a contract requiring a certain amount be paid when a certain percentage of the work has been completed)
- progress or AIA G702 structure

Creating a Set Price Invoice

Sometimes you need to get an invoice out the door quickly. This is usually for non-time-and-materials billings — perhaps a small, short-term job that doesn't require an estimate. For example, suppose a customer phones you to come out and fix a hole in a wall and you tell her you'll come and fix it today. Since she's a good customer who frequently refers your company to others, you agree to do the job for a flat $250. In this case, there's no estimate and the invoice is billed based on a set price.

Here's how you would enter a set price invoice:

- Click **Home**, then click **Create Invoices**, or from the **Customers** menu, choose **Create Invoices**.
- From the pull-down **Customer:Job** list, select the customer. The Bill To section will fill in automatically if you completed that part of the customer record. See our example in Figure 13-1.
- Enter **P.O. No.** if necessary.
- From the pull-down **Terms** list, select the appropriate term. We've used Net 10 in our example.
- From the pull-down **Class** list, select **Revenue - Job Related**.
- Click in the **Item** column and select an item from the drop-down list. Keep in mind that your items represent job phases. **Description** will fill in automatically if you entered it when you set up the item. Change description to fit the job. For this example, we used item 18 Interior Wall with a description of Fix hole in wall of guest bedroom, and a rate of $250.00.

Figure 13-1

In the Create Invoices window, enter each item you want to appear on a printed invoice. Make sure the Customer:Job and Bill To address are correct.

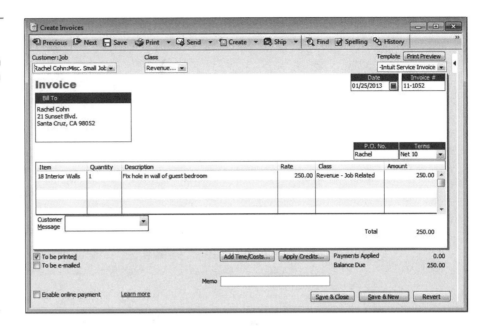

▌ Enter **Quantity** and **Rate** if necessary. Amount will be calculated automatically.

If a term you normally use isn't on the drop-down list, you can add it. There are two types of terms — a standard term, which requires payment within a certain number of days, or a date driven term, which requires payment by a certain date. To add a standard term:

▌ From the pull-down Terms list, choose **Add New**. See our example in Figure 13-2.

▌ In the New Terms window, in **Terms**, enter a name for the new term.

▌ Click **Standard**.

▌ In **Net due in**, enter the number of days the customer has to pay the invoice.

▌ In **Discount percentage is** and **Discount if paid within**, enter a discount percentage and number of days required for the early payment discount if you offer such a discount.

▌ Click **OK** to create the new term.

Figure 13-2

Use the New Terms window to define the terms on your invoices. Use a Standard term to require payment within a number of days.

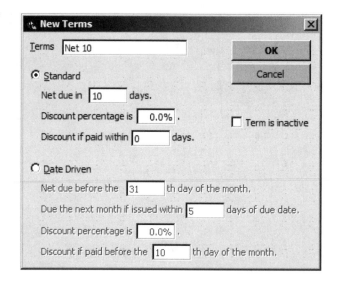

Figure 13-3

Use a Date Driven term to require payment by a certain date.

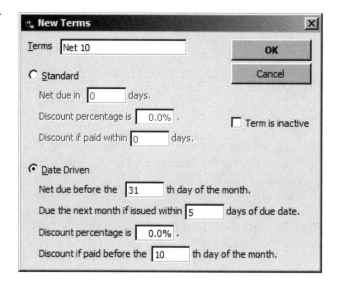

A date driven term is set up the same way, except you click Date Driven and enter the day of the month that the invoice is due. In our example, we want all invoices paid by the last day of the month, so we entered 31, as shown in Figure 13-3. You can also push back the due date if the invoice is issued late in the month, so your customers have plenty of time to pay their bills on time.

Now let's get back to the invoice. After entering all items:

▌ In the Create Invoices window, click the **Print** icon to print the invoice.

When you're satisfied the invoice is correct:

▌ Click **Save & Close** to close the invoice window. The invoice will automatically be added to Accounts Receivable.

Creating a Time-and-Materials or Cost-Plus Invoice

A time-and-materials contract means that you agree to complete a job for the documented project costs plus the labor costs (at certain rates). A cost-plus contract means the customer is billed for documented costs, plus a fee (generally a percent of the documented costs). These arrangements have the least risk and the least reward. You're essentially working for wages. It's very important to make sure all expenses are being covered with these types of contracts. Any costs that slip through the cracks and don't get billed are a complete loss that won't be recovered.

Before creating a time-and-materials invoice, enter the job costs incurred. Also enter timecards for the employees who worked on the job. Information on how to enter job-related costs is in Chapter 14. For information on how to enter payroll, see Chapter 15.

In this example, we'll show you how to enter a time-and-materials invoice for a job. At this point you should have already entered bills and assigned the costs to the job, as well as processed payroll, if you have employees.

To create a new time-and-materials invoice:

▌ Click **Home**, then click **Create Invoices**, or from the **Customers** menu, choose **Create Invoices**.

▌ From the pull-down **Customer:Job** list, select the customer. In our example, we use the Jose & Marie Sanchez: Cottage — New Construction job. If you made an estimate before preparing the invoice, you'll see a dialog box that prompts you to either select or exclude outstanding billable time and costs. Click on **Select the outstanding billable time and costs to add to this invoice**. Click **OK**.

▌ In the Choose Billable Time and Costs window, click the **Time** tab if you're charging for payroll costs and using time tracking. Put a check in the first column of each line you want to add to the invoice. See Figure 13-4.

▌ In the Choose Billable Time and Costs window, click the **Items** tab. Put a check in the first column of each line you want to add to the invoice. In our example, shown in Figure 13-5, we checked Roof Framing, Excavation materials, Exterior Trim & Decks, and Siding.

Figure 13-4

The Time tab displays a list of all time charged to the job by employees.

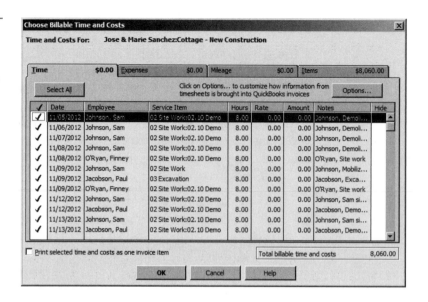

Figure 13-5

Use the Items, Expenses, and Time tabs to create the line items of a time-and-materials invoice.

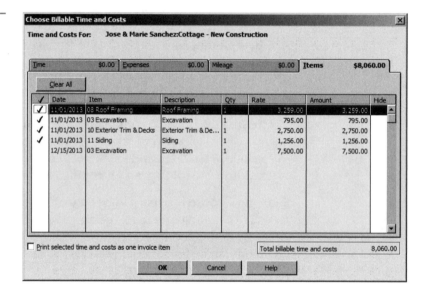

▌ If you want the selected time and costs to appear as one item on the invoice, click **Print selected time and costs as one invoice item**.

▌ Click **OK**.

▌ Back in the Create Invoices window, enter the rate you charge for the employee in the **Rate** column. Amount is calculated from the rate.

▌ Click **Print** to print the invoice.

Figure 13-6

A completed time-and-materials invoice.

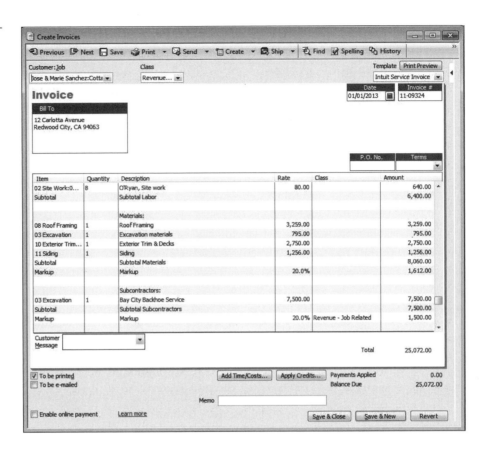

When you're satisfied that the invoice is correct:

▌ Click **Save & Close** to close the invoice window. The invoice will automatically be added to Accounts Receivable.

Your completed time-and-materials invoice will be similar to the example we show in Figure 13-6.

Creating a Fixed-Price Contract Invoice

A fixed-price (also called lump sum) contract means that, except for change orders, you agree to complete the job as specified in the plans and contract documents for an agreed amount. You assume the entire risk if the job goes over budget. But you also have the opportunity to exceed your estimated profit if you can bring the job in under the contract amount.

When using a fixed-price contract, bill a specified amount of the contract price at designated stages of the job. The specified amount is typically less than the total contract price. As an example, you might have a billing schedule like this one:

Invoice #1: 40% of contract payable at start of rough framing

Figure 13-7

Use this item when you create an invoice for a fixed-price contract.

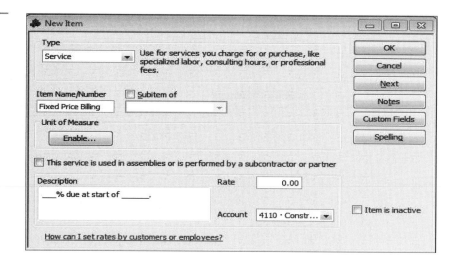

Invoice #2: 20% of contract payable at start of drywall

Invoice #3: 30% of contract payable at start of final flooring

Invoice #4: 10% of contract payable at start of signing punch list

The customer or the lender usually makes an inspection to authorize a billing against the contract.

When invoicing for a fixed-price contract, first create an item so you can enter the percentage. Here's how to create the item:

- Click **Home**, then click **Items & Services**, or from the **Lists** menu, choose **Item List**. In the Item List window, pull down the **Item** menu and choose **New**.

- For **Type**, select **Service**.

- In **Item Name/Number**, enter **Fixed Price Billing**. See Figure 13-7.

- In **Description**, enter a generic description. This description will automatically fill in on the invoice when you use the item. In the example shown in Figure 13-7, we used "_% due at start of __." You can fill in the blanks in this description when you complete the invoice the item appears on.

- In **Account**, select your Construction Income account. In our example, we used 4110 Construction Income.

- Click **OK**.

To create a fixed-price invoice:

- Click **Home**, then click **Create Invoices**, or from the **Customers** menu, choose **Create Invoices**.

Figure 13-8

A completed fixed-price contract invoice.

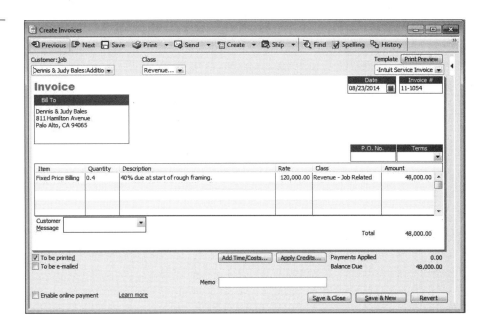

▌ From the **Customer:Job** drop-down list, select a customer. For our example, we've used Dennis and Judy Bales: Addition. If you made an estimate before preparing the invoice, you'll see a dialog box that tells you there's an estimate for the job and asks if you want to create the invoice based on that estimate. Click **Cancel**.

▌ From the pull-down **Class** list, select **Revenue - Job Related**.

▌ Click in **Item** and from the pull-down **Item** list, select **Fixed Price Billing**.

▌ In **Quantity**, enter as a decimal the percentage of the contract you're currently billing.

▌ In **Description**, change the blank lines to percent and job phase. See Figure 13-8.

▌ In **Rate**, enter the full contract amount. Amount will be computed by multiplying the percentage entered in Quantity by the full contract amount.

▌ Click **Print**. Check the printed invoice carefully to make sure it's correct. Then print two copies so you have one for your customer file.

▌ Click **Save & Close**.

Creating a Progress Invoice

A progress invoice, or AIA G702, has many line items on the invoice. Typically, the estimate matches the summary job phases discussed in Chapter 12, Estimating. This type of invoice is used for larger jobs and state

Figure 13-9

QuickBooks lets you choose to invoice from an existing estimate or start the invoice from scratch.

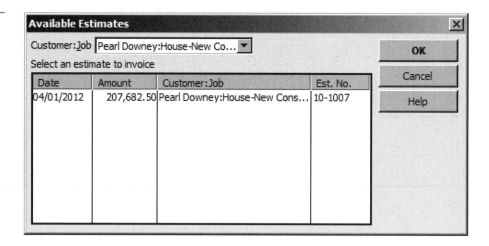

or government work, which usually requires a special AIA G702 invoice structure.

These two steps must be completed before creating a progress invoice:

1. Create an estimate for the job using items. See Chapter 12 if you need information on creating estimates.

2. Make sure the **Progress Invoicing preference** is active.

To turn on the progress invoice preference:

▌ From the **Edit** menu, choose **Preferences** and click the **Jobs & Estimates** icon and the **Company Preferences** tab.

▌ Click **Yes** to answer the question **Do You Do Progress Invoicing?**

▌ Click **OK**.

Now, to create a progress invoice:

▌ Click **Home**, then click **Create Invoices**, or from the **Customers** menu, choose **Create Invoices**.

▌ From the drop-down **Customer:Job** list, select the customer. For our example, we've used Pearl Downey: House - New Construction.

▌ If you're following our example, you'll see a dialog box that allows you to select an estimate for the customer, as shown in Figure 13-9. At this point you'll need to select the estimate you want to create a progress invoice against.

▌ Select **OK**.

▌ This takes you to the Create Progress Invoice Based On Estimate window shown in Figure 13-10. Now you have to decide how you want to use the estimate to create the invoice. Make your selection here based on the type of contract you have with the customer. For our example, we select the last option — Create invoice for selected items or for different percentages of each item.

▌ Click **OK**.

Figure 13-10

When you use an existing estimate to create an invoice, you have three choices for how to create the invoice.

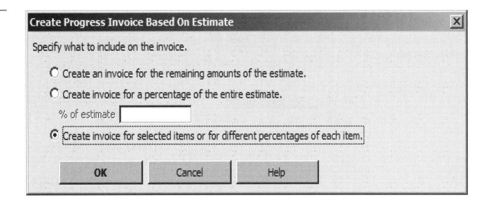

Figure 13-11

Use this window to choose which items from an estimate to include in an invoice.

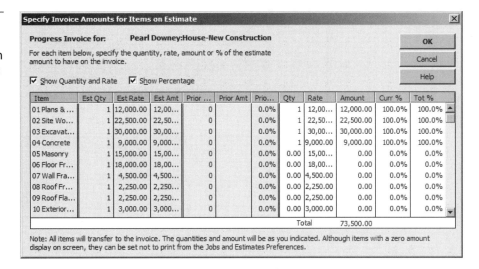

This brings up the Specify Invoice Amounts for Items on Estimate window. Here you enter the amount, percentage, quantity, and/or rate due for each item you want to appear on the invoice. To specify invoice amounts from an estimate:

▌ In the **Curr %** column for the item, enter the new percentage. Amount will fill in based on the new percentage. In our example shown in Figure 13-11, we invoiced 100% of Plans & Permits, Site Work, Excavation and Concrete.

▌ Or, in the **Amount** column for the item, enter the new amount. Curr% will fill in based on the new amount.

▌ In the **Quantity** column for the item, enter the new quantity.

▌ In the **Rate** column for the item, edit to enter the new rate.

▌ Click **OK** to get back to the Create Invoices window.

▌ Back in the Create Invoices window, click **Print** to print the invoice, shown in Figure 13-12.

Figure 13-12

This is an example of a completed progress invoice.

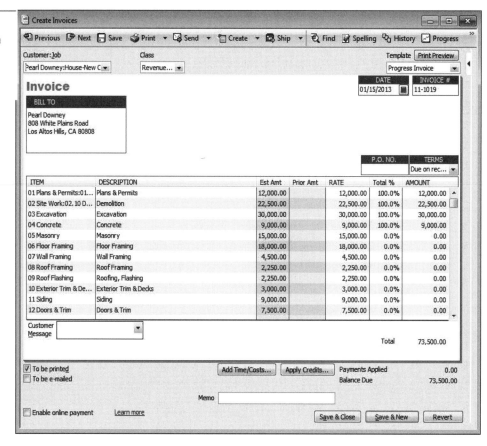

Check your printed invoice carefully. When you're satisfied that the invoice is correct:

▌ Click **Save & Close** to close the invoice window. The invoice will automatically be added to Accounts Receivable.

Tracking Change Orders on Estimates

With the Contractor Edition of QuickBooks, you can track change orders.

Whenever you modify items in an existing estimate, you have the option to save your changes as a change order in the description field at the bottom of the estimate form.

The change order specifies exactly what changed, the dollar amount of each change, and the net dollar change to the estimate. You may then wish to print the estimate form for the customer for final approval. (You cannot print the change order by itself.)

Figure 13-13

To create a change order in the Contractor Edition, you simply change an existing estimate.

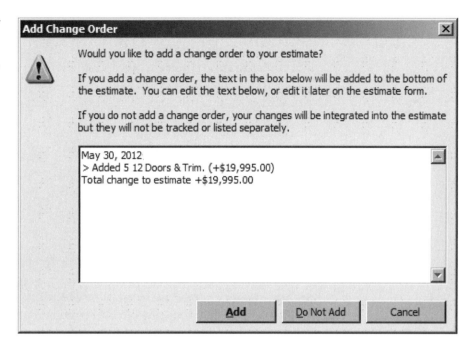

To Track Change Orders on an Estimate

1. Change your estimate as usual.

2. Save your changes.

3. QuickBooks displays the Add Change Order window, in which you can do one of the following:

▌ Click **Add** to add the displayed text to the bottom of the estimate. See Figure 13-13.

If you don't like the way the change order appears, you can edit the text in the Add Change Order window before clicking **Add**, or you can edit the change order on the estimate form later.

▌ Click **Do Not Add** if you want the estimate to be updated with your changes without explicitly listing the change order at the bottom of the form.

▌ Click **Cancel** to return to the estimate form and reconsider your changes.

Tip: If you want to save your original estimate before creating a change order, right-click in the Create Estimates window and choose Duplicate Estimate. Either save and edit the duplicate estimate, or display and edit the original estimate. Note that if you edit the duplicate estimate before you save it, a change order won't be created. Change orders are generated only on existing estimates that have previously been saved.

Reviewing and Changing an Estimate

1. Display the estimate. From the **Customer** menu, select **Create Estimates**. Hit **Previous** button until you find the estimate you want to modify.

2. Click **Print** to create a copy of the original estimate for your records. (Optional)

3. Enter your changes on the estimate form. QuickBooks automatically recalculates totals.

4. Save your changes.

How to Handle Retainage

Sometimes you'll be required to hold back 10 percent of your total progress payments (billing only for 90 percent of the contract price) as a retainer until you've completed the project satisfactorily. After the job is complete and it's agreed that you can collect the retainage, you can bill the customer for the remaining 10 percent of the project cost. Here's how to handle this type of billing:

Step 1— Setting Up an Account for Retentions Receivable

First, set up an asset account for retainage. If you used our example Chart of Accounts, the asset account number for retainage is 1320 - Retentions Receivable. If you don't have an asset account for retentions receivable, follow these steps to create a new account:

▌ Click **Home**, then click the **Chart of Accounts** icon, or from the **Lists** menu, choose **Chart of Accounts**.

▌ In the lower part of the Chart of Accounts list window, click **Account** and choose **New**.

▌ Select the account type. Click **Continue**. See Figure 13-14 for an example of creating a Retentions Receivable account.

▌ Fill in the information for the Retentions Receivable account.

▌ Click **Save & Close**.

Step 2 — Setting Up an Item for Retentions Receivable

If you don't have an item for Retentions Receivable, follow these steps to create a new item:

▌ Click **Home**, then click the **Items & Services** icon, or from the **Lists** menu, choose **Item List**.

▌ Click **Item** in the lower part of the Items List window. From the pull-down menu choose **New**. See Figure 13-15 for an example of creating a Retention item.

Figure 13-14

Use the New Account window to create an account for retentions receivable.

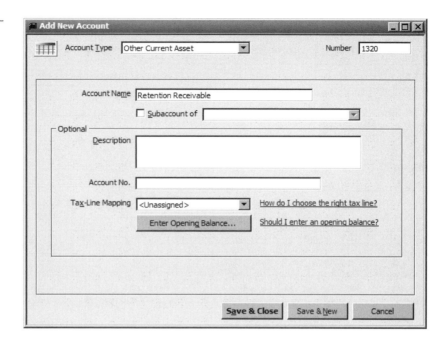

Figure 13-15

Use the New Item window to create an item for retention.

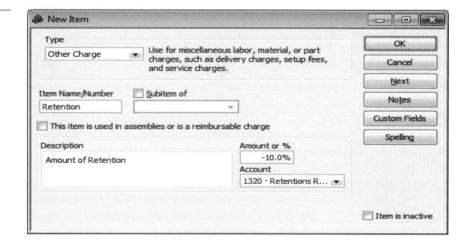

▌ In **Type**, select **Other Charge**.

▌ Fill in the fields for the Retentions item.

▌ Click **OK** to create the new item.

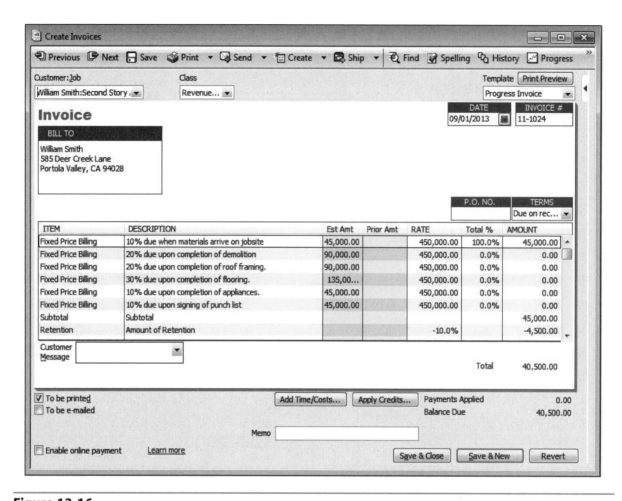

Figure 13-16

When you include a retention amount on an invoice, the balance due on the invoice is lowered by that amount.

Step 3 — Including the Retention on an Invoice

To include the retention on an invoice:

▌ Create an invoice for the job in the usual way.

▌ In the Create Invoices window, click on a blank line in the **Item** column and select the **Subtotal** item from the pull-down Item list. This will subtotal the invoice.

▌ Then select the **Retention** item from the pull-down Item list. The retention item will automatically deduct 10% from the subtotal line listed above. In Figure 13-16, the original amount of the invoice was $45,000. We entered a retainage of −$4,500. The final amount of the invoice ends up to be $45,000 − $4,500 = $40,500.

▌ Click **Save & Close**.

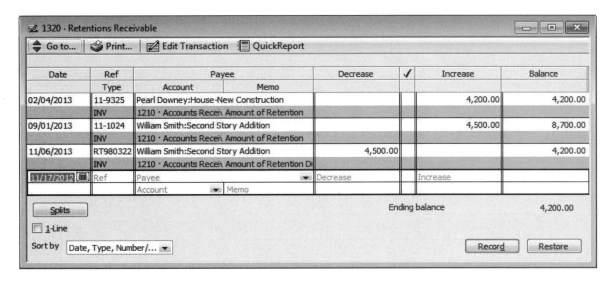

Date	Ref	Payee		Decrease	✓	Increase	Balance
	Type	Account	Memo				
02/04/2013	11-9325	Pearl Downey:House-New Construction				4,200.00	4,200.00
	INV	1210 · Accounts Recei\ Amount of Retention					
09/01/2013	11-1024	William Smith:Second Story Addition				4,500.00	8,700.00
	INV	1210 · Accounts Recei\ Amount of Retention					
11/06/2013	RT980322	William Smith:Second Story Addition		4,500.00			4,200.00
	INV	1210 · Accounts Recei\ Amount of Retention D(					
11/17/2013 ▦	Ref	Payee	▼	Decrease		Increase	
		Account ▼	Memo				

Splits   ☐ 1-Line   Sort by Date, Type, Number/... ▼

Ending balance   4,200.00

Record   Restore

Figure 13-17
The Retentions Receivable register shows transactions in the Retentions Receivable account.

Recalling Who Owes You a Retention and How Much You're Owed

An easy way to determine the amount is to look at the register of your Retentions Receivable account. If you used our *company.qbw* data file to set up your company, you can use the memorized Retentions Receivable Report to see this information. This report will summarize who owes you for retention and how much they owe. You'll find more information on this report in Chapter 17, Reports. Otherwise, to see your retentions receivable:

▌ Click **Home**, then click **Chart of Accounts**, or from the **Lists** menu, choose **Chart of Accounts**.

▌ In the Chart of Accounts list window, select your **Retentions Receivable** account. In our example shown in Figure 13-17 it's 1320 - Retentions Receivable.

▌ From the bottom of the Chart of Accounts window, click **Activities** and choose **Use Register** from the pull-down menu. You will see a register that shows all the activity in the Retentions Receivable account. See Figure 13-17.

▌ Click the **X** in the upper right of the window to close the register.

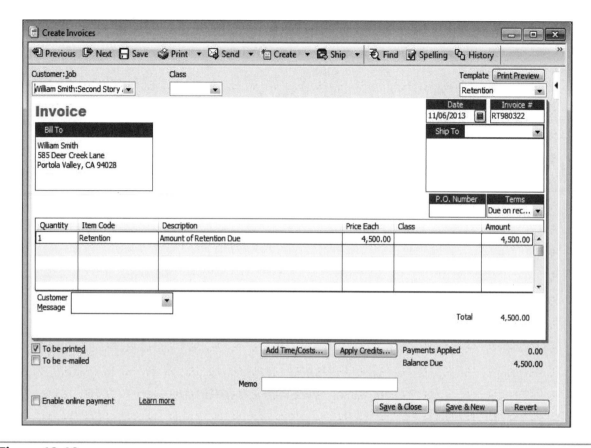

Figure 13-18
When you bill for retention, create a new invoice for just the retention.

Invoicing for Retention

When you're ready to bill for the retention, create a new invoice that contains only the retention item.

▌ Create an invoice for the job in the usual way. See Figure 13-18.

▌ From the Template pull-down list, select **Retention**.

▌ Click in the **Item Code** column and select **Retention** from the pull-down list.

▌ In **Amount**, enter the total amount of the retention held to date as a positive number.

▌ Click **Save & Close**.

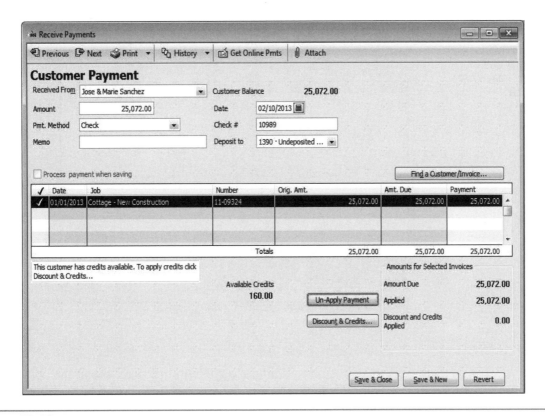

Figure 13-19
Use the Receive Payments window to record each payment you receive from a customer.

Recording a Payment You Receive

When you create and send an invoice to a customer, QuickBooks creates a record in the Accounts Receivable register. When you receive a payment from the customer, you record receipt of the payment in the Receive Payments window.

To record a payment:

▌ Click **Home**, then click **Receive Payments**, or from the **Customers** menu, choose **Receive Payments**.

▌ In the Receive Payments window, select the customer from the pull-down **Received From** list. In our example shown in Figure 13-19, we show receipt of a payment from customer Jose & Marie Sanchez.

▌ Fill in the date you received the customer's payment, the amount paid, the payment method, and the check number if the customer paid by check.

Figure 13-20

Use the Payments to Deposit window to record each payment you deposit.

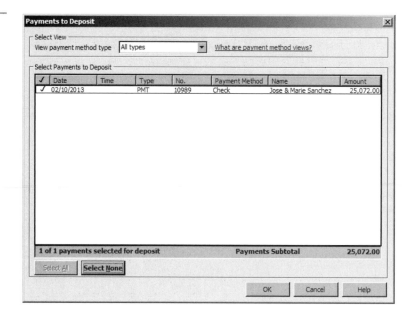

■ If you want to hold the payment until you deposit the check, select your Undeposited Funds account in the **Deposit to** field. In our example, it's account 1390. We'll show you how to record the deposit in the next section. If you want to bypass the Undeposited Funds account and deposit the payment directly in a bank account, select the appropriate account in the **Deposit to** field.

■ Click **Save & Close** to record the payment and close the window.

Recording a Deposit

Before you record the deposit of a customer payment, record the payment using the steps in the previous section. When you record the deposit of the payment, it will be transferred from Undeposited Funds to your bank account. Enter non-customer payments you want to deposit here, also.

To record a deposit:

■ Click **Home**, then click **Record Deposits**, or from the **Banking** menu, choose **Make Deposits**.

Note: If you don't see anything listed on the Make Deposits screen, you probably didn't select the Undeposited Funds account in the Deposit to field when you received the customer's payment (see previous section).

■ In the Payments to Deposit window, click each customer check you're depositing. In our example shown in Figure 13-20, we select the payment from Jose & Marie Sanchez.

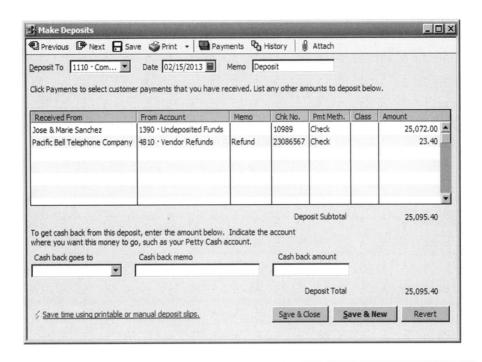

Figure 13-21
You can also use the Make Deposits window to record non-customer payments you deposit.

▌ Click **OK** to proceed to the Make Deposits window.

▌ In the Make Deposits window, add any non-customer payments that you'll be depositing. In our example shown in Figure 13-21, we deposit a refund from Pacific Bell Telephone Company for $23.40.

▌ Click **Save & Close** to record the deposit.

Recording a Job Deposit

A job deposit is money that belongs to the customer, but is held until contractual obligations are fulfilled. In other words, it's money in your hand, but you still need to earn it. Don't record it as income. Record it as a liability even though the funds are deposited into your checking account. When the customer agrees you can apply the deposit to the job costs, or defaults on the contract, record the deposit as income.

To record a deposit as a liability:

▌ Click **Home**, then click **Create Sales Receipts**, or from the **Customers** menu, choose **Enter Sales Receipts**.

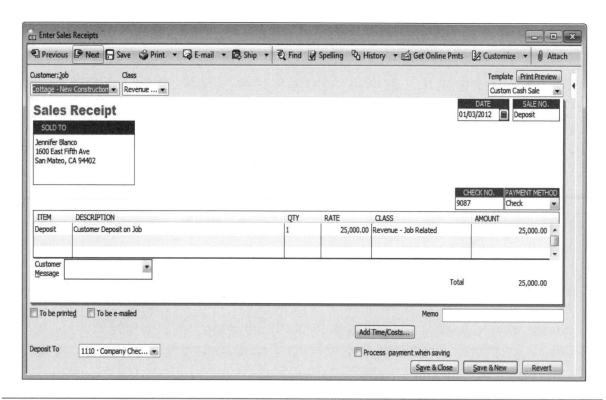

Figure 13-22
Use the Enter Sales Receipts window to record a job deposit as a liability.

■ From the pull-down **Customer:Job** list in the Enter Sales Receipts window, select the customer. In our example shown in Figure 13-22, we enter a customer deposit for $25,000 from Jennifer Blanco.

■ In **Class**, select **Revenue - Job Related**.

■ In **Date**, enter the date you deposited the funds.

■ In **Sale No.**, enter **Deposit**.

■ Select **Payment Method** from the drop-down list.

■ In the **Item** column, select **Deposit** from the drop-down Item list. In **Quantity**, enter **1**. Enter **Rate**.

■ To print a message on the receipt, select a message from the **Customer Message** drop-down list. To add a new message, click **Add New** and create your own personalized message.

■ Click the **Print** icon to create the receipt for your customer.

■ At the very bottom of the Enter Sales Receipts window, click **Deposit To**. From the pull-down Account list, select the **Checking** or **Savings** account you want to put the funds in. Make sure you deposit

Figure 13-23

This Create Invoices window shows a deposit deducted from a final billing.

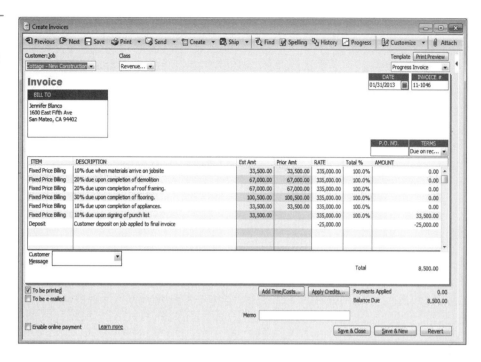

this check by itself, not as part of a group deposit. When you reconcile the Checking or Savings account in QuickBooks, you want this deposit to be listed alone.

▌ Click **Save & Close** to record the deposit.

To apply the deposit to an invoice:

▌ Follow the usual steps for creating an invoice for the customer.

▌ At the end of the invoice items, enter a deposit item using a negative rate. In our example shown in Figure 13-23, we subtracted $25,000 from the Jennifer Blanco:Cottage Progress invoice.

▌ Click **Save & Close** to create the invoice.

Now you know how to process invoices to customers in QuickBooks.

Chapter 14

Payables

We've based the information in this chapter on the accrual method of accounting discussed in Chapter 13. The advantages of this accounting method, as it relates to Accounts Payable, are:

▌ job cost reports will include unpaid vendor bills

▌ Accounts Payable Report will help track the vendors you owe money to

▌ profitability reports will be more accurate

Here's what we're going to discuss in this chapter:

1. entering purchase orders

2. using purchase orders to track multiple draws and committed costs

3. entering bills for job-related and overhead expenses without purchase orders

4. selecting bills for payment

5. printing checks

6. payables and vendor workers' comp reports

To get job and non-job expenses into your accounting system accurately and completely, enter who you're paying and what you're paying for. Be sure to enter a memo or note about each expense and put a record of the transaction in the proper account. Then QuickBooks reports will accurately reflect all your expenses.

You should already have set up the Chart of Accounts and other lists in QuickBooks before going through this chapter. You can open the *sample.qbw* file and use it to follow the examples in this chapter. Then you can try out the steps without affecting any actual company information.

Figure 14-1

Use purchase orders to track items that you've ordered and check against what you receive.

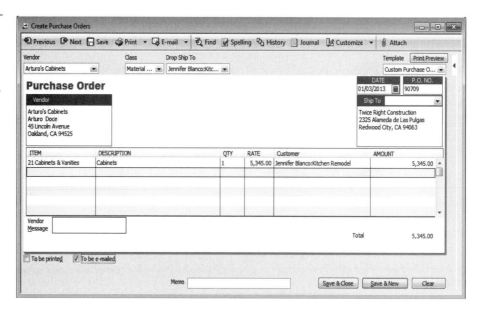

Creating and Using Purchase Orders

Purchase orders in QuickBooks are a record of what has been ordered. Purchase orders let you compare what you order with what you receive. For example, suppose Twice Right Construction ordered cabinets from Arturo's Cabinets and created the purchase order shown in Figure 14-1. QuickBooks will track the order date and the amount quoted for the cabinets. Then Twice Right doesn't have to rely on memory for this information.

Let's look at how to create a purchase order:

> ▌ Click **Home**, then click the **Purchase Orders** icon, or from the **Vendors** menu, choose **Create Purchase Orders**.

If you don't see the command Create Purchase Orders in the Vendors menu, you need to turn on purchase order tracking. To do this:

> ▌ From the **Edit** menu, choose **Preferences**.
>
> ▌ Click **Items & Inventory**.
>
> ▌ Click the **Company Preferences** tab.
>
> ▌ Select **Inventory and purchase orders are active**.
>
> ▌ Click **OK**.

Now, back to our purchase order.

> ▌ In the top part of the form, enter the Vendor, the Ship To address (job site), the Class (materials), Date, PO number, and vendor's address.

Figure 14-2

Use a purchase order to enter the parts of a multiple-payment draw schedule.

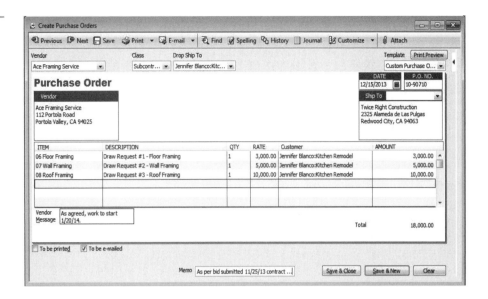

▌ Click in the **Item** column and select the items you're ordering from the pull-down list. Change the Description, Quantity, and Rate fields as necessary.

▌ Click in the **Customer** column and select the customer you're ordering materials for from the pull-down Customer list.

▌ In **Memo** enter a brief description about this PO. This is important because the memo will appear when you move the PO into a vendor bill.

▌ Click **Save & Close** or **Save & New** to enter another PO.

Using Purchase Orders to Track Multiple Draws and Committed Costs (Buyouts)

In QuickBooks, you can assign each line item of a purchase order to a job. This feature lets you use the purchase order to track multiple payment draws and committed costs to subcontractors. Let's look at multiple draws first.

Multiple Draw Schedules

Suppose you want to track an agreement like the one we made with Ace Framing Serivce for a three-part draw. As soon as you make this type of agreement or contract, you should enter the draw schedule as a purchase order. In Figure 14-2 you'll see an example showing the purchase order where Twice Right Construction entered a three-part draw to Ace Framing for floor (Draw #1), wall (Draw #2), and roof (Draw #3) framing.

Figure 14-3

Use the Open Purchase Orders window to see a list of the open POs for a vendor.

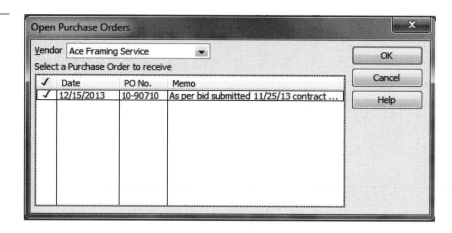

When Twice Right received Ace Framing's first bill for Draw #1 — Floor Framing, they used that same purchase order to record the payment of the first draw. Here are the steps:

▌ Click **Home**, then click **Receive Inventory**, **Receive Inventory with Bill**, or from the **Vendors** menu, choose **Receive Items and Enter Bill**.

▌ In the Enter Bills window, from the pull-down **Vendor** list, select the appropriate vendor. In our example it's Ace Framing.

▌ You'll see the Open PO's Exist window, with a warning that open purchase orders exist for the vendor. Click **Yes** here to tell QuickBooks that you want to use an existing PO.

▌ In the Open Purchase Orders window, a list of open purchase orders is displayed. Click in the ✓ column to select the appropriate open PO. In our example shown in Figure 14-3, we checked the PO dated 12/15/2013.

▌ Click **OK**.

Back in the Enter Bills window, as shown in Figure 14-4:

▌ In **Date**, enter the date on the vendor's bill.

▌ In **Ref. No.**, enter the vendor's invoice number.

▌ In **Amount Due,** enter the amount you plan to pay the vendor (or the draw). In our example, Twice Right will pay $3000, which is 100 percent of Draw #1 - Floor Framing.

▌ In **Qty,** enter 1 for any draw that you want to pay now. If you only want to pay half of the draw, enter 0.5 in Qty. If you don't want to pay any of the draw, enter 0.

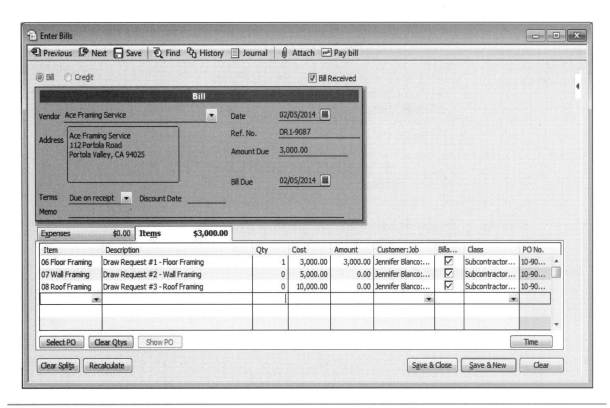

Figure 14-4
In this Enter Bills window, Twice Right will pay the first draw to Ace Framing.

▌ The **Amount** column will calculate automatically. In our example, it's $3,000 for Draw #1. The amount shown on the Items tab should be the same as the amount you're paying. The amounts for the other draws you're not paying will be 0.00.

▌ Click **Save & Close**.

Committed Costs

You can also use a purchase order and the same method to track what you've committed to pay a subcontractor. For example, suppose you have a subcontractor who bid a project out at a certain price and you want to track the bid price to compare it to his final bill. To do this, set up a purchase order at the beginning of the project and compare it to the final bill you receive from the subcontractor. In our example in Figure 14-5, Twice Right used a PO to track the bid price (contract price) from Blue Dolphin Plumbing for rough and finish plumbing. When Blue Dolphin Plumbing submits their bill, Twice Right can compare the original bid price to the original purchase order.

Figure 14-5

Use a PO to track a bid price from a subcontractor.

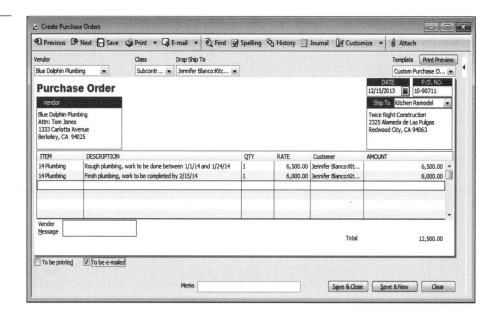

Tracking Unfilled Purchase Orders

QuickBooks has a built-in report to track purchase orders that haven't been filled. Run this report to list all subcontractors who haven't completed or submitted bills on a project. To generate this report:

▌ Click the **Report Center**, or from the **Reports** menu, choose **Purchases** and then **Open Purchase Orders by Job**.

▌ In the Modify Report: Open Purchase Orders by Job window, click **OK**.

Important note! You may have a problem with this report if you make a partial payment to a subcontractor. The amount remaining after the partial payment will clear from the report unless you enter a number less than 1 in the Qty column in the Enter Bills window. To avoid this reporting problem, always enter a number *less than 1* when you release part of a PO. For example if you pay $1,500 of a $3,000 bid, enter 0.5 in Qty.

Entering Bills Without Purchase Orders

Entering Bills for Job-Related Expenses

Suppose you don't have the need (or time) to enter a purchase order before you get a vendor bill. In this case, skip entering the purchase order and enter the bill directly. Figure 14-6 is an example of a bill Twice Right got from Eric Savage Electrical Company for $2,300 that they hadn't entered a purchase order for. To record the $2,300 and get the cost into job cost

Figure 14-6

Use the Items tab on the Enter Bills window to record job-related expenses.

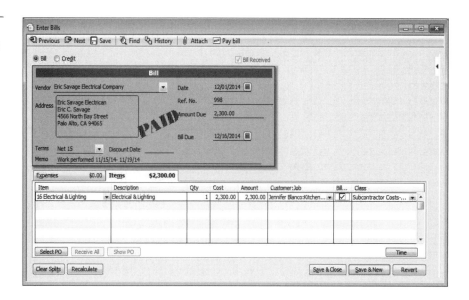

reports, they'll enter a bill in QuickBooks. It's important to enter job-related costs on the Items tab.

To enter a bill for a job-related expense:

▌ Click **Home,** then click **Enter Bills,** or from the **Vendors** menu, choose **Enter Bills**.

▌ Fill in the **Bill** form in the top half of the window.

▌ In **Memo**, enter a memo that tells what the bill is for. This memo will appear on billing reports such as A/P Aging Summary and Vendor Balance Detail. If you pay the bill by check and you *didn't* enter an account number when you set up the vendor's account, QuickBooks puts the memo in the Memo field on the check. If you *did* enter an account number when you set up the vendor's account, QuickBooks puts the account number in the Memo field of the check.

▌ Click the **Items** tab. Always enter job-related expenses on the Items tab of the Enter Bills window.

▌ Click in the **Item** column and select the items for the bill from the pull-down list.

▌ Edit **Description** and **Amount** if necessary.

▌ Click in the **Customer:Job** column and select the customer from the pull-down list.

▌ Click in the **Class** column and select the class from the pull-down list.

▌ Click **Save & Close** to record the bill.

Figure 14-7
Use the Expenses tab on the Enter Bills window to record overhead expenses. Make sure you enter the correct account.

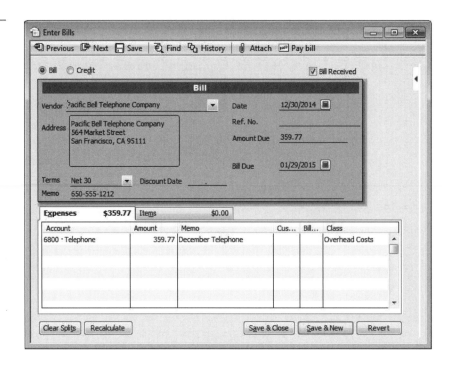

Entering Bills for Overhead Expenses

Non-job-related expenses are overhead expenses for things such as telephone, electricity, office supplies, etc. Enter a bill for any expense when you receive the bill, even if you charged it to a credit card or you have an account with the company. Then you'll have the costs in your books as soon as it's been charged.

To enter a bill for an expense that's not a job-related expense:

▌ Click **Home,** then click **Enter Bills**, or from the **Vendors** menu, choose **Enter Bills**. In our example shown in Figure 14-7, we show a bill from the phone company.

▌ Fill in the **Bill** form in the top half of the window.

▌ In **Memo** (not the Memo column on the Expenses tab), enter a memo that describes the bill. This memo will appear on billing reports such as the A/P Aging Summary. If you pay the bill by check and you *didn't* enter an account number when you set up the vendor's account, QuickBooks puts the memo in the Memo field on the check. If you *did* enter an account number when you set up the vendor's account, QuickBooks puts the account number in the Memo field of the check.

▌ Click the **Expenses** tab. Always use the **Expenses** tab of the **Enter Bills** window for non-job-related expenses.

▌ Make sure each bill entered is associated with the proper account. That's the best way to get useful and accurate reports of your expenses. Click in the **Account** column and select the appropriate expense account(s) from the pull-down list. If you're paying a bill with multiple items and you need to split the amount over more than one expense account, change the amount that's automatically entered in the first line to match the line item in the bill. Then tab to the second line and make the entry for the next line item. Continue this way for each line item.

▌ In the **Memo** column, enter a description or account number (you won't have a Customer:Job for non-job-related expenses).

▌ Click **Save & Close** to record the bill.

Selecting Bills for Payment

The Pay Bills feature in QuickBooks lets you select bills to pay. This is usually called a check run. In the construction industry, check runs usually happen every Friday or on the last day of the current month and the 15th day of the following month. In this section, we'll explain how to select bills to pay. In the next section, we'll explain how to print checks using check stock.

To select bills for payment:

▌ Click **Home,** then click **Pay Bills**, or from the **Vendors** menu, choose **Pay Bills**. QuickBooks will list all unpaid bills or all bills due for the date range you enter.

▌ At the top of the Pay Bills window, next to **Show bills,** select **Due on or before** to enter a date to cover all the bills that you want to pay. Or select **Show all bills**.

▌ Click in the ✓ column to select each bill you want to pay. As you select the bills, compare the total in the **Amt To Pay** column against the total shown for **Ending Balance** in the Payment section of the Pay Bills window. Make sure there is enough money in the checking account to cover all the bills you've selected to pay.

▌ To pay only part of a particular bill, change the amount shown in the **Amt To Pay** column. In our example shown in Figure 14-8, Twice Right paid $1,000 of the $2,300 owed to Eric Savage Electrical.

▌ In the Payment Method section of the Pay Bills window select **To be printed**. From the pull-down Method list, select **Check**.

▌ To record the payments, click **Pay Selected Bills**.

▌ The Payment Summary window will appear. If you're ready to print checks, click the **Print Checks** button. Otherwise, click **Done**.

Figure 14-8

Select the bills you want to pay in the Pay Bills window.

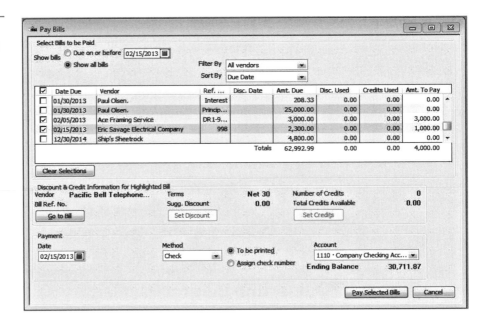

Figure 14-9

Select the checks you want to print in the Select Checks to Print window.

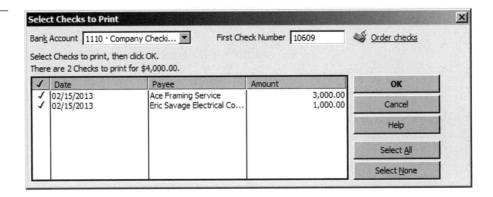

Printing Checks

To print your checks:

▌ From the **File** menu, choose **Print Forms** and then **Checks**. or click the **Print Checks** icon.

▌ Put a check mark in front of each check you want to print. See Figure 14-9.

▌ Click **OK** to print the checks.

Be sure you have blank check stock in your printer, and that the number in the First Check Number field matches the first number on your checks in the printer.

Figure 14-10

Use the Additional Info tab on the Edit Vendor window to create custom fields.

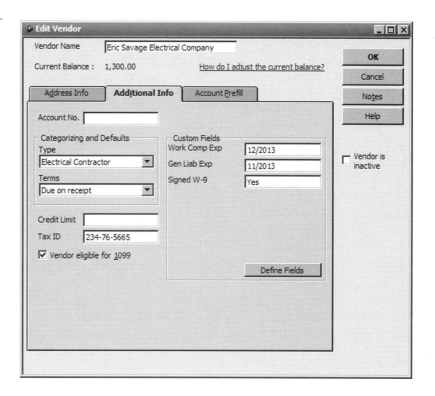

Vendor Workers' Comp Reports

Staying on top of the workers' comp expiration dates for subcontractors is a constant headache. As a matter of policy, never issue a purchase order, let alone pay a bill, to a subcontractor who hasn't supplied you with a current certificate of insurance for workers' comp. A workers' comp audit can cost you dearly if you can't show that your subcontractors had coverage at the time they provided their services. You can easily create a custom field in your vendors list to hold the date each subcontractor's workers' comp expires. You may find it helpful to get a report of your vendors and their workers' comp expiration dates. The *sample.qbw* file on the Download with this book has the custom field Work Comp Exp created for vendors. You'll find more information on the Vendor Workers' Comp Expirations report in Chapter 17, Reports.

Here's how to create a custom field:

▌ Click the **Vendor Center** icon on the menu bar, or from the **Vendors** menu, choose **Vendor Center**.

▌ In the **Vendor Center** window, right click any vendor and choose **Edit Vendor**.

▌ Click the **Additional Info** tab. The example in Figure 14-10 shows the Work Comp Exp custom field.

▌ In the lower right of the Custom Fields area, click **Define Fields**.

Figure 14-11

Use the Set up Custom Fields for Names window to name a custom field and select who the field will be used for.

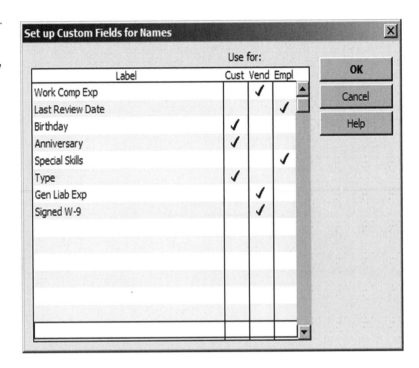

In the Set up Custom Fields for Names window, under the Label column, enter the field names you want to create. See Figure 14-11.

In the columns to the right, check to select who you're using the custom field for.

Click **OK** in the Define Fields window.

If you're using the QuickBooks Premier Contractor edition, you don't need to create this custom field. You can track insurance expiration dates on the Additional Info tab. See Figure 8-5 in Chapter 8, Vendors & Subcontractors.

Adding a Custom Field to Purchase Order Forms

To add a custom field to your purchase order forms:

From the **Lists** menu, choose **Templates**. In Figure 14-12, we show the Templates list.

Double click **Custom Purchase Order** in the **Name** column.

Click **Additional Customization** to get a window like the one shown in Figure 14-13.

Figure 14-12

The Templates list shows the existing templates.

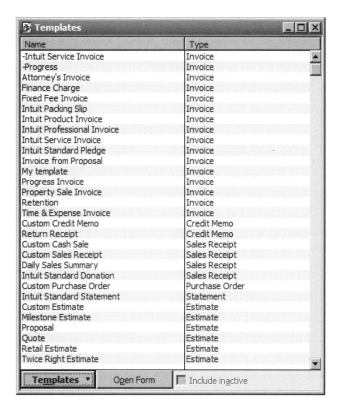

Figure 14-13

Use the Header tab window to select which fields you want to see in the Purchase Order window and which fields you want printed on your purchase orders.

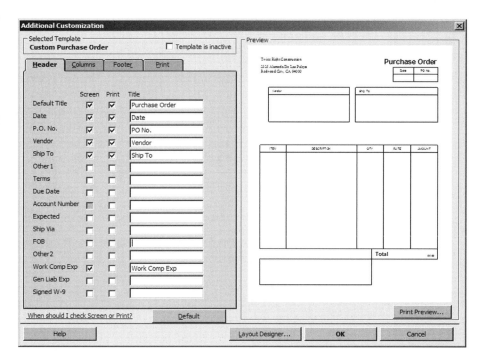

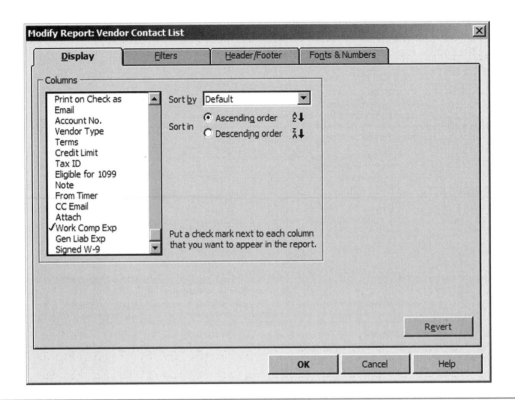

Figure 14-14
Use the Display tab of the Modify Report: Vendor Contact List window to select the columns you want to appear in a Vendor Contact list.

> ▌ Select the check box next to **Work Comp Exp**. You can also specify if you want the custom field printed on the purchase order, if you want it to appear only on the screen, or if you want both. Usually you'll choose to see the custom field only on the screen.
>
> ▌ Click **OK** to add the field to the purchase order form.

Preparing a Vendor Report on a Custom Field

Here's how to include a custom field on a vendor report:

> ▌ Click the **Report Center**, or from the **Reports** menu, choose **Vendors & Payables**, then **Vendor Contact List**.
>
> ▌ On the **Display** tab of the Modify Report: Vendor Contact List window, under the **Columns** box, scroll through the list to select only **(left margin)**, **Vendor**, **Phone**, **Contact**, and **Workers Comp Exp**. See Figure 14-14.
>
> ▌ Click **OK** to see a report like the Vendor Contact List we show in Figure 14-15.

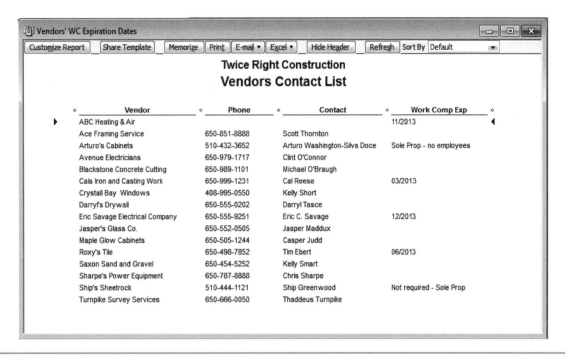

Figure 14-15
This Vendor Contact List report shows the custom field Workers' Comp Expires.

Now that you've finished entering bills and writing checks, proceed to payroll, Chapter 15. Even if you don't have employees, read through this chapter because we've included a special section on how to enter time for sole proprietors and partnerships.

Payroll

The ability to handle payroll is one of QuickBooks best features. It has tremendous flexibility, which is also why setting it up can be somewhat frustrating.

In this chapter we'll show you how to:

- enter a timesheet

- process payroll

- print payroll checks

And, if your company is a sole proprietorship or partnership, we'll show you how to enter and process owner's time to jobs so it's included on your job cost reports. But before we begin, make sure you have all your payroll items set up. You'll find information on payroll items back in Chapter 5.

Entering a Timesheet

Before creating a payroll check for an employee, you should complete a timesheet in QuickBooks to assign the hours the employee worked during the pay period to a customer: job, service item (job phase), payroll item and workers' compensation code. You get this information from the weekly timesheet completed by the employee or the supervisor in charge of the project. TIP: Keep in mind that some states require that employees sign their timecard if someone else fills it out.

Before you process payroll the first time, we suggest opening the *sample.qbw* file that comes with this book. We'll walk you through entering a weekly timesheet and processing payroll. The employee we'll be using first is Joe Bliss. In our sample company world, he's filled out and turned in a timecard for the week ending December 23, 2012. To begin, we're going to enter the information on his timecard into QuickBooks.

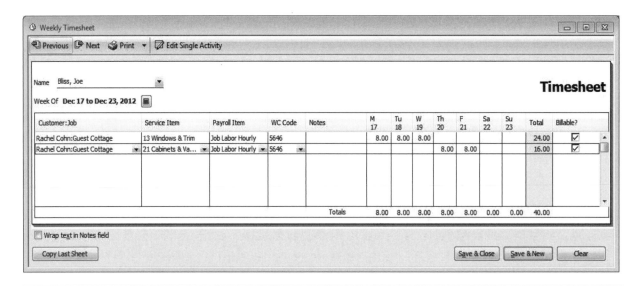

Figure 15-1
The QuickBooks timesheet assigns the hours worked to a Customer:Job, Service Item, and Payroll Item.

To enter a timesheet:

▌ Click **Home**, and **Enter Time**, then click the drop arrow and select **Use Weekly Timesheet**, or from the **Employees** menu, choose **Enter Time**, and then **Use Weekly Timesheet**.

▌ From the **Name** drop-down list, select the employee name. Figure 15-1 shows our Weekly Timesheet example for employee Joe Bliss.

You'll see the current week displayed below the employee name. Make sure you're entering time for the correct week. To move to different weeks:

▌ Click **Previous** or **Next**. To quickly move to a particular date, click the calendar icon at the end of the "Week Of" field. In our example, it's the week of December 17, 2012.

Let's look at the Weekly Timesheet in Figure 15-1 in detail.

The Customer:Job column represents the customer and job. As you see, Joe Bliss worked on the Rachel Cohn:Guest Cottage.

The Service Item column represents the job phases the employee worked on. For more information on job phases, see Chapter 4, Items. In our example, Joe worked on different job phases during the week. On Monday through Wednesday he worked on Rachel Cohn:Guest Cottage installing windows and trim. Then on Thursday and Friday Joe installed cabinets.

Figure 15-2

Warning window for a payroll item that hasn't been set up.

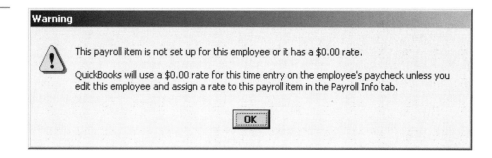

The contents of the Payroll Item column depend on whether or not you're using payroll items to track workers' compensation. In our example, we use workers' compensation codes as Payroll Items in QuickBooks. This lets us print a report later to help us fill out our workers' compensation report.

Entering a Payroll Item Not on an Employee's Payroll Info Tab

If you enter a payroll item that isn't on the employee's Payroll Info tab, you'll get a warning like the one shown in Figure 15-2. The Payroll Info tab is a part of an employee's record. To fix this problem:

▌ Click the **Employee Center** on the menu bar, or from the **Employees** menu, choose **Employee Center**.

▌ In the Employee Center window, double-click the employee you're entering the timecard for.

▌ From the **Change Tabs** dropdown list, choose **Payroll and Compensation Info**.

▌ In the Earnings section of the Edit Employee window, click in the **Item Name** column and select the item(s) you need from the pull-down Payroll Item list. Our example in Figure 15-3 shows the Payroll Info tab for Joe Bliss.

▌ Click **OK**.

Returning to the Weekly Timesheet (Figure 15-1), the Notes column is extremely important if you'll be billing a customer for an employee's labor on a time-and-materials basis. If you use QuickBooks to generate an invoice for the customer, make sure you fill in Notes with the exact text you want the customer to see on the invoice. The text you enter here will appear as a description on the invoice.

To the right of the Total column is the Billable column. Put a checkmark in the box for any time that is billable on a time-and-materials job.

Figure 15-3

Payroll items for an employee are listed in the Earnings box of the employee's data record.

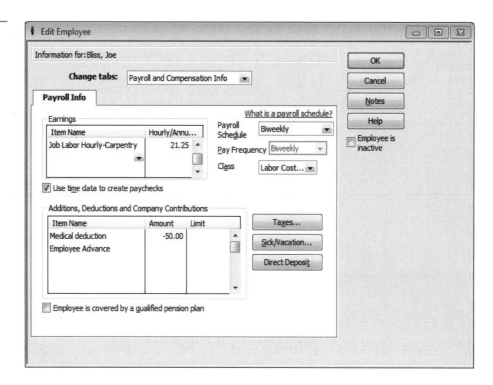

Now back to what to enter on the timesheet:

▌ Enter, on a different line, the hours worked on each job and the job phase.

▌ Enter the time for the week.

▌ Click the billable column boxes as necessary for the jobs.

▌ Click **Save & Close** to record the timesheet.

Any report generated before processing payroll will show only the hours entered, not the dollar amounts for those hours. After processing payroll, the dollar amounts associated with the hours will appear on reports.

Processing Employee Payroll

Before processing payroll, you should enter a timesheet for each employee. But before you can process payroll for the first time, you need to follow the setups outlined below to setup the payroll module.

To setup payroll:

▌ From the **Employee** menu, choose **Payroll**, **Turn on Payroll in QuickBooks**. You'll then simply walk through the steps.

Figure 15-4 shows you three options for setting up payroll.

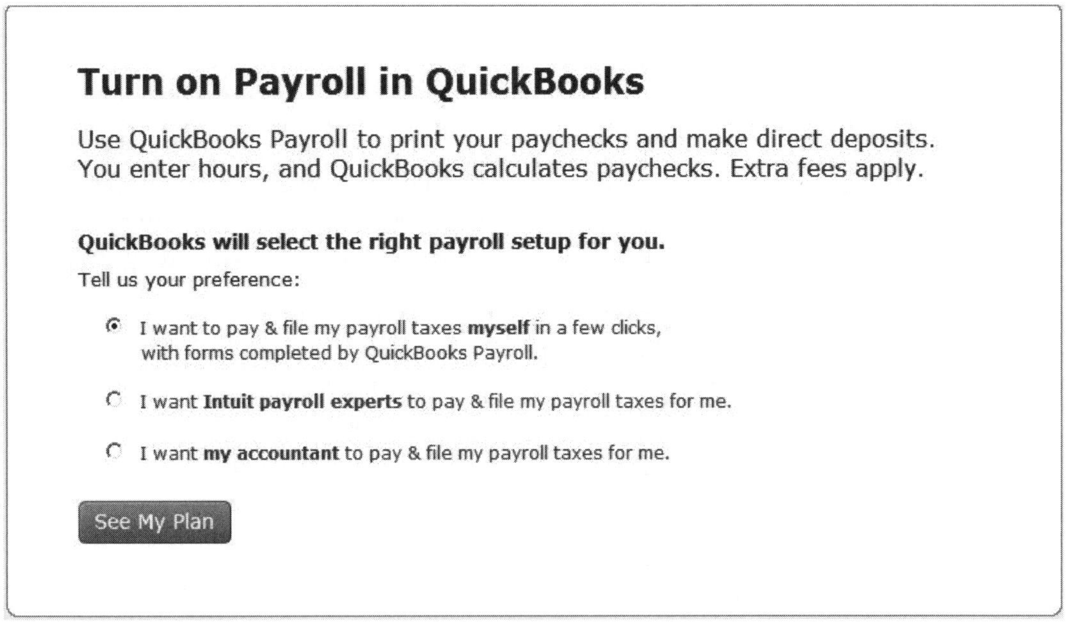

Turn on Payroll in QuickBooks

Use QuickBooks Payroll to print your paychecks and make direct deposits. You enter hours, and QuickBooks calculates paychecks. Extra fees apply.

QuickBooks will select the right payroll setup for you.

Tell us your preference:

- ⊙ I want to pay & file my payroll taxes **myself** in a few clicks, with forms completed by QuickBooks Payroll.

- ○ I want **Intuit payroll experts** to pay & file my payroll taxes for me.

- ○ I want **my accountant** to pay & file my payroll taxes for me.

[See My Plan]

Figure 15-4
The QuickBooks Payroll Services window displays your payroll options.

Option 1: "I want to pay and file my payroll taxes **myself** in a few clicks, with forms completed by QuickBooks Payroll."

Explanation — If you select this option, you'll be responsible for processing payroll in QuickBooks, paying *all* liabilities and processing the appropriate federal and state payroll forms in a timely manner. This is also called 'Enhanced Payroll' by Intuit, the makers of QuickBooks.

Option 2: "I want **Intuit payroll experts** to pay and file my payroll taxes for me."

Explanation — Similar to the option above, but the *Intuit payroll service* processes all payroll tax payments *and* they'll send all your payroll reports to the IRS and your state(s). This option is good for the person who has little or no experience with payroll or for someone who's looking for a hassle-free payroll system. Keep in mind that you'll still enter timesheets and process payroll, and then electronically send the payroll information to Intuit. They'll pay your payroll taxes and file the appropriate reports. This option is often referred to as 'Assisted Payroll' by Intuit.

Option 3: "I want **my accountant** to pay and file my payroll taxes for me."

Explanation — Here, "Accountant" is your *bookkeeper or in-house accountant*. With this option, you pay for payroll tax tables, and can print checks from QuickBooks (use direct deposit). You take

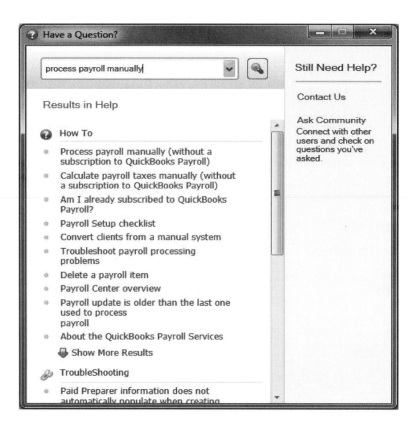

Figure 15-5
If you have a payroll service and want to get your labor cost to jobs, set up the QuickBooks payroll module to manually calculate payroll.

on all the responsibility of paying the payroll taxes to the proper authority. All payroll reports must be completed manually. This option should only be used for an *advanced* payroll specialist.

You can choose to calculate the payroll manually. Follow the steps below if you use a payroll service and just want to use QuickBooks payroll to get labor costs included in job costs. To enable manual payroll calculations:

▌ From the **Help** menu, select **QuickBooks help**.

▌ In the search menu bar, type in **process payroll manually**. Under the "How To" click on the topic **Process payroll manually (without a subscription to QuickBooks Payroll)**. See Figure 15-5. The help article will come to the screen. Follow the instructions.

▌ This will bring up a recommendation from QuickBooks. Look down at **Item #1**, and click on **manual payroll calculations**. QuickBooks will ask you if you're sure (look for the highlighted area). Click on **Set my company file to use manual calculations**.

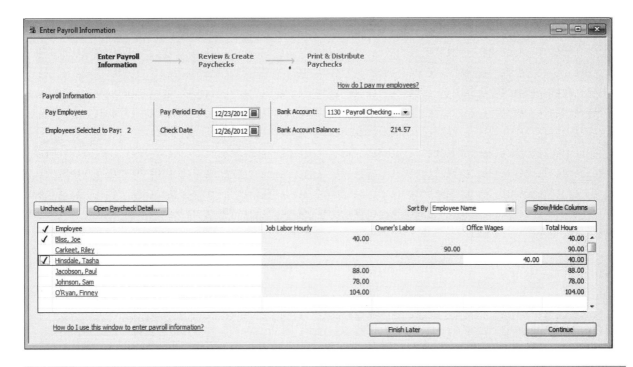

Figure 15-6
Put a check mark next to each employee to be paid.

If you select this option, you need to manually calculate the payroll taxes for each employee every time you run a payroll check. No table tables are included, but you can enter a payroll check issued after the fact by your payroll processing company.

Once you have set up the payroll module, follow the steps below to process payroll.

▌ Click **Home**, then click the **Pay Employees** icon, or from the **Employees** menu, select **Pay Employees**.

▌ In the Enter Payroll Information window, select the correct Bank Account you'll use for the checks. In our example shown in Figure 15-6, we used our 1130 Payroll Checking Account.

▌ Enter **Check Date** and **Pay Period Ends** date.

If hours don't show up for an employee even though you know you've entered time for that employee, you probably didn't enter the pay period ending date correctly. To make sure all time you entered on a previous timesheet shows up, you must enter a date after the last date that shows up on the previous timesheet you entered. For example, in Figure 15-1, the last date on the timesheet next to "Week Of" is 12/23/2012. To pick up all the time on that timesheet, the date you enter into the Pay Period Ends box must be 12/23/2012. Also, the date must not conflict with the next timesheet you enter.

Figure 15-7

Use the Preview Paycheck window to make sure you enter all costs for an employee correctly.

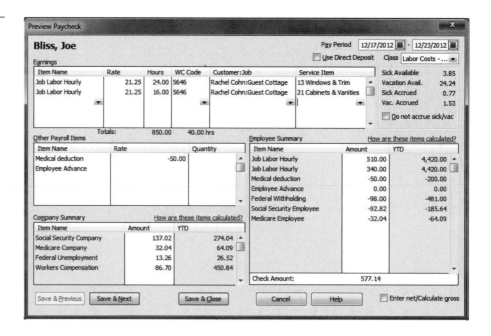

■ Check the box in the leftmost column next to the employee name for each employee you're paying.

■ Next you'll review each paycheck for accuracy.

Using the Preview Paycheck Window

The Preview Paycheck window allows you to review each person's paycheck for accuracy. Under the Employee column of the Enter Payroll Information window, click on each employee name to get to the Preview Paycheck window.

The Preview Paycheck window displays the information that was entered on the timecard.

The hours for each payroll Item, Customer:Job, and Service Item entered will show in the Earnings box. The information in the Earnings box comes directly from the Weekly Timesheet. Our example shown in Figure 15-7 is the Preview Paycheck window we get using the timesheet shown in Figure 15-1.

Verify that the information in the Earnings box is correct. If any information isn't correct, click Cancel to close the Preview Paycheck window right away. Then return to the employee's timesheet and make the necessary changes. If you make changes in the Earnings box in the Preview Paycheck window, the timecard won't be automatically changed. Make any corrections directly on the timesheet.

Entering Payroll Additions and Deductions

You use the Other Payroll Items box to track additions to an employee's pay (bonus) and deductions from an employee's pay (medical or dental). In our example, we deducted $50 from Joe's paycheck for medical insurance. To do this, in the Preview Paycheck window:

▌ Click in the **Item Name** column under the **Other Payroll Items** box and select the addition or deduction from the pull-down Item Name list.

▌ In the **Rate** column, enter the amount of the addition or deduction. Check to make sure you've entered the information correctly. To enter a deduction, enter a negative number in the **Rate** column. In our example in Figure 15-7, we deducted $50 for medical insurance from Joe Bliss's check.

▌ Be sure to check your entries in the Employee Summary box.

One of the benefits of Enhanced Payroll is workers' compensation tracking. Having QuickBooks calculate workers' comp is an important feature for contractors because each time a payroll check is created in QuickBooks, it will put the cost of workers' comp on the job cost report under the appropriate phase of the job. It tracks the amount you owe the workers' compensation company, and it creates the reports needed to properly pay your monthly, quarterly or annual premiums for workers' comp.

Note: Once you turn this feature on, you'll see a new column on the timesheet and payroll check labeled WC Code. This new field allows QuickBooks to gather the appropriate hours and calculate the workers' comp cost for you.

Before this feature can be used, you'll need to turn it on in Preferences:

▌ From the **Edit** menu, select **Preferences**, click on **Payroll & Employees, Company Preferences**, Click on **Workers Compensation Button**, add a check mark to the **Track Workers Comp**.

▌ From the **Employee** menu, select, **Workers Comp, Set-up Workers Comp**.

The Setup Wizard will aid you in entering the name of your policy holder, policy number, and effective date, as well as setting each employee to the correct workers' comp codes.

Figure 15-8

Print Paychecks window.

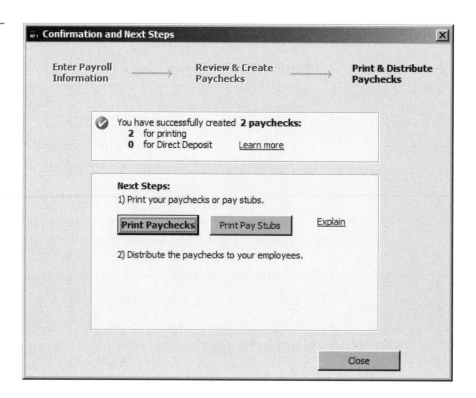

In order to complete the workers' comp setup wizard, you'll need your current policy information in front of you, including a workers' comp code list and rates. If you need to go back and edit any of the entries you entered while setting the workers' comp defaults, go to the **List menu, Workers Comp List**.

Check the employee's information in the Preview Paycheck window again. If everything is correct:

▌ Click **Save & Next**. Preview each paycheck.

Once all paychecks have been reviewed:

▌ Click **Continue** in the **Enter Payroll Information** window.

▌ Give the paychecks a final review in the **Review and Create Paychecks** window.

▌ When everything looks correct, click **Create Paychecks**.

▌ A payroll confirmation window is displayed. See Figure 15-8.

▌ If you're ready to print the paychecks, click **Print Paychecks**. If not, click **Close**. Follow the steps below to print the checks when you are ready.

Figure 15-9
Put a check mark next to each check you're ready to print.

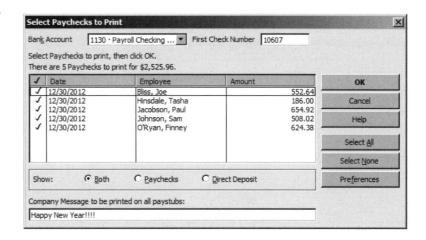

Printing Employee Checks

To print the employee checks:

▌ From the **File** menu, choose **Print Forms** and then **Paychecks**.

▌ Select the paychecks to print, as shown in our example in Figure 15-9.

▌ Click **OK** to print the checks.

Allocating Sole Proprietor or Partner's Time to a Job

One of the most common questions we hear is "How do I, as an owner, allocate my time to a job?" Simply enter your time on a timecard and then process payroll. When you process payroll, deduct the dollars back out by creating a zero check. Entering the timecard and processing payroll will add the hours, and the dollars associated with those hours, to job cost reports. But be sure payroll items have been set up for Owner's Labor and Owner's Labor Deduction. See Chapter 5 if you need help setting up a payroll item.

Entering a Timesheet for an Owner

For each pay period, enter the owner's time on a timesheet just as you would a regular employee. Let's go through an example for Riley Carkeet, the sole proprietor of Twice Right Construction. To enter a timesheet for an owner or partner:

▌ Click **Home**, and **Enter Time**, then click the dropdown arrow and select **Use Weekly Timesheet**, or from the **Employees** menu, choose **Enter Time**, and then **Use Weekly Timesheet**.

▌ From the **Name** drop-down list, select the owner. Figure 15-10 shows our Weekly Timesheet example for Riley Carkeet.

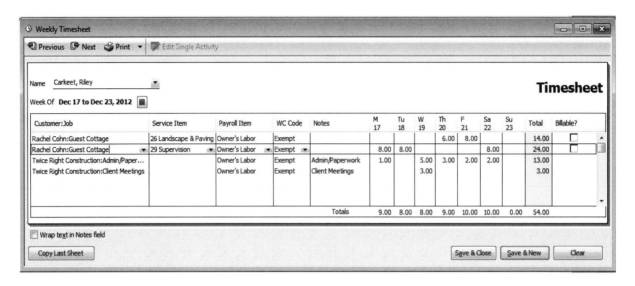

Figure 15-10
When entering a timesheet for an owner, the payroll item must be Owner's Labor.

▌ Select the appropriate week. In our example, it's December 17 - December 23, 2012.

▌ Enter a different line for the hours worked on each job and phase.

▌ In the **Payroll Item** column of each line on the timesheet, select the payroll item **Owner's Labor**. Always use this item when entering owner's time. The Owner's Labor item is set up to post to an equity account (account 3999 Owner's Time to Jobs in our *sample.qbw* file). If you select a payroll item that doesn't post to the appropriate equity account, the owner's labor costs won't appear properly in your job cost reports.

▌ Click the invoice icons as necessary for the jobs.

▌ Click **Save & Close** to record the owner's time.

Processing an Owner's Time

To process payroll allocating owner's time to jobs:

▌ Click **Home,** then click the **Pay Employees** icon, or from the **Employees** menu, choose **Pay Employees**.

▌ From the pull-down Bank Account list, select your **Adjustment Register** account. Since you're creating a zero check, you don't want it showing up in the regular bank account. Use the Adjustment Register to hold transactions with zero amounts. In our example shown in Figure 15-11, we use 1111 Adjustment Register account.

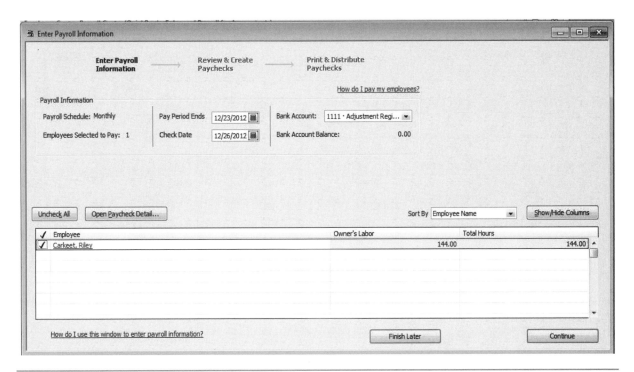

Figure 15-11
Use your Adjustment Register account when you process an owner's paycheck.

▌ Enter the **Pay Period Ends** and **Check Date**.

▌ Click in the checkmark column next to the owner's name.

▌ Under the Employee column of the **Enter Payroll Information** window, click on the owner's name to get to the Preview Paycheck window.

Now you'll see the Preview Paycheck window for the owner's timesheet. Figure 15-12 shows our example for Riley Carkeet. Be sure to select Owner's Labor Deduction in the Other Payroll Items box. To do this:

▌ In the **Item Name** column, under the **Other Payroll Items** box, select the payroll item **Owner's Labor Deduction**.

▌ In the **Rate** column enter –100%.

▌ Make sure **Check Amount** is 0.0 when you finish entering these amounts. It's important that you clear all taxes in the Company Summary and Employee Summary boxes to zero as well.

▌ Click **Save & Close**.

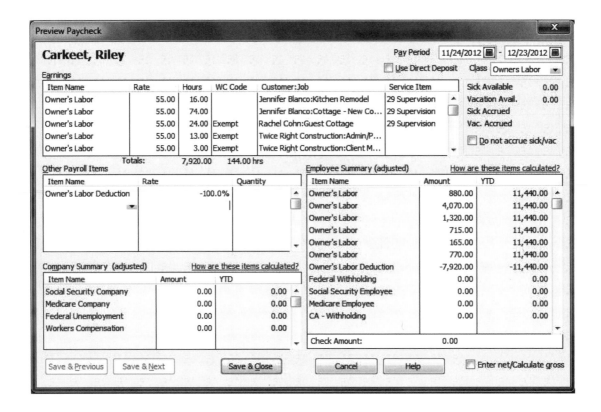

Figure 15-12
When processing payroll for an owner, make sure the Owner's Labor Deduction and rate are entered correctly. It's important that the Check Amount is 0.00.

▌ Click **Continue** in the Enter Payroll Information window.

▌ In the Review and Create Paychecks window, click **Create Paychecks**.

▌ Click **Close.**

In this chapter, we gave you a great deal of information. We told you how to:

▌ enter timesheets

▌ process payroll

▌ allocate workers' comp costs to jobs

▌ get owner's time into job cost reports

If you feel a bit overwhelmed by all the information we've presented, keep in mind that you don't have to take all of this in at one time. For example, you can simply process payroll first and then add workers' comp costs later. Then you can add owner's time when you have payroll and workers' comp figured out. In other words, you can take things one step at a time.

Chapter 16

Using QuickBooks on a Cash Basis

QuickBooks can be used on a cash basis or an accrual basis. You can start on a cash basis and later change to an accrual basis. All you have to do is change one option in your Reports & Graphs preferences.

In the previous two chapters we discussed receivables and payables on the accrual basis. That's what most contractors will use. But if you're a small operator with few or no employees, or no time to do bookkeeping, you're probably running your business on a cash basis.

If you're just starting your business, you may feel more comfortable starting to use QuickBooks on a cash basis. Although this may be an easier way to get up and running, try to change to the accrual method as soon as possible. Accrual-based reports will give you a more timely and accurate picture of your finances, job status, and operating status. Since QuickBooks has the ability to switch reporting between cash and accrual, you can file your tax returns on a cash basis, and get management reports on the more accurate accrual basis.

So let's look at the cash basis of accounting. To report an expense, simply write a check and log it in. To report income, deposit money in the bank and log in the deposit. It's easy and fast. You don't have to enter a bill or invoice and then tell the computer it has been paid. The downside, of course, is that the computer isn't tracking who you owe money to, or who owes you money. Also, your reports don't include expenses that you haven't paid or invoices you haven't issued to customers.

To tell QuickBooks that you want to operate on a cash basis:

▎ From the **Edit** menu, choose **Preferences**.

▎ Click the **Reports & Graphs** icon. See Figure 16-1.

▎ Click the **Company Preferences** tab.

▎ Select **Cash** for the Summary Reports Basis.

▎ Click **OK**.

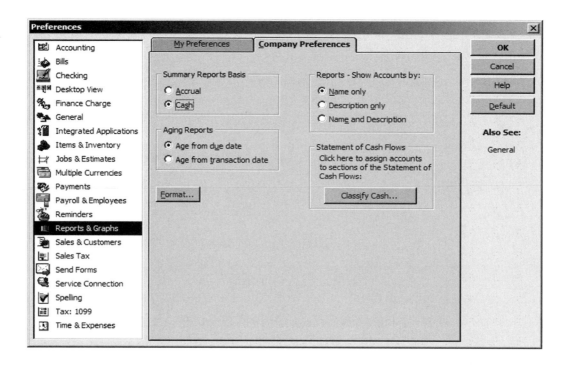

Figure 16-1
Use the Reports & Graphs Preferences window to let QuickBooks know you operate on a cash basis.

How to Record a Check

To record a check:

> ▌ Click **Home**, then click **Write Checks**, or from the **Banking** menu, choose **Write Checks**.

Now let's look at Figure 16-2 to see what you would need to enter here:

> ▌ In **Bank Account**, select the correct bank account.
>
> ▌ In **No.**, enter the check number if it's a handwritten check. Otherwise, check the **To be printed** box.
>
> ▌ In **Date**, enter the date of the check.
>
> ▌ In **Pay to the Order of**, enter payee name or select the name from the drop-down vendor list.
>
> ▌ In **$**, enter the check amount. The Dollars field will fill in automatically.

Figure 16-2
The QuickBooks Write Checks window looks similar to a regular paper check.

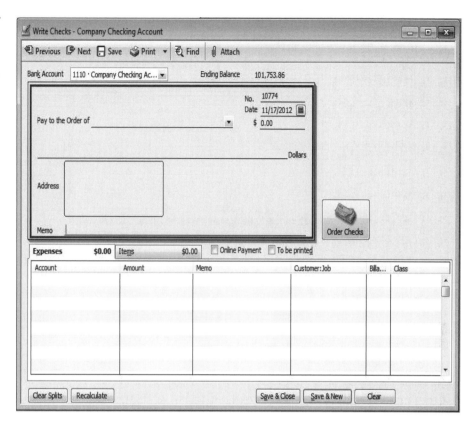

Using the Items Tab to Record a Job-Related Cost

You should always use the Items tab to enter job-related costs. Our example in Figure 16-3 shows the Items tab of a check to Pella Windows for the job-related cost of windows for Jennifer Blanco:Kitchen Remodel.

To record a check for a job-related cost in a Write Checks window:

▌ Click the **Items** tab. Click in the **Item** column and select the appropriate items from the drop-down list.

▌ In **Qty**, enter the quantity of the item. Amount will be calculated automatically.

▌ Select **Customer:Job** from the pull-down Customer:Job list.

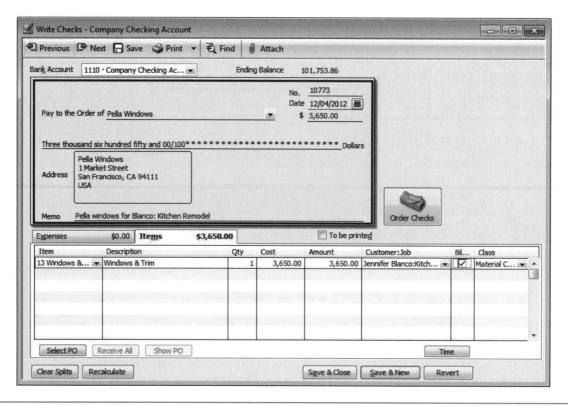

Figure 16-3

It's important to use the Items tab when you write checks for job-related expenses.

▌ Put a check in the Billable column if you are billing the item amount to your client.

▌ In **Class**, select the appropriate class from the pull-down Class list.

If you're splitting the total payment to the vendor over more than one job (or if the payment covers more items), click in the next line and make the additional entry(s) using the same procedure.

▌ Click **Save & Close**.

Using the Expenses Tab to Record an Overhead Expense

Always use the Expenses tab to enter overhead costs. Our example in Figure 16-4 shows check number 10774 to Acme Fast Fuel for gasoline, which is an overhead expense.

To enter an overhead expense check in a Write Checks window:

▌ Click the **Expenses** tab.

▌ Click in the Account column and select the correct expense account from the drop-down list. In our example, we used 6101 - Gas & Oil.

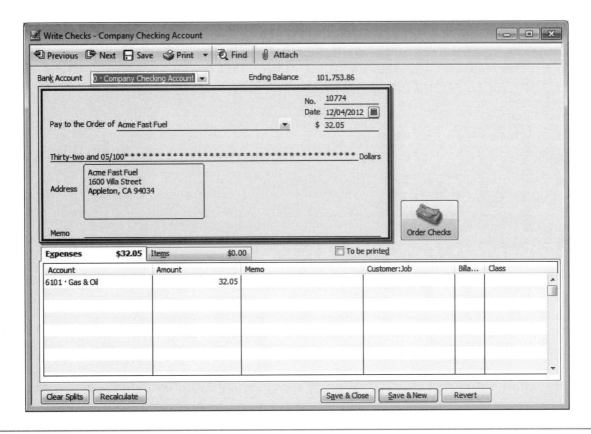

Figure 16-4
Use the Expenses tab when you write checks for overhead expenses.

If you're splitting the total payment to the vendor over more than one expense account, click in the next line and make the additional entry(s) using the same procedure.

When the check entry is complete:

▌ Click **Save & Close** to record the check.

How to Record a Deposit

Deposits to your checking account are recorded in the Make Deposits window. To record a deposit:

▌ Click **Home**, then click the **Record Deposits** icon, or from the **Banking** menu, choose **Make Deposits**.

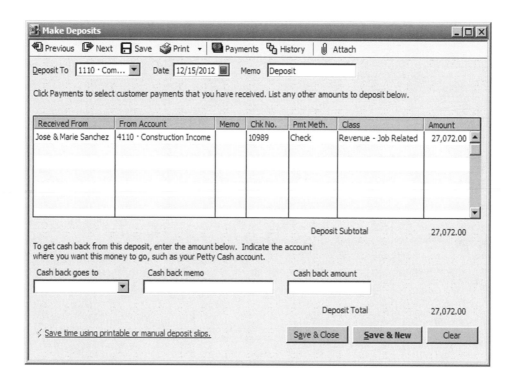

Figure 16-5
The Make Deposits window shows all checks that are ready to be deposited.

Look at Figure 16-5 for an example deposit:

▌ In the Make Deposits window, in **Deposit To**, select your checking account from the pull-down list. If you have multiple checking accounts, make sure you select the correct one.

▌ In **Date**, enter the date of the deposit.

▌ In **Received From**, use the pull-down list to select who you've received the check from.

▌ In **From Account**, select the correct account for the deposit from the pull-down list. Usually this is an income account.

▌ In **Chk No.**, enter the check number.

▌ In **Pmt Meth.**, select payment method from the pull-down list.

▌ In **Class**, select the correct class for the deposit from the pull-down list. Usually, you'll use Revenue - Job Related. If the deposit isn't job related, you can skip this.

▌ In **Amount**, enter the deposit amount.

▌ Click **Save & Close** to record the deposit.

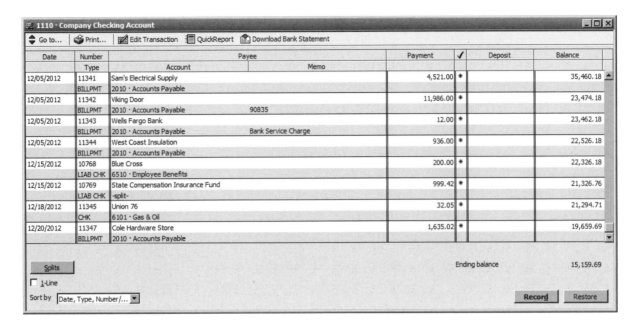

Figure 16-6
Your checking account register shows all your payments, deposits, and your account balance.

Checking Your Transactions with the QuickBooks Register

QuickBooks has a register you can use to look at all your recorded transactions listed. Use the register to get a quick look at all the checks you've written over a certain time. Or you can use it to get your checkbook account balance.

To open the Checking Register:

▌ Click **Home**, then click **Chart of Accounts**, or from the **Lists** menu, choose **Chart of Accounts**.

▌ In the Chart of Accounts list, double-click your checking account to bring up the register. See Figure 16-6.

This register will show payments, deposits, and the current balance of your checking account.

Now that you've learned how to enter transactions on a cash basis, keep in mind that running your construction company on a cash basis isn't the best way to run the business. As soon as possible, switch to an accrual basis of accounting so job cost reports will always be up to date.

Chapter 17

Reports

As a contractor, you need up-to-the-minute information on job costs — but "up-to-the-minute" means different things to different contractors. If you typically run jobs that last only a week or so, you'll probably want to analyze your job costs daily. That's the only way to keep up with them. If your jobs run months or years, you don't need to get job cost reports so frequently; once a month may be sufficient for longer jobs.

In this chapter, we'll cover:

▌ how to customize existing reports

▌ how to use the memorized reports in the *sample.qbw* and *company.qbw* data files on the Download that comes with this book

▌ how to use the project reports in QuickBooks

Finding and learning to use reports will give you more insight into the day-to-day status of your jobs. Learning how to modify reports will give you the power to create reports that are meaningful to you and more specific to your business.

We added the memorized reports in *sample.qbw* and *company.qbw* to give you construction-specific reports you can use on a day-to-day basis.

How to Customize Reports

Use the Modify Report window to select information you want to include in the report. For example, you may want to get a report for just one job, or you may want to change a report to include an invoice or check number. When a report is displayed, you'll see the Modify Report window blocking the report. To view the report, click OK. To retrieve the Modify Report window, click Customize Report in the top left corner of the report window. You can see this button in Figure 17-1, where we show a Job Profitability Detail report.

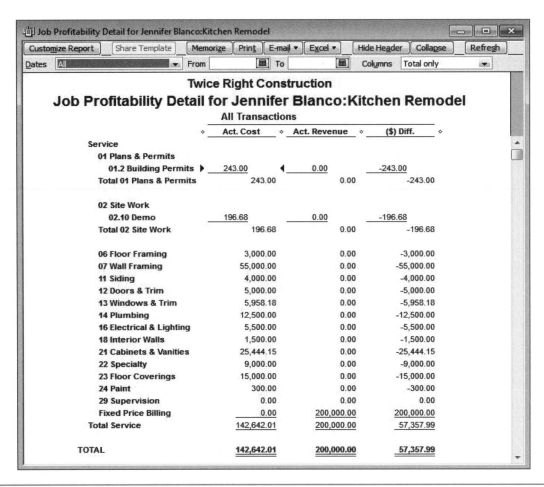

Figure 17-1
To change a report, click the Customize Report button located in the top left corner of the report window.

The Display Tab on the Modify Report Window

In general, you use the Display tab of a Modify Report window to select the date range and the columns you would like to see on a report. Figure 17-2 shows the Display tab column settings for the Job Profitability Detail report in Figure 17-1. It's worth noting here that the Display tab options change depending on the report you're customizing. For example, in Figure 17-2, a date range and column options can be specified for a Job Profitability Report. In Figure 17-3, columns can be added/deleted and sorting details specified for a Customer Phone List.

Figure 17-2

The Display tab window lets you specify which dates and columns will be on the report.

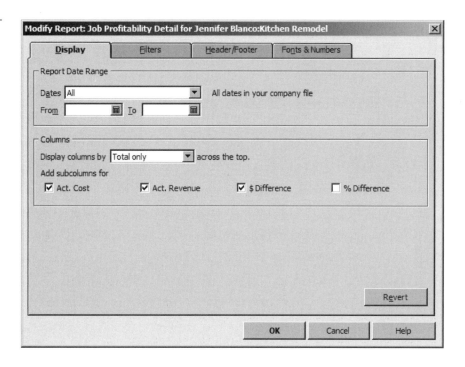

Figure 17-3

The Display tab window changes depending on the type of report you're generating.

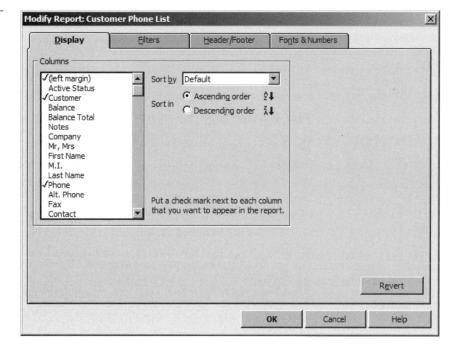

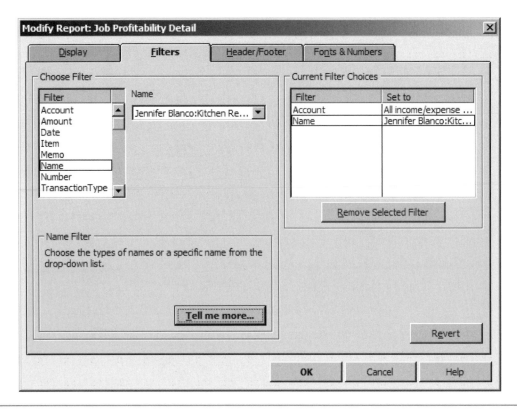

Figure 17-4
The Filters tab window lets you pick which data is on your report.

The Filters Tab on the Modify Report Window

The Filters tab on the Modify Report window lets you specify which specific records will appear in a report. You can define the accounts, customers:jobs, classes, transaction types, payees, dates, transaction amounts, and/or memo contents that each record must match before it's included in the report. In Figure 17-4, we show a Filters tab window to get a report for a particular job — Jennifer Blanco:Kitchen Remodel. At the right side of the Filters tab window under Current Filter Choices, you'll see a list of the current filters for the report.

The Header/Footer Tab on the Modify Report Window

The Header/Footer tab on the Modify Report window lets you customize your report and modify your header and footer information. When memorizing a new report, you'll use this tab to change the report's title.

Figure 17-5

The Memorized Report List in *sample.qbw* and *company.qbw*.

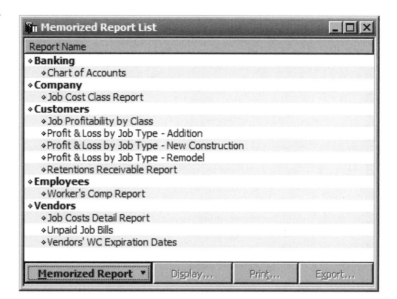

Memorized Report List

Report Name
- ◆**Banking**
  - ◆Chart of Accounts
- ◆**Company**
  - ◆Job Cost Class Report
- ◆**Customers**
  - ◆Job Profitability by Class
  - ◆Profit & Loss by Job Type - Addition
  - ◆Profit & Loss by Job Type - New Construction
  - ◆Profit & Loss by Job Type - Remodel
  - ◆Retentions Receivable Report
- ◆**Employees**
  - ◆Worker's Comp Report
- ◆**Vendors**
  - ◆Job Costs Detail Report
  - ◆Unpaid Job Bills
  - ◆Vendors' WC Expiration Dates

Memorized Report ▼   Display...   Print...   Export...

Using Our Memorized Reports

Memorizing a report is easy — but creating the report may take some time. Determining exactly what combination of modifying and filtering will give you the report you want can be a bit of a brain twister. Also, you have to be absolutely consistent and accurate when you enter transactions. If you enter a transaction incorrectly, it may not be in the reports when, or where, it should be. You don't want to make a good decision based on bad information.

We defined and memorized the reports we discussed in this section in the *company.qbw* and *sample.qbw* data files included on the Download that comes with this book. We hope you can make good use of these reports in managing your business. We based the reports on the *sample.qbw* data file. If you've changed the file or are using other data files, review the reports to make sure they show what you need.

To display a list of the memorized reports in *sample.qbw* or *company.qbw*:

▌ Open *sample.qbw* or *company.qbw*.

▌ Click **Report Center**, then **Memorized**, or from the **Reports** menu, choose **Memorized Reports** and then **Memorized Report List**. See Figure 17-5.

▌ To generate a memorized report, select the report and click **Display**.

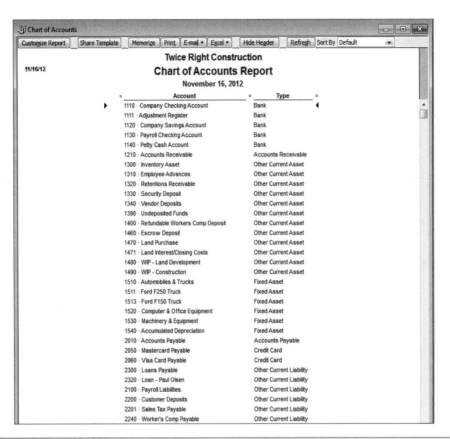

Figure 17-6
A memorized Chart of Accounts Report.

If you didn't use the *sample.qbw* or *company.qbw* data file to set up your QuickBooks company file, you may want to memorize some of the reports in this section in your own company file.

We'll step through creating and memorizing each report.

If you set up your company file using *company.qbw*, skip the information on memorizing each report. All the memorized reports are already set up for you.

Now let's look at each memorized report.

Chart of Accounts Report

The memorized Chart of Accounts Report simplifies the QuickBooks built-in Chart of Accounts Report. It looks similar to the one included in Chapter 3. Use this report to help define which accounts you have set up in your Chart of Accounts. Figure 17-6 shows a memorized Chart of Accounts Report.

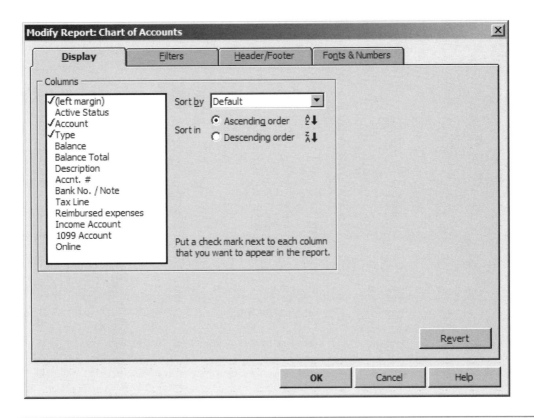

Figure 17-7
Choose the columns to appear in the Chart of Accounts Report.

Memorizing the Chart of Accounts Report — To memorize the Chart of Accounts Report in your QuickBooks data file:

▌ Click **Report Center**, or from the **Reports** menu, choose **List**, then **Account Listing**.

▌ Now select the columns in the Display tab of the Modify Report window, as shown in Figure 17-7. Select only **(left margin)**, **Account**, and **Type** from the Columns list. Be sure to scroll down the list to deselect other columns on the list.

▌ Click the **Header/Footer** tab. In **Report Title**, enter **Chart of Accounts Report**.

▌ Click **OK**.

▌ In the report window, click **Memorize**.

▌ In the **Memorize Report** window, enter **Chart of Accounts**.

▌ Click **OK**.

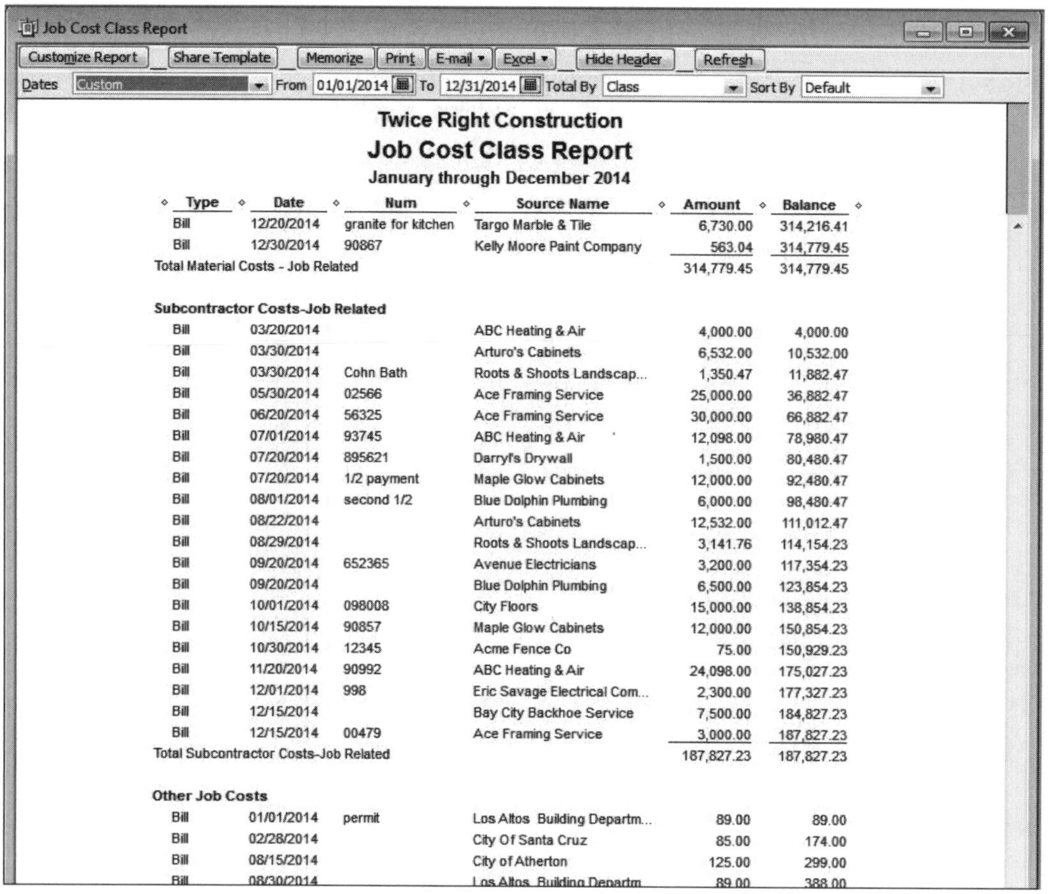

Job Cost Class Report

Customize Report | Share Template | Memorize | Print | E-mail | Excel | Hide Header | Refresh

Dates Custom From 01/01/2014 To 12/31/2014 Total By Class Sort By Default

Twice Right Construction

Job Cost Class Report

January through December 2014

Type	Date	Num	Source Name	Amount	Balance
Bill	12/20/2014	granite for kitchen	Targo Marble & Tile	6,730.00	314,216.41
Bill	12/30/2014	90867	Kelly Moore Paint Company	563.04	314,779.45
Total Material Costs - Job Related				314,779.45	314,779.45
Subcontractor Costs-Job Related					
Bill	03/20/2014		ABC Heating & Air	4,000.00	4,000.00
Bill	03/30/2014		Arturo's Cabinets	6,532.00	10,532.00
Bill	03/30/2014	Cohn Bath	Roots & Shoots Landscap...	1,350.47	11,882.47
Bill	05/30/2014	02566	Ace Framing Service	25,000.00	36,882.47
Bill	06/20/2014	56325	Ace Framing Service	30,000.00	66,882.47
Bill	07/01/2014	93745	ABC Heating & Air	12,098.00	78,980.47
Bill	07/20/2014	895621	Darryl's Drywall	1,500.00	80,480.47
Bill	07/20/2014	1/2 payment	Maple Glow Cabinets	12,000.00	92,480.47
Bill	08/01/2014	second 1/2	Blue Dolphin Plumbing	6,000.00	98,480.47
Bill	08/22/2014		Arturo's Cabinets	12,532.00	111,012.47
Bill	08/29/2014		Roots & Shoots Landscap...	3,141.76	114,154.23
Bill	09/20/2014	652365	Avenue Electricians	3,200.00	117,354.23
Bill	09/20/2014		Blue Dolphin Plumbing	6,500.00	123,854.23
Bill	10/01/2014	098008	City Floors	15,000.00	138,854.23
Bill	10/15/2014	90857	Maple Glow Cabinets	12,000.00	150,854.23
Bill	10/30/2014	12345	Acme Fence Co	75.00	150,929.23
Bill	11/20/2014	90992	ABC Heating & Air	24,098.00	175,027.23
Bill	12/01/2014	998	Eric Savage Electrical Com...	2,300.00	177,327.23
Bill	12/15/2014		Bay City Backhoe Service	7,500.00	184,827.23
Bill	12/15/2014	00479	Ace Framing Service	3,000.00	187,827.23
Total Subcontractor Costs-Job Related				187,827.23	187,827.23
Other Job Costs					
Bill	01/01/2014	permit	Los Altos Building Departm...	89.00	89.00
Bill	02/28/2014		City Of Santa Cruz	85.00	174.00
Bill	08/15/2014		City of Atherton	125.00	299.00
Bill	08/30/2014		Los Altos Building Departm...	89.00	388.00

Figure 17-8

A memorized Job Cost Class Report.

Job Cost Class Report

The memorized Job Cost Class Report shows, in detail, all revenue and costs separated by class. This report is a Transaction Detail by Account report sorted by these classes: Labor, Materials, Subcontractor, Equipment Rental, and Other. The bold column header at the top left of each section is the class. See Figure 17-8.

Memorizing the Job Cost Class Report — To memorize the Job Cost Class Report in your QuickBooks data file:

- Click **Report Center**, or from the **Reports** menu, choose **Accountant & Taxes**, and then **Transaction Detail by Account**.
- Select the columns in the Display tab of the Modify Report window, as shown in Figure 17-9. Select only **(left margin), Type**, **Date**, **Num**, **Source Name**, **Amount**, and **Balance**. Scroll down to the bottom of the list to find Source Name, Amount, and Balance.

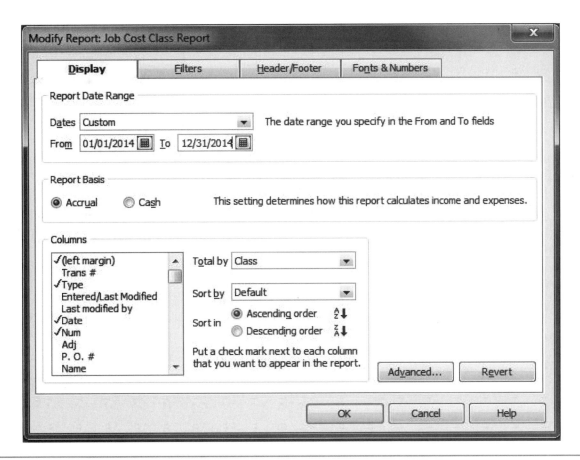

Figure 17-9
In the Total by field, select Class to group and subtotal transactions by job cost class.

▌ In **Report Date Range**, enter the date range you're interested in. Usually this would be for a given month or year. Our example in Figure 17-9 uses the fiscal year 1/1/2014 to 12/31/2014.

▌ In **Total By**, select **Class** from the pull-down list.

▌ Click on the **Filters** tab. In the **Filter** list, click on **Account**. In the drop-down **Account** list, select **All cost-of-sales accounts**.

▌ In the **Filter** list, click on **Class**. In the drop-down **Class** list, select **Multiple classes**. In the **Select Class** window, click on: **Labor, Materials, Subcontractor, Equipment, and Other Job Costs**. Click **OK**.

▌ Click **OK**.

▌ In the report window, click **Memorize**.

▌ In the **Memorize Report** window, enter **Job Cost Class Report**.

▌ Click **OK**.

Figure 17-10

To filter a report for a specific job, select the job from the Name drop-down list.

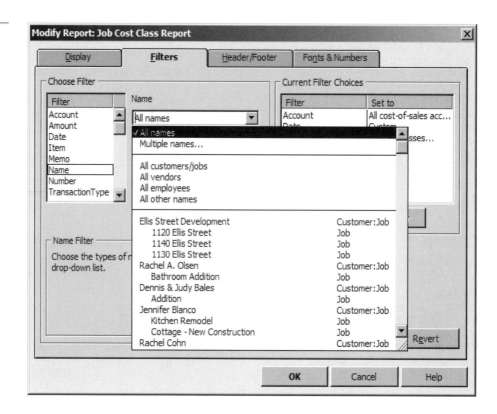

Often you'll want to know the job-related labor costs for just one job. To do this:

▌ Click the **Modify Report** button when you have a Job Cost Class report on your screen.

▌ Click the **Filters** tab.

▌ In the Filters tab window, select **Name** from the Filter list. See Figure 17-10.

▌ From the Name drop-down list, select the **Customer:Job** you're interested in.

▌ Click **OK**.

Profit & Loss by Job Type

In Chapter 7 we discussed using job types such as Residential, Commercial, or Remodel. This report lets you evaluate profitability for the jobs that fall into each job type. This information will help you decide whether or not to continue with a particular line of work. For example, if your commercial jobs aren't as profitable as your residential jobs, you may decide to focus on residential. Figure 17-11 shows a memorized Profit & Loss by Job Type Report.

Figure 17-11

To get an accurate analysis of your business, create a P & L by Job Type for each of your job types.

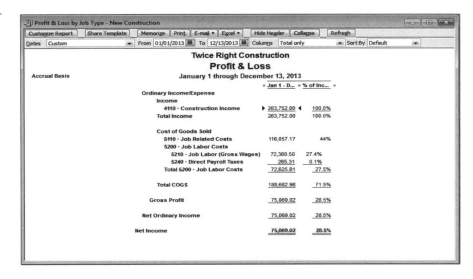

Figure 17-12

Use the Modify Report window to specify a date range for the report. Typically, your date range will be a calendar year.

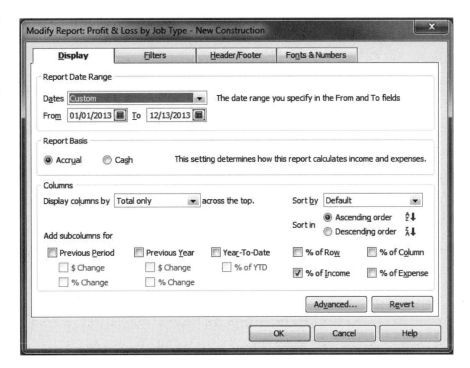

To memorize the Profit & Loss by Job Type report:

▌ Click **Report Center**, or from the **Reports** menu, select **Company & Financial**, and then **Profit & Loss Standard**.

▌ In **Report Date Range**, enter the date range you are interested in. Usually your date range will be a year. See Figure 17-12.

▌ Click on **% of Income**.

Figure 17-13

Filter the report using Job Type. In this example, our report will show how well we did on remodels.

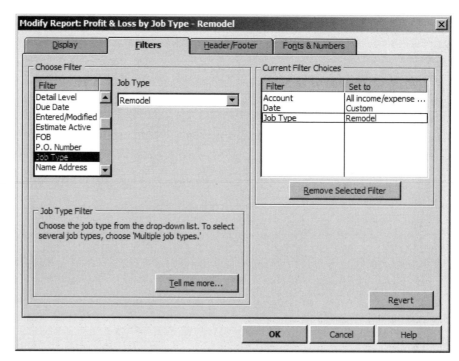

■ Click on the **Filters** tab. In the **Filter** list, click on **Job Type**. In the drop-down **Job Type** list, select the job type you want to use in your report. In our example, we select **Remodel**. See Figure 17-13.

■ Click on the **Header/Footer** tab. In Report Title, enter a name for the report such as **Profit & Loss by Job Type - Remodel**.

■ Click **OK**.

■ In the report window, click on **Memorize**. Enter a name for the memorized report.

■ Click **OK**.

Retentions Receivable Report

The Retentions Receivable Report lists all the customers that owe you for retention. See Figure 17-14.

Memorizing the Retentions Receivable Report — To memorize the Retentions Receivable Report in your QuickBooks data file:

■ Click **Report Center**, or from the **Reports** menu, choose **Customers & Receivables**, and then **Customer Balance Summary**.

■ In **Report Date Range**, enter the date range you're interested in. Usually this would be for a given month or year.

Figure 17-14

A memorized Retentions Receivable Report.

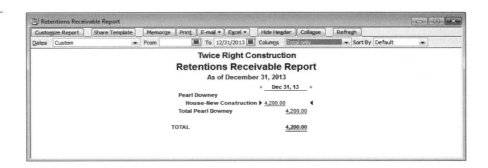

Figure 17-15

The Report Filters window showing some of the settings for the Retentions Receivable Report.

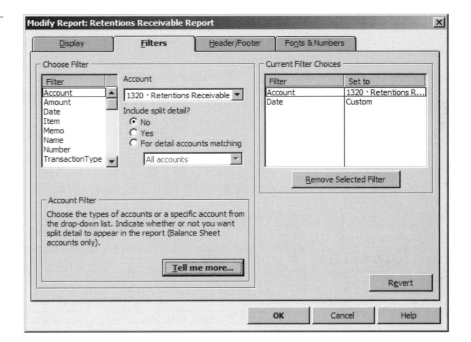

▌ Click the **Filters** tab.

▌ In the Filters tab window, select **Account** from the Filter list.

▌ From the pull-down Account list, select your **Retentions Receivable** account. In our example shown in Figure 17-15, the account is 1320 - Retentions Receivable.

▌ Click **OK**.

▌ In the report window, click **Memorize**.

▌ In the **Memorize Report** window, enter **Retentions Receivable Report**.

▌ Click **OK**.

Figure 17-16

A memorized Job Profitability by Class report.

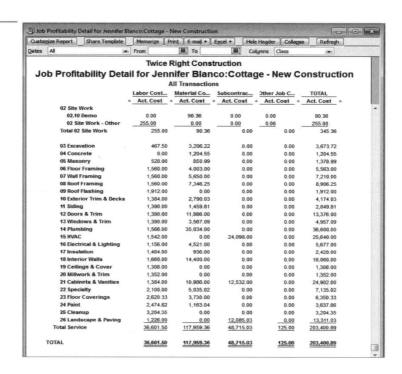

Job Profitability by Class Report

The memorized Job Profitability by Class report breaks down all costs for a single job by these classes: Labor, Material, Subcontractor, Equipment, and Other. Figure 17-16 shows an example of a memorized Job Profitability Detail report.

Memorizing the Job Profitability by Class Report — To memorize the Job Profitability by Class Report in your QuickBooks data file:

▌ Click **Report Center**, or from the **Reports** menu, choose **Jobs, Time & Mileage**, then **Job Profitability Detail**. The Filter Report by Job window will appear. Select a Customer:Job and click **OK**.

▌ Set the columns area in the Display tab of the Modify Report window as shown in Figure 17-17.

▌ Click on the **Filters** tab. Select **Class** from the Filter list.

▌ From the pull-down Class list, select **Multiple classes** to bring up the pop-up window showing all your classes, as shown in Figure 17-18.

▌ Select the classes Labor Costs - Job Related, Material Costs - Job Related, Subcontractor Costs - Job Related, Equip Rental Costs - Job Related, and Other Job Costs. Your class names may be slightly different.

▌ Click **OK** to close the Select Class window.

Figure 17-17

In the Columns section, select Display columns by Class.

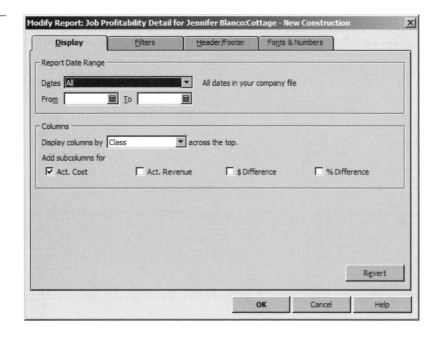

Figure 17-18

Filter your report to include only the classes you want displayed.

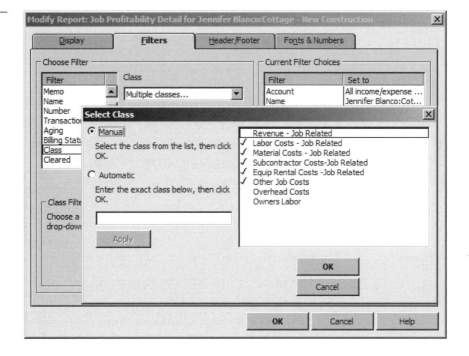

▌ Click on **OK** to display the report.

▌ Click **Memorize** in the report window.

▌ In the Memorize Report window, enter Job Profitability by Class.

▌ Click **OK**.

Workers Compensation by Code and Employee

Customize Report | Share Template | Memorize | Print | E-mail | Excel | Hide Header | Refresh

Dates Custom From 01/01/2013 To 01/31/2013

Twice Right Construction

Workers Compensation by Code and Employee

January 2013

	Jan 13							
	Gross Wages	OT Premium	WC Wages	Hours	WC Rate	WC Premium	Exp. Mod.	Adj. WC Premium
5188 - Plumbing								
Jacobson, Paul	231.00		231.00	11	9.10	21.02	100.0%	21.02
Johnson, Sam	264.00		264.00	12	9.10	24.02	100.0%	24.02
O'Ryan, Finney	42.50		42.50	2	9.10	3.87	100.0%	3.87
Total 5188 - Plumbing	537.50		537.50	25		48.91		48.91
5190 - Electrical								
O'Ryan, Finney	212.50		212.50	10	10.02	21.29	100.0%	21.29
Total 5190 - Electrical	212.50		212.50	10		21.29		21.29
5475 - Painting								
Jacobson, Paul	352.00		352.00	16	4.20	14.78	100.0%	14.78
Johnson, Sam	187.50		187.50	10	4.20	7.88	100.0%	7.88
O'Ryan, Finney	340.00		340.00	16	4.20	14.28	100.0%	14.28
Total 5475 - Painting	879.50		879.50	42		36.94		36.94
5646 - Carpentry								
Jacobson, Paul	3,630.00		3,630.00	165	10.20	370.25	100.0%	370.25
Johnson, Sam	2,992.00		2,992.00	136	10.20	305.21	100.0%	305.21
O'Ryan, Finney	3,060.00		3,060.00	144	10.20	312.12	100.0%	312.12
Total 5646 - Carpentry	9,682.00		9,682.00	445		987.58		987.58
9891 - Admin Office								
Hinsdale, Tasha	1,200.00		1,200.00	80	0.90	10.80	100.0%	10.80
Total 9891 - Admin Office	1,200.00		1,200.00	80		10.80		10.80
9899 - Supervision								
O'Ryan, Finney	85.00		85.00	4	10.12	8.60	100.0%	8.60
Total 9899 - Supervision	85.00		85.00	4		8.60		8.60
TOTAL	12,596.50		12,596.50	606		1,114.12		1,114.12

Figure 17-19

A Payroll Summary by Employee report, customized to report on workers' compensation.

Workers' Compensation Report

The memorized Workers' Comp Report lists the allocated payroll transactions by workers' compensation category. However, you must have used workers' comp codes as payroll items to use this report. The totals displayed cover the report dates you select. Figure 17-19 shows a memorized Workers' Comp Report.

Memorizing the Workers' Comp Report — To memorize the Workers' Comp Report in your QuickBooks data file:

- Click **Report Center**, or from the **Reports** menu, choose **Employees & Payroll**, and then **Payroll Summary**.
- On the Display tab of the Modify Report window, change the date range of the report to match the dates your Workers' Compensation Insurance carrier asks for, as shown in Figure 17-20.
- Click **OK**.
- Click **Memorize** in the report window.
- In the Memorize Report window, enter **Workers' Comp Report**.
- Click **OK**.

Figure 17-20

Set the dates for the Workers' Comp Report in this window.

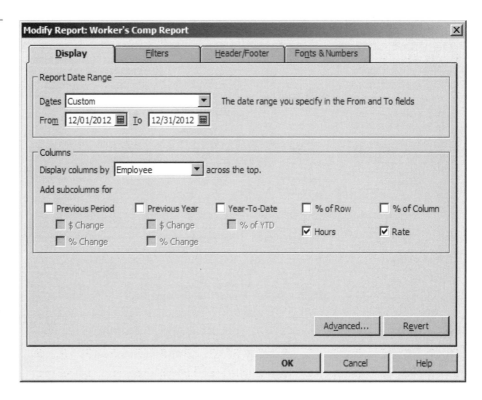

Job Costs Detail Report

The memorized Job Costs Detail report lists and totals all job cost trans-actions for any job you select, and summarizes the transactions by job phase. Figure 17-21 shows an example of a memorized Job Costs Detail report.

Memorizing the Job Costs Detail Report — To memorize the Job Costs Detail report in your QuickBooks data file:

▮ Click **Report Center**, or from the **Reports** menu, choose **Accountant & Taxes**, and then **Transaction Detail by Account**.

▮ From the pull-down Dates list, select **All**.

▮ Now select the columns in the Display tab of the Modify Report window, as shown in Figure 17-22. Select only **(left margin)**, **Type**, **Date**, **Num**, **Source Name**, **Debit**, and **Credit**. Scroll down to the bottom of the list to find Source Name, Debit, and Credit.

▮ From the **Total by** pull-down list, select **Item detail**.

▮ Click the **Filters** tab.

▮ Under **Filter**, select **Account**.

Figure 17-21

A memorized Job Costs Detail report.

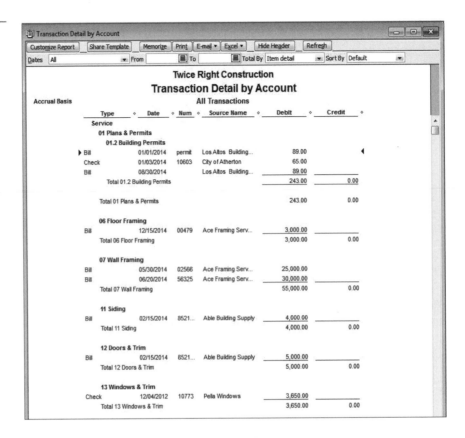

Figure 17-22

Choose the columns to appear in the Job Costs Detail report.

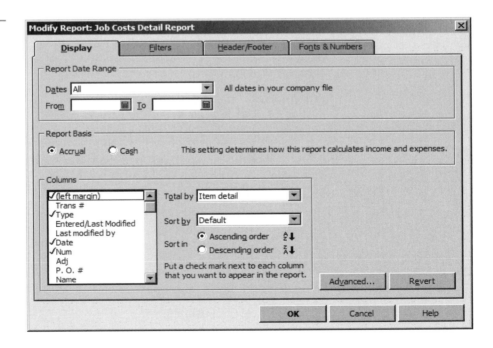

Figure 17-23

Choose the transaction types to include in the Job Costs Detail report.

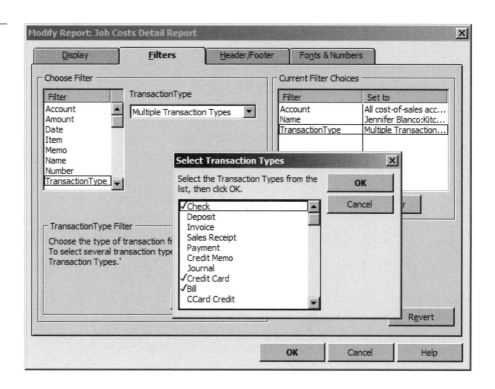

▮ From the pull-down Account list, select **All cost-of-sales accounts**.

▮ Under **Filter**, select **Transaction Type**.

▮ From the pull-down Transaction Type, select **Multiple Transaction Types** and then select **Check**, **Credit Card**, **Bill**, **CCard Refund**, **Bill Credit**, **Bill CCard**, **Item Receipt**, and **Paycheck**. See Figure 17-23.

▮ Click **OK** to close the Select Transaction Type window.

▮ Under **Filter**, select **Name**. In the **Name** drop-down list, select the job you wish to report on.

▮ Click the **Header/Footer** tab, and in the **Report Title**, change to **Job Costs Detail Report**.

▮ Click **OK**.

▮ Click **Memorize** in the report window.

▮ In the Memorize Report window, enter **Job Costs Detail**.

▮ Click **OK**.

Figure 17-24

A memorized Unpaid Job Bills report.

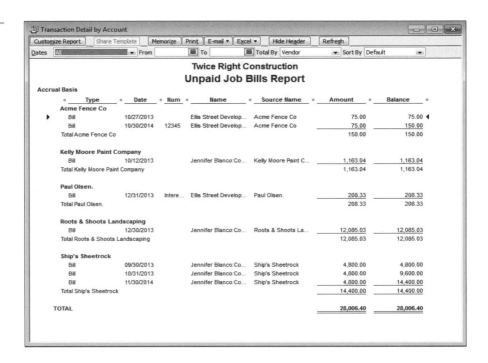

Unpaid Job Bills

This report will list and total all unpaid job expenses. Transactions are grouped and subtotaled by vendor, which are the bold headings on the report. Figure 17-24 shows an example of a memorized Unpaid Job Bills report.

Memorizing the Unpaid Job Bills Report — To memorize the Unpaid Job Bills report in your QuickBooks data file:

▌ Click **Report Center**, or from the **Reports** menu, choose **Accountant & Taxes**, and then **Transaction Detail by Account**.

▌ In **Dates**, select **All**.

▌ Now select the columns in the Display tab of the Modify Report window, as shown in Figure 17-25. Select only **(left margin)**, **Type**, **Date**, **Num**, **Name**, **Source Name**, **Amount**, and **Balance**. Scroll down to the bottom of the list to find Source Name, Amount, and Balance.

▌ In **Total by**, select **Vendor** from the pull-down list.

▌ Click the **Filters** tab.

▌ Under **Filter**, select **Account** and then from the pull-down Account list, select **All cost-of-sales accounts**. See Figure 17-26.

▌ Under **Filter**, select **Transaction Type** and then from the pull-down Transaction Type list, select **Bill**.

▌ Under **Filter**, select **Paid Status** and then **Open**, as shown in Figure 17-27.

Figure 17-25

Choose the columns to appear in the Unpaid Job Bills report.

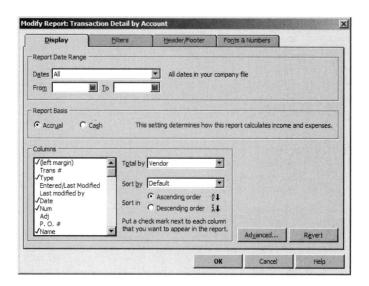

Figure 17-26

Choose the accounts to include in the Unpaid Job Bills report.

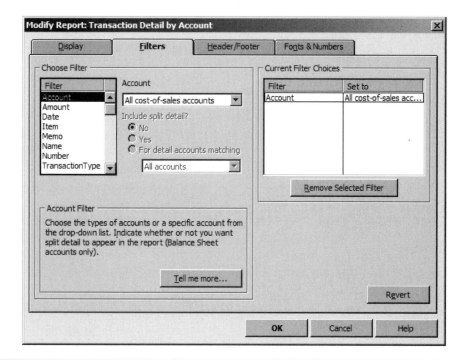

Figure 17-27

Choose the status of the transactions to include in the Unpaid Job Bills report.

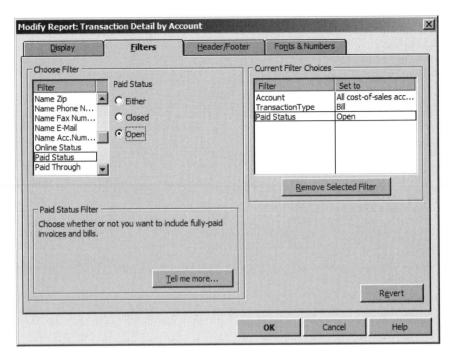

I Click the **Header/Footer** tab. In the **Report Title** change to **Unpaid Job Bills Report**.

I Click **OK**.

I Click **Memorize** in the report window.

I In the Memorize Report window, enter **Unpaid Job Bills**.

I Click **OK**.

Vendors' WC Expiration Dates

The memorized Vendor Workers' Comp Expiration Dates report lists all subcontractors, with the phone, contact name, and workers' comp expiration date. If you've made an entry into the custom field for "work comp exp," that date will display in the far right column. Refer back to Chapter 14 for more information on creating and using the "work comp exp" custom field. Figure 17-28 shows a memorized Vendors' WC Expiration Dates report.

Memorizing the Vendors' WC Expiration Dates Report — To memorize the Vendor's WC Expiration Dates report in your QuickBooks data file:

I Click **Report Center**, or from the **Reports** menu, choose **Vendors & Payables** and **Vendor Contact List**.

I Now select the columns in the Display tab of the Modify Report window, as shown in Figure 17-29. Select only **(left margin)**, **Vendor**, **Phone**, **Contact**, and **Work Comp Exp**. We've scrolled down to the bottom of the list to show Work Comp Exp in the list, but it won't be there if you didn't set up a custom field for it.

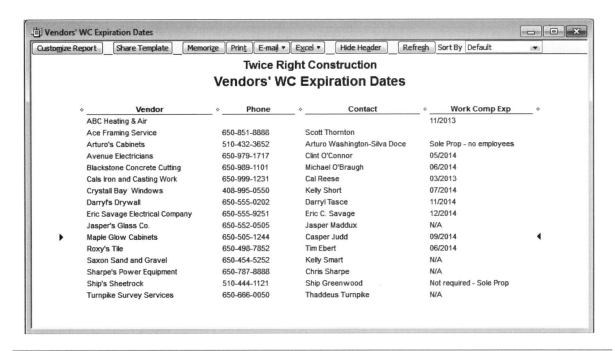

Figure 17-28
A memorized Vendors' WC Expiration Dates report.

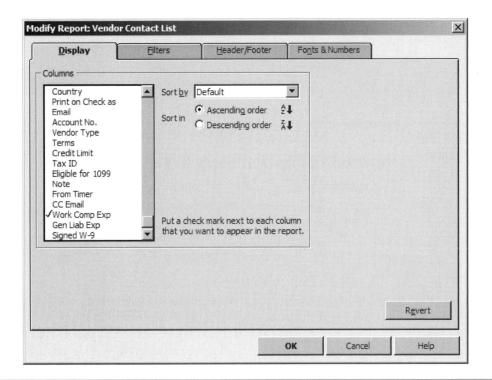

Figure 17-29
Choose the columns to appear in the Vendors' WC Expiration Dates report.

▌ Click the **Header/Footer** tab. In **Report Title**, type **Vendors' WC Expiration Dates.**

▌ Click **OK**.

▌ Click **Memorize** in the report window.

▌ In the Memorize Report window, enter **Vendors' WC Expiration Dates**.

▌ Click **OK**.

Using Jobs, Time & Mileage Reports

Use the built-in QuickBooks Jobs, Time & Mileage project reports to help you bill customers, analyze how well each job is progressing financially, and identify problem jobs before it's too late. We'll discuss what each report shows, how to use the report in your business, and when to run it. We'll also show you a sample printout of each report. We didn't discuss the Item Profitability, Item Estimates vs. Actuals, Profit & Loss by Job, or Time by Item reports because they aren't useful to contractors.

To run a project report:

▌ Click **Report Center**, or from the **Reports** menu, choose **Jobs, Time & Mileage** and select the report by name.

When the Modify Report window appears, you can usually accept the default values and just click **OK** to create the report. In some cases you'll want to specify a time period for the report.

When running certain reports, such as the Job Profitability Detail report, you'll be asked to select the job you want to run the report for in the Filter Report by Job window.

Job Profitability Summary Report

The Job Profitability Summary report lists every job you're working on. This report lists the jobs by name, actual job costs to date, actual revenue or total amount of invoicing to date, and in the last column, dollar difference. Dollar difference is the actual costs to date minus the total amount billed to the job. Figure 17-30 shows an example of a Job Profitability Summary.

Use this report to help invoice customers. Since the report gives you a good idea of where each project's actual costs are in relation to invoicing, you can use it to get an idea of how much to bill on each job. For example, if you invoice each week on a lump sum basis, this report will help analyze exactly what the costs are to date and how much you've invoiced so far. Use this information to bill each job so your costs and profits are covered and the job is at or below its estimated cost.

Figure 17-30

Use the Job Profitability Summary report to help you when you invoice customers.

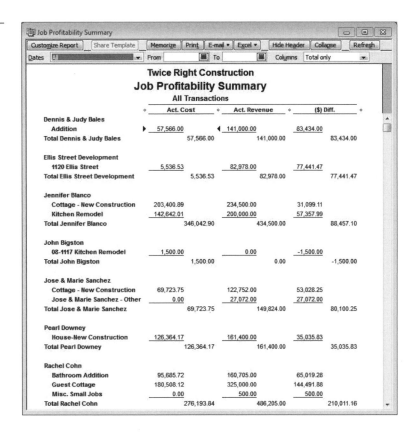

If 100 percent of a job has been invoiced, the report will tell you how profitable it was. For example, if the actual cost of a job is $15,000 and you invoiced $17,000, the $2,000 difference is profit.

Print (and check) this report before invoicing a customer.

Job Profitability Detail Report

The Job Profitability Detail report shows one job, broken down by job phases (items). It tells you the actual job costs to date, actual revenue or total amount of invoices to date, and in the last column, the dollar difference. Dollar difference is the actual costs to date minus the total amount invoiced for each job phase, in dollars. Figure 17-31 shows a sample Job Profitability Detail report.

Use this report to help invoice a job on a percentage-complete basis by phase. Since this report gives you a good idea of where each project's actual costs are in relation to its billings, it'll help you decide how much to invoice by phase. For example, if you invoice a job based on how much work has been completed on each phase of construction, use this report to analyze exactly what the costs are to date by job phase and how much you've previously invoiced. Then you can quickly produce a billing for the job by phase of construction.

Figure 17-31

The Job Profitability Detail report breaks down a particular job by item.

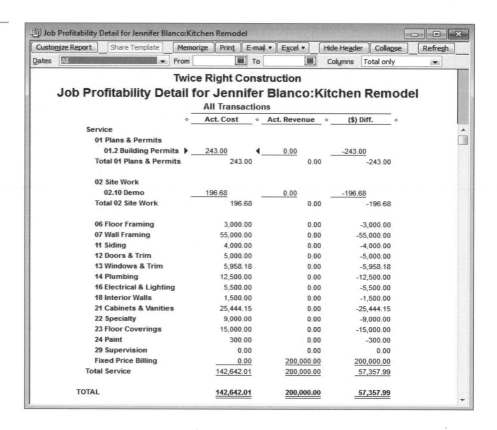

If 100 percent of the job is invoiced, the report will give you an idea of each job's profitability by phase. For example, if phase 01 - Plans and Permits actual costs is $1,992.93 and its actual revenue is $2,275, then the profit is $282.07.

Print this report before invoicing a customer. It'll help ensure a job's actual costs aren't running too high or low in relation to its billings.

Job Estimates vs. Actuals Summary Report

The Job Estimates vs. Actuals Summary report tells you how each job is progressing, and which jobs are over, or under, their estimated costs. It's a handy report for quick reference, especially if you have many small jobs that last a short time. Print the report often to check actual versus estimated costs. Use this report to adjust estimated costs if you find that certain types of jobs consistently have lower profit margins. Figure 17-32 shows an example of a Job Estimates vs. Actuals Summary.

Figure 17-32

Print this report often to check actual vs. estimated costs.

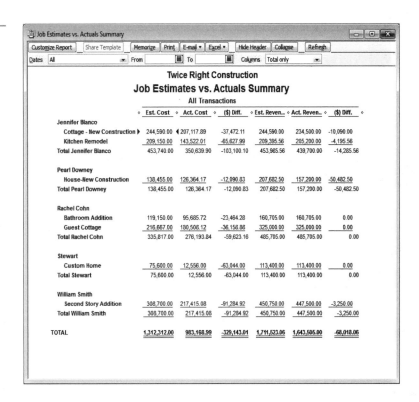

If you tend to have larger projects with many phases that span several months or years, this report may not be as useful to you as the next one, Job Estimates vs. Actuals Detail report.

Job Estimates vs. Actuals Detail Report

The Job Estimates vs. Actuals Detail report shows, by job phase, how each job is progressing, and which part of a job is in danger of running over estimated costs. Figure 17-33 shows a sample Job Estimates vs. Actuals Detail report.

This is a handy report for quick reference, especially if you have jobs that last a long time and you need to track them by job phase. You can also use this report to help estimate future jobs. It'll give you a good idea of which phases were over, or under, estimate.

Print this report once a week and give it to the Project Manager. Then he can see which part or parts of his project are over, or under, estimate while there's still time to make adjustments.

Figure 17-33

The Job Estimates vs. Actuals Detail report breaks down a particular job by item.

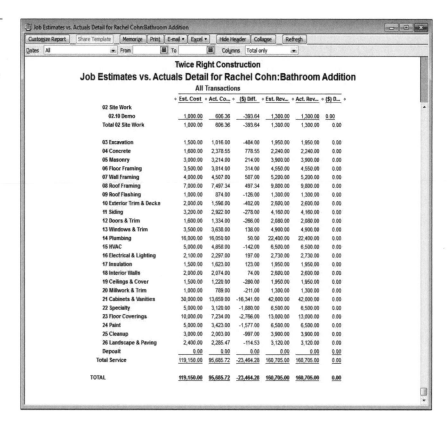

Figure 17-34

Use the Job Progress Invoices vs. Estimates report to check that the jobsite progress matches the percentage of progress.

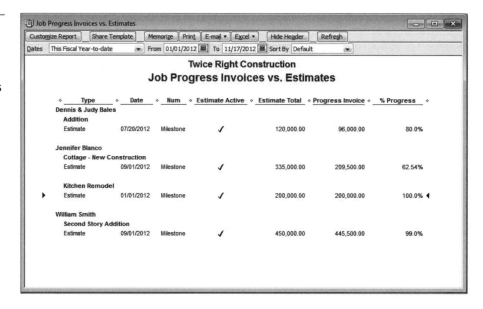

Job Progress Invoices vs. Estimates Report

The Job Progress Invoices vs. Estimates report lists each customer:job, job status, estimate total, amount invoiced to date, and percentage complete. Figure 17-34 shows a sample Job Progress Invoices vs. Estimates report.

This report gives you an idea of how much has been invoiced to date and what percentage that amount is of the total estimated costs. It's important to run this report from time to time to check whether the actual job progress matches up with the percentage progress. For example, if you get a project status report from the field each week, compare the estimated field percentage complete to the % Progress on this report. They should be similar. If the information from the field estimates a higher percentage complete than the % Progress report, you may be behind in invoicing the customer. If the % Progress report has a higher percentage complete than the actual field progress estimate, you may have invoiced more than you should have.

You may need to adjust job status as work progresses. To do this:

▍ Click the **Customer Center** icon on the menu bar, or from the **Customers** menu, choose **Customer Center**.

▍ Double-click the job.

▍ Click the **Job Info** tab.

▍ In **Job Status**, select the new status from the pull-down list.

▍ Click **OK**.

Unbilled Costs by Job Report

This report is handy if customers are invoiced on a time-and-materials basis. It gives a list of all project costs (except labor costs) that haven't been assigned to a job. Use this report to double-check that you've invoiced all costs on a time-and-materials basis to a job. Figure 17-35 shows an example of an Unbilled Costs by Job report.

Time by Job Summary Report

This report lists each job, with detailed information for the job and phase. It's particularly useful if a job seems to be running over budget and you suspect that time has been mistakenly allocated to the wrong job or phase. Figure 17-36 shows an example of a Time by Job Summary report.

Open Purchase Orders by Job Report

In Chapter 14 we described how to use purchase orders to track committed costs or subcontractors' bids. This report will help you figure out how much you still have outstanding on those committed costs or subcontractors' bids.

QuickBooks has a built-in report for tracking purchase orders that haven't been filled (in other words, a report listing all subcontractors who haven't completed or submitted bills on a project). Figure 17-37 shows an example of an Open Purchase Orders by Job report.

Figure 17-35

An Unbilled Costs by Job report.

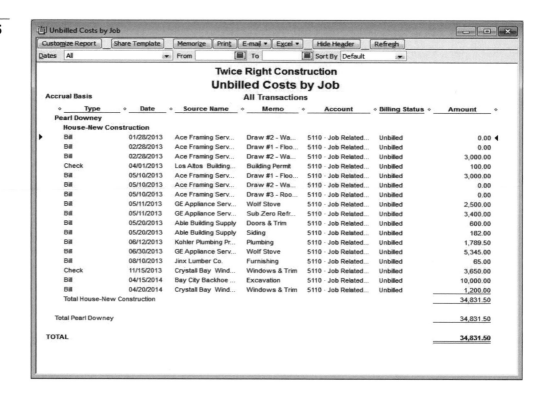

Figure 17-36

The Time by Job Summary report.

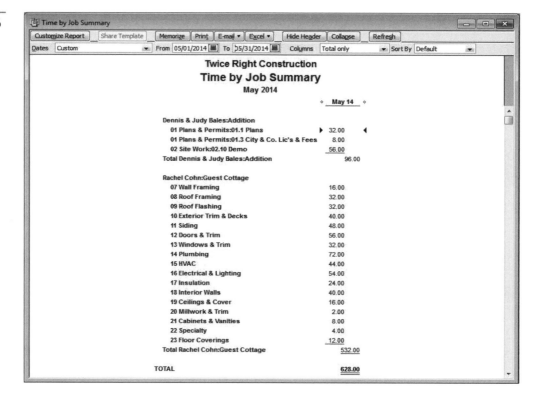

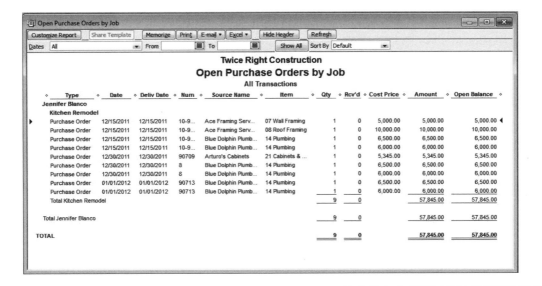

Figure 17-37

An Open Purchase Orders by Job report.

Important! It's worth noting here that you may have a problem with this report if you make partial payments to subcontractors. The problem occurs when you release a portion of the original PO. The remaining amount will clear from the report if you don't enter a quantity *less than 1* in the quantity field. In other words, to avoid reporting problems, always enter an amount less than 1 when releasing only a portion of the PO. For more information, see Chapter 14 under the heading Using Purchase Orders to Track Multiple Draws and Committed Costs Buyouts.

The Delivery Date represents the day you were told the goods would arrive (for example, special order windows or doors) or the date the services were to start (the date the plumber or electrician said he would start work).

Time by Job Detail Report

This report lists each employee and his/her time on each job phase, subtotaled by job. Use this report to doublecheck that the time was entered correctly for each timecard, to calculate the total hours spent on a job, or to see who's spending time on specific jobs. Figure 17-38 shows an example of a Time by Job Detail report.

Time by Name Report

This report lists all employees and the hours each worked during a certain period. Use this report to find out how many hours each person has worked, and on which job, during a time period. Figure 17-39 shows part of a sample Time by Name report.

Figure 17-38

A Time by Job Detail report.

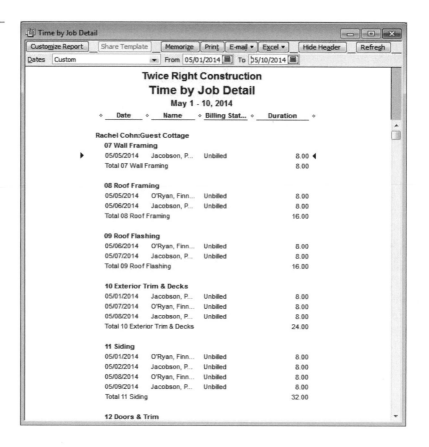

Figure 17-39

A Time by Name report.

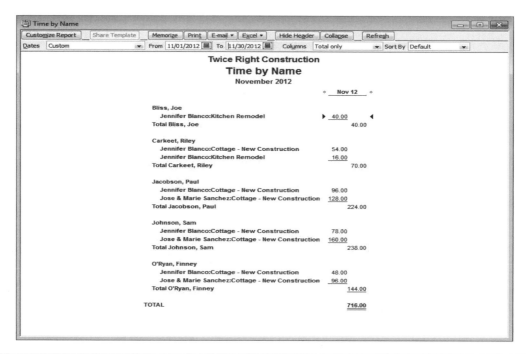

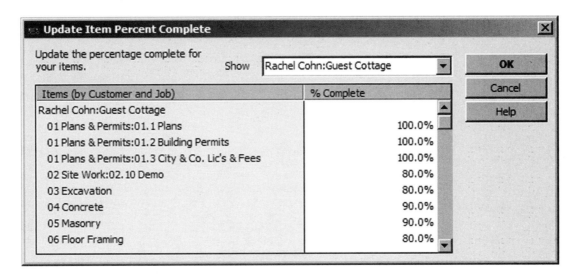

Figure 17-40
Enter the percent complete for each job phase.

Using Reports in QuickBooks Premier Contractor Edition

Some valuable reports are included in the Contractor Edition of QuickBooks. We've outlined two important reports below.

To run these reports:

❚ Click **Report Center**, or from the **Reports** menu, choose **Contractor Reports** and select the report by name.

Cost to Complete by Job Detail

The Cost to Complete by Job Detail report is excellent for giving you an idea of where you stand on any given job, based on the percentage complete, by phase, of the project.

❚ When running this report, you will be prompted to filter the report. Select the appropriate Customer:Job and click **OK**.

❚ Enter the percent complete for each job phase in the % Complete column. See Figure 17-40. Click **OK**.

❚ In the Modify Report window, click **OK** to display the report. See Figure 17-41.

Unpaid Bills by Job

The Unpaid Bills by Job report sorts all unpaid bills by job. If you pay your vendors when you receive a check from a customer and need to know which bills are outstanding for a job, print this report. See Figure 17-42.

Figure 17-41

A Cost to Complete by Job Detail report.

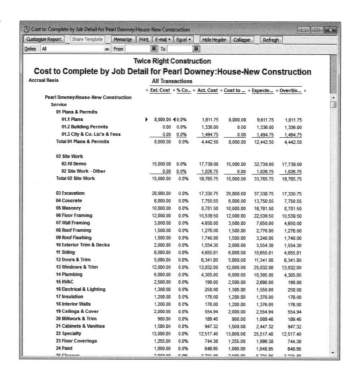

Figure 17-42

An Unpaid Bills by Job report.

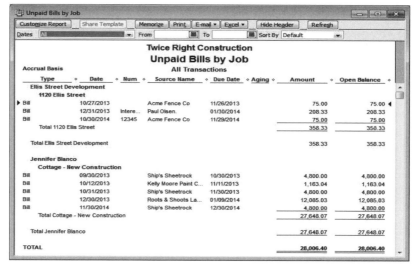

In this chapter we showed you how to modify, filter, and memorize reports. We also explained the built-in QuickBooks project reports.

Along with these reports, you should set up procedures to check data entry accuracy. As an example, you need to be sure all customers are being invoiced and that Accounts Receivable are in balance. The same applies to bills and Accounts Payable. These procedures can be broken down into end-of-month procedures and end-of-year procedures. The next chapter will walk you through those procedures, step-by-step.

Chapter 18

End of Month and End of Year Procedures

In this chapter, we'll explain procedures to be completed at the end of each month and at the end of each fiscal year. Keep in mind that QuickBooks doesn't force you to close out any month or year. We're simply suggesting what you should do to make sure that the information you've entered into QuickBooks is accurate. We also suggest printing out several reports to analyze how well your business is doing financially.

End of Month Procedures

Let's look first at what to do at the end of each month:

▌ reconcile all checking, savings, credit card, and loan accounts with your bank statement

▌ run reports to make sure all transactions are correct

▌ print monthly reports

▌ back up data and close the month

Reconcile Each Checking Account

QuickBooks makes bank account reconciliation simple, so you won't have any excuse for putting it off. Set aside the time and do it every month. Reconciling your bank account will catch any errors you or your bank have made, and serve as a check of your accounting. Be sure to reconcile all savings, credit card, and loan accounts too. Here's how to reconcile a checking account:

▌ Click **Home**, then click **Reconcile**, or from the **Banking** menu, choose **Reconcile**.

▌ At the Begin Reconciliation window, in **Account**, select your checking account from the pull-down list. In our example shown in Figure 18-1, it's 1110 Company Checking Account.

▌ In **Statement Date**, enter the ending date on the bank statement.

▌ In **Ending Balance**, enter the amount on the bank statement (usually called New Balance or Balance this Statement).

Figure 18-1

Use the Begin Reconciliation window to select your checking account and enter all relevant information.

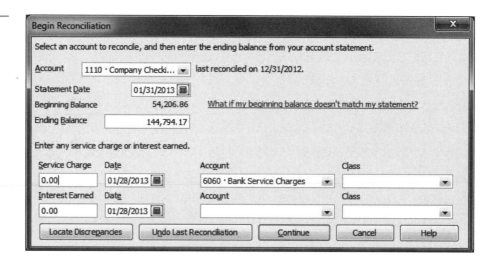

- In **Service Charge**, enter the amount listed on the statement, and the date the service charge was posted. In **Account**, select the expense account **Bank Service Charges** in your Chart of Accounts pull-down list.

- In **Interest Earned**, enter the amount listed on the statement, and the date any interest was posted. In **Account**, select the income account **Interest Income** in your Chart of Accounts pull-down list.

- Click **Continue**.

At the Reconcile window (Figure 18-2), verify each deposit, credit, check, payment, and service charge to make sure it's the same as the corresponding amount on the bank statement. If an amount is different, find the problem and correct it before continuing. To make a correction, double-click the transaction and make the appropriate changes. If the bank made an error, make sure they correct it. If you find an amount on the bank statement that isn't listed in the Reconcile window, it may mean you forgot to enter it. Enter the transaction before continuing with the reconciliation.

When your records match the bank statement, Ending Balance and Cleared Balance will be the same, and Difference will be zero.

- Click **Reconcile Now** to complete the reconciliation.

Now you'll get a dialog box asking what type of reconciliation report you would like to print:

- Select **Detail**.

- Click **Print**.

File the printed reconciliation report and bank statement together, or set up a three-ring binder to store the reports.

Figure 18-2

Use the Reconcile window to clear checks and deposits according to your bank statement.

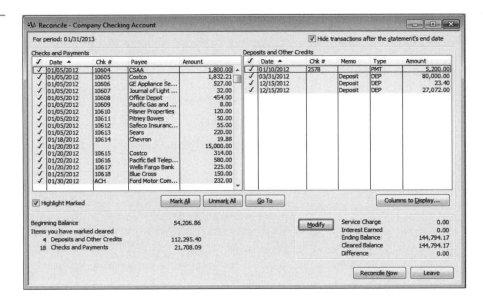

Run Reports to Make Sure All Transactions Are Correct

Run these reports to ensure all transactions have been entered accurately and correctly:

▌ Transaction Detail by Account

▌ A/R Aging Detail

▌ A/P Aging Detail

On each report, check every transaction to make sure it's accurate and posted to the correct account. Correct any mistakes before continuing. From any report window, double-click a transaction to open it. You'll see a window showing the original transaction where any necessary corrections can be made.

Now let's look at each one of these reports.

Transaction Detail by Account — The Transaction Detail by Account report lists each account in your Chart of Accounts and all transactions on each account. Use this report to find any transactions that have been posted to the wrong account. For example, all checks written to the phone company should be posted to the Telephone account. If a check for office supplies shows up under the Telephone account, you'll need to correct the transaction. Here's how to get the Transaction Detail by Account report:

▌ Click **Report Center**, or from the **Reports** menu, choose **Accountant & Taxes**, and then **Transaction Detail by Account**.

▌ In **Dates**, select **Custom**. In **From** and **To**, enter the month you're closing. In the examples we show here, we've used the month of November.

Figure 18-3

The Display tab window lets you specify which dates and columns will be on the Transaction Detail by Account report.

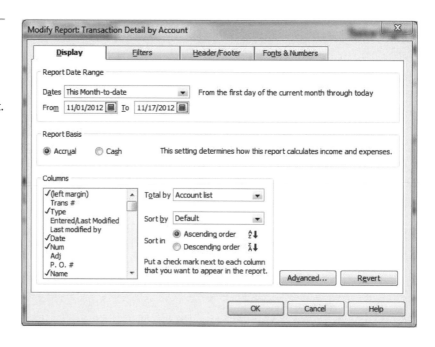

▌ In the Display tab of the Modify Report window, under the Columns box, select only **(left margin)**, **Type**, **Date**, **Num**, **Name**, **Memo**, **Class**, **Clr**, **Amount**, and **Balance** as shown in Figure 18-3. You'll have to scroll down to the bottom of the list to find Memo, Class, Clr, Amount, and Balance.

▌ Click **OK**.

Figure 18-4 shows an example of this customized Transaction Detail by Account report. Check the transactions on your own report and correct any that are in error.

A/R Aging Detail Report — The A/R Aging Detail report lists all unpaid customer invoices as of the last day of the month you're closing. Use it to show any invoices that have been posted twice, missing invoices, and payments that haven't been applied to an invoice. You'll know there's a mistake if you see a payment with a negative amount. To fix this problem, double-click the negative payment amount, and at the bottom of the Customer Payment window, select the invoice this payment should be applied to.

Here's how to get an A/R Aging Detail report like the example we show in Figure 18-5:

▌ Click **Report Center**, or from the **Reports** menu, choose **Customers & Receivables**, and then **A/R Aging Detail**.

▌ In the Display tab of the Modify Report window, in **Dates**, select **Custom**. In **From** and **To**, enter the month you're closing. See Figure 18-6.

Figure 18-4

A sample Transaction Detail by Account report you can create in QuickBooks.

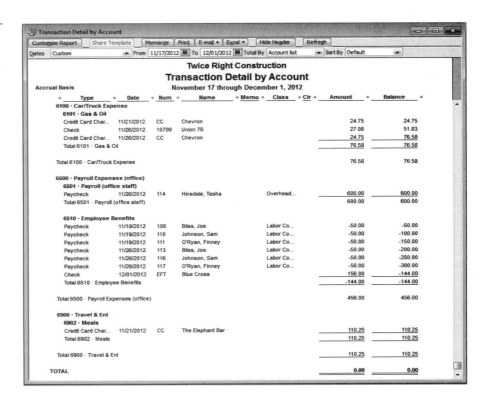

Figure 18-5

A sample A/R Aging Detail report you can create in QuickBooks.

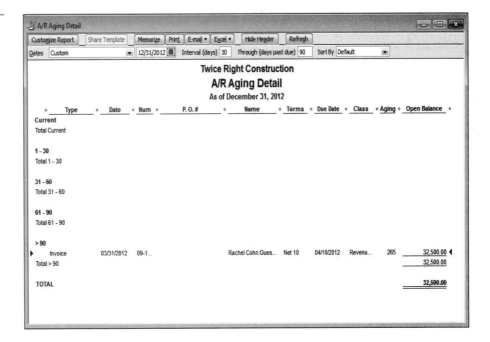

Figure 18-6

The Display tab window lets you specify which dates and columns will be on the A/R Aging Detail report.

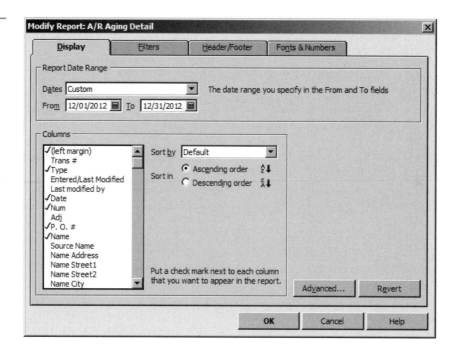

▌ Under the Columns box, select only **(left margin)**, **Type**, **Date**, **Num**, **P.O. #**, **Name**, **Terms**, **Due Date**, **Class**, **Aging**, and **Open Balance** as shown. You'll have to scroll down to the bottom of the list to find Terms, Due Date, Class, Aging and Open Balance.

▌ Click **OK**.

Check all transactions on the report and correct any errors.

A/P Aging Detail Report — The A/P Aging Detail report lists all unpaid vendor bills as of the last day of the month you're closing. Use it to show any missing bills or bills that have been posted twice.

Here's how to get an A/P Aging Detail report like the one in Figure 18-7:

▌ Click **Report Center**, or from the **Reports** menu, choose **Vendors & Payables**, and then **A/P Aging Detail**.

▌ In the Display tab of the Modify Report window, in **Dates**, select **Custom**. In **From** and **To**, enter the month you're closing. See Figure 18-8.

▌ Under the Columns box, select only **(left margin)**, **Type**, **Date**, **Num**, **Name**, **Due Date**, **Aging**, and **Open Balance**. You'll have to scroll down to the bottom of the list to find Due Date, Aging, and Open Balance.

▌ Click **OK**.

Check all transactions on the report and correct as necessary. Be sure to watch out for missing bills and bills that have been posted twice.

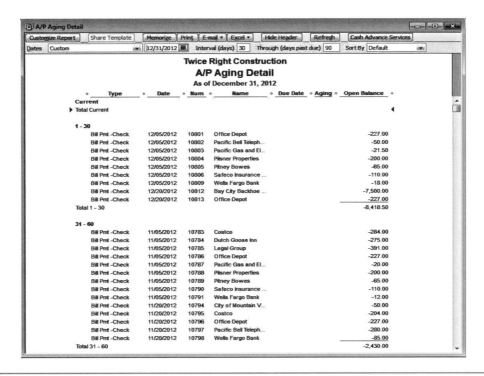

Figure 18-7
A sample A/P Aging Detail report you can create in QuickBooks.

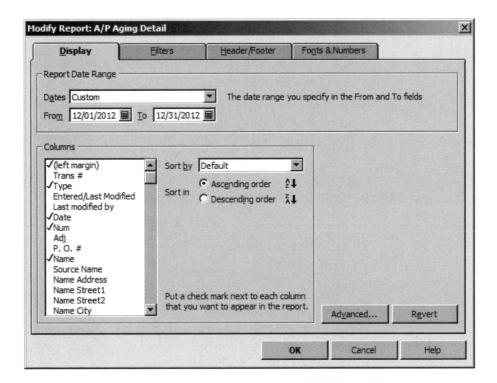

Figure 18-8
The Display tab window lets you specify which dates and columns will be on the A/P Aging Detail report.

Printing and Filing Monthly Reports

Now you're ready to print these reports for the month you're closing. To print the Transaction Detail by Account and the A/R and A/P Aging Detail reports, just follow the same steps used to open and correct the reports, and then click Print in each report window.

You'll also want to print financial statements for the month. To do that:

▮ Click **Report Center**, or from the **Reports** menu, choose **Company & Financial**, and then **Balance Sheet Standard**.

▮ Click **OK** to close the Modify Report window, then click **Print**.

▮ Click **Report Center**, or from the **Reports** menu, choose **Company & Financial**, and then **Profit & Loss YTD Comparison**.

▮ Click **OK** to close the Modify Report window, then click **Print**.

Back Up Data and Close the Month

When you've made sure everything is correct, follow these steps to back up your data:

▮ From the **File** menu, choose **Create Backup**.

▮ Select **Local backup** and select the **Options** button.

▮ Click **Save it Now**. Click **Next**.

▮ In the **Backup Options** window, select a location for your backup file. Typically, you'd select an external backup drive, a USB flash drive, or a CD drive to store the backup.

▮ Once you've selected the right backup destination in the box at the top, select the **OK** button.

▮ Back at the **Create Backup** screen, select **Finish**.

Now you're ready to close and lock yourself out of making changes to the accounting period you just completed.

▮ From the **Edit** menu, choose **Preferences**.

▮ Click the **Accounting** icon in the left hand scroll bar.

▮ Click the **Company Preferences** tab.

▮ In the Closing Date area, click on **Set Date/Password** and enter the last day of the month just closed. This will cause a warning to display if you're making any entries into the closed month. You may also want to set a password to prevent any unauthorized change of transactions in closed months.

▮ Click **OK**.

Reading and Understanding Your Financial Reports

It's important to analyze how well your business is doing before filing reports. The rest of the work up to this point was just that, work. Now we get to have a little fun. Let's analyze the past to change the future. You can pinpoint overexpenditures and figure out, finally, what your overhead percentage is running.

Balance Sheet

The Balance Sheet lists:

▊ company assets (things your company owns)

▊ liabilities (funds your company owes)

▊ capital or equity (assets minus the liabilities or the amount of equity you've built up in the business)

There are two things to look for in this report. First, make sure everything is listed on the report. Are your checking account, savings account, company vehicles, large equipment, and so on, listed as assets? Then check the liabilities. Are all loans, lines of credit, and payroll taxes you owe listed?

Second, analyze the report. Keep in mind this is the report the bank will look at to determine how well you manage your business, as well as its stability and growth. The bank will be looking closely at the assets in relation to the liabilities. The bank wants to know if your company is solvent. In other words, if you stopped business today, could your company sell its assets and pay off all its liabilities and have a few bucks left over? The bank wants to see total assets of two times your total liabilities, give or take a few dollars.

Balance Sheet Comparison (Optional Report for Analysis)

It's best if you analyze the Balance Sheet over two periods — for example first quarter 2013 and second quarter 2013 (or better yet, year to year).

If you've been using QuickBooks for more than one quarter, print the Balance Sheet Comparison report to see how you did this quarter compared to last quarter. To print this report:

▊ Click **Report Center**, or from the **Reports** menu, choose **Company & Financial**, and then **Balance Sheet Prev Year Comparison**.

▊ Click **OK** to close the Modify Report window, then click **Print**.

On this report, check to see:

▊ Are the assets increasing?

▊ Are the liabilities decreasing?

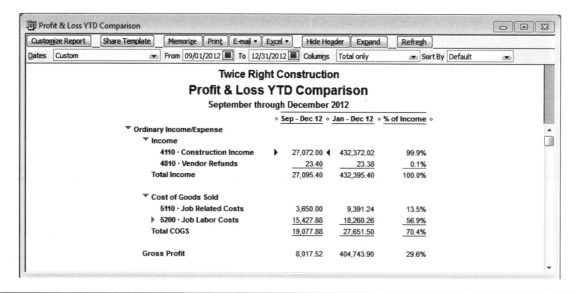

Figure 18-9
A sample Profit & Loss YTD Comparison report for the last quarter of 2012.

▌ If the liabilities increased, the assets should have increased as well.

▌ Is the value of the business (assets minus liabilities) increasing or decreasing?

If it's decreasing, something is wrong. Give the problem your immediate attention.

Profit & Loss YTD Comparison Report

The Profit & Loss YTD Comparison report shows how much income your company has generated versus its expenses for the same time period. It's obvious here that you want to be generating more income than expenses, and the bottom line or net income/loss needs to be positive. This report will also list total job costs and overhead percentage. In Figure 18-9, we show an example of the report, modified to include the % of Income column.

Take a look at the Total Cost of Goods Sold (COGS) row and check the percentage in the column titled % of Income. In the construction business, this percentage averages about 40 to 60 percent. If your percentage is lower, good for you! That means more money is going in your pocket. You're spending less on construction-related costs than the average construction company.

Now scroll down to the Total Expense row (not shown in our sample) and check the percentage in the column titled % of Income. This is the percentage of income spent on overhead costs — costs not associated with a job, such as office rent, telephone, postage, and utilities. If your percentage is 10, it means

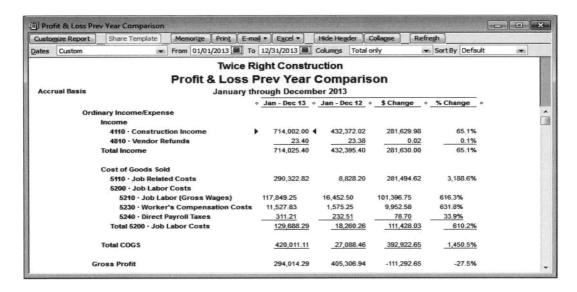

Figure 18-10
A sample Profit & Loss Previous Year Comparison report comparing 2012 with 2013.

that for every $100.00 you generate in revenue, you spend $10.00 for overhead costs. In the construction business, the average is about 8 to 12 percent.

To print this report:

▌ Click **Report Center**, or from the **Reports** menu, choose **Company & Financial**, and then **Profit & Loss YTD Comparison**.

▌ Click **% of Income** box.

▌ Click **OK** to close the Modify Report window, then click **Print**.

Profit & Loss Prev Year Comparison Report

Again, like the Balance Sheet, it's best if you analyze the Profit & Loss over two years. If you've been using QuickBooks for more than one year, print the Profit & Loss Prev Year Comparison report to see how you did this year compared to last year. In Figure 18-10, we show an example of a report comparing 2012 with 2013.

This report will tell you how well you did this year compared to last year. First, compare your Total Income. Has it increased or decreased from last year? Second, compare Total COGS — where COGS = Job Costs. Have your job-related costs gone up or down? Why would that be? Third, look at Total Expense. Have your expenses gone up or down? Are you spending more money this year than last? Where are you spending less?

File the monthly reports in the company accounting binder for the appropriate year. Label the tabs in the binder according to the names of the reports — Balance Sheet and Profit & Loss, for example.

To print this report:

▌ Click **Report Center**, or from the **Reports** menu, choose **Company & Financial**, and then **Profit & Loss Prev Year Comparison**.

▌ Click **OK** to close the Modify Report window, then click **Print**.

End of Year Procedures

In QuickBooks you don't have to end the current year before starting a new year. To close a year:

▌ follow the procedures in the previous section to close each month

▌ write off bad debts

▌ print financial reports, file them, and give a copy to your tax preparer

▌ back up your QuickBooks file, close and lock the year

Write Off Bad Debts and Run the Aging Detail Reports

At the end of the year write off any bad debts from customers that aren't going to pay. To do this, create a credit memo for each customer invoice that won't be paid. This clears the invoice out of Accounts Receivable and decreases net profit by the amount of the unpaid invoice.

A/R Aging Detail Report — Run the A/R Aging Detail report, making sure the **To** and **From** dates are both the last day of the fiscal year. Make sure every invoice listed was actually outstanding as of the last day of your fiscal year. Check that all customer payments have been entered.

Write Off Bad Debts — Write off any bad debts from customers who aren't going to pay. To do this, create a credit memo for each customer invoice that won't be paid. This clears the invoice out of Accounts Receivable and decreases net profit by the amount of the unpaid invoice. To begin, create an expense account for the bad debt:

▌ Click **Home**, then click the **Chart of Accounts** icon, or from the **Lists** menu, choose **Chart of Accounts**.

▌ Pull down the **Account** menu and choose **New**.

▌ Select the **Expense** category. Click **Continue**.

Figure 18-11

Here's an example of how to set up a Bad Debt account.

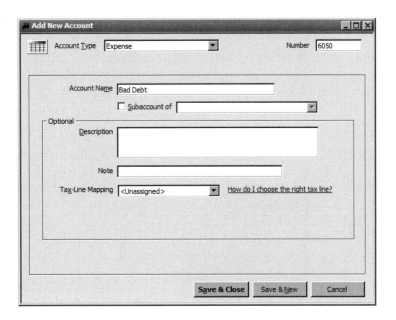

▌ Fill in the Add New Account window as shown in Figure 18-11. We've used 6050 as our Bad Debt account.

▌ Click **Save & Close**.

Next, create an Item for bad debt:

▌ Click **Home**, then click the **Items & Services** icon, or from the **Lists** menu, choose **Item List**. In the Item List window, pull down the **Item** menu and choose **New**.

▌ Fill in the New Item window as shown in Figure 18-12. Link the item to the Bad Debt expense account you created above.

▌ Click **OK**.

Next, create a credit memo to offset the amount the customer will not be paying:

▌ Click **Home**, then click the **Refunds & Credits** icon, or from the **Customers** menu, choose **Create Credit Memo/Refunds**.

▌ Enter the **Customer:Job**.

▌ Enter the date as the last day of the year or the last day of your fiscal year.

Figure 18-12

Here's an example of how to create a Bad Debt item linked to a Bad Debt account.

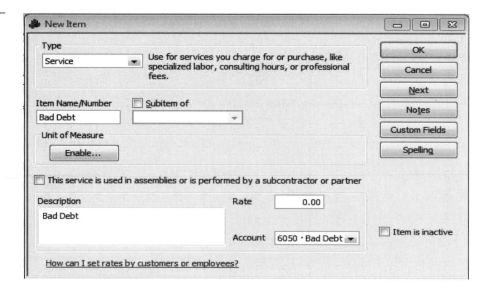

- In the **Credit No.** field, enter **Bad Debt**.

- Under **Item**, select **Bad Debt** from the pull-down Item list.

- In **Amount** enter the amount the customer was invoiced but will not be paying you. See Figure 18-13.

- Click **Save & Close**.

Now you'll be prompted with an Available Credit dialog box. See Figure 18-14.

- Select **Apply to an invoice**.

- Click **OK**.

Finally, in the Apply Credit to Invoices window:

- Put a checkmark in the left hand column to apply the credit to the appropriate invoice(s). See Figure 18-15.

- Click **Done**.

A/P Aging Detail Report — Run the A/P Aging Detail report, making sure the **To** and **From** dates are the last day of the last fiscal year and the last day of the present. If there are duplicates or mistakes, fix them before you close the year.

Figure 18-13

Use a credit memo to record the bad debt.

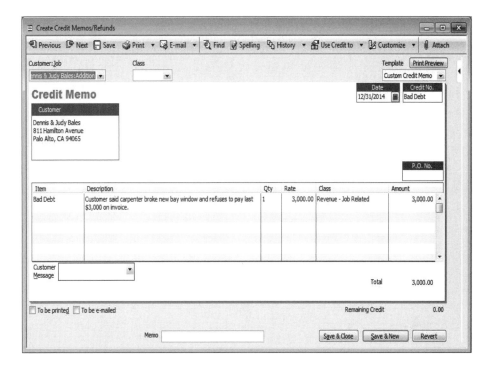

Figure 18-14

The Available Credit dialog box.

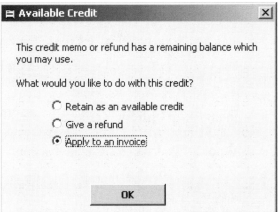

Figure 18-15

Apply the credit to the appropriate invoice(s).

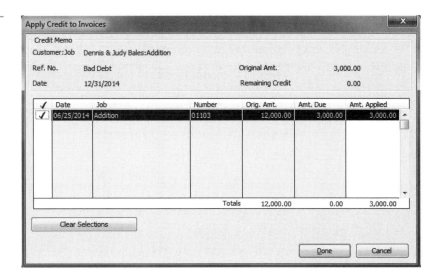

Print Your Annual Reports

At the close of your fiscal year, print the Balance Sheet, Profit & Loss statement, and aging reports for the year you're closing.

▌ Click **Report Center**, or from the **Reports** menu, choose and print these reports:

▌ Company & Financial, Balance Sheet Standard

▌ Company & Financial, Profit & Loss Standard

▌ Customers & Receivables, A/R Aging Detail

▌ Vendors & Payables, A/P Aging Detail

File the annual reports in the company accounting binder for the appropriate year. Label the tabs in the binder according to the names of the reports — Balance Sheet, Profit & Loss, for example.

Make a copy of the Balance Sheet and Profit & Loss reports for your tax preparer.

Back Up Your Data Files and Close the Year

To back up your end of the year data:

▌ From the **File** menu, choose **Create Backup**.

▌ Select **Local backup** and select the **Options** button.

▌ Click **Save it Now**. Click **Next**.

▌ In the **Backup Options** window, select a location for your backup file. Typically, you'd select an external backup drive, a USB flash drive, or a CD drive to store the backup.

▌ Once you've selected the right backup destination in the box at the top, select the **OK** button.

▌ Back at the **Create Backup** screen, select **Finish**.

Now you're ready to close and lock yourself out of making changes to the period you just completed.

▌ From the **Edit** menu, choose **Preferences**.

▌ Click the **Accounting Preferences** icon in the left hand scroll bar.

▌ Click the **Company Preference** tab.

▌ In the Closing Date area, click on **Set Date/Password** and enter the last day of the year just closed. This will cause a warning to display if you're making any entries into the closed month. You may also want to set a password to prevent any unauthorized change of transactions in closed months.

▌ Click **OK**.

In this chapter, you learned what to do at month end and at year end. You saw how to reconcile your bank statements, print financial reports, and review transactions to make sure they were entered correctly. The next chapter is for builders who develop land. If you're a builder, be sure to go through this chapter. If you're a remodeling contractor and you don't develop land, nor plan to, you may want to just skim over the next chapter. But read the conclusion. It's pertinent to all contractors.

Chapter 19

Real Estate Development

As a spec builder or developer, you need an accounting system that handles some specialized tasks. You need to track money borrowed and spent to purchase land, improve that land, and then build on the improved land. You also need to record the sale of the property. In this chapter, we'll look at how to use QuickBooks to easily deal with these matters.

New Accounts

First, you may need to add a few new accounts to your Chart of Accounts. For information on setting up accounts, see Chapter 3. Here are the new accounts you'll need:

Account number	Name	Type
1111	Adjustment Register	Bank
1460	Escrow Deposit	Other Current Asset
1470	Land Purchase	Other Current Asset
1471	Land Interest/Closing Costs	Other Current Asset
1480	WIP — Land Development	Other Current Asset
1490	WIP — Construction	Other Current Asset
2300	Loans Payable	Other Current Liability
2400	Land Acquisition Loan	Other Current Liability
2405	Land Development Loan	Other Current Liability
2410	Construction Loan	Other Current Liability

▌ *Adjustment Register* — Use the Adjustment Register account to temporarily record the transaction where you pay off one loan with another loan. For example, a development loan may pay off a land loan, or a construction loan may pay off a development loan. You'll see later exactly how to use this account to temporarily record loans that have been paid off during escrow closing. In our example Chart of Accounts, we use 1111 Adjustment Register.

▌ *Escrow Deposit Account* — Use the Escrow Deposit account if you're required to place a deposit with an escrow company when you purchase land. Usually you write a check to the escrow company to open up an escrow account. In our example Chart of Accounts, we use 1460 Escrow Deposit.

▌ *Land Purchase Accounts* — Use the Land Purchase accounts to keep track of the original purchase price of any land you purchase for development and costs related to that purchase. In our example Chart of Accounts, we use 1470 Land Purchase and 1471 Land Interest/Closing Costs.

▌ *WIP — Work in Process Accounts* — Use the WIP accounts to keep track of the costs of developing and building on a property. These accounts will appear on your balance sheet as assets, even though you use them for costs. In real estate development, you have to hold your costs until you sell the property. Then you match the sale of the building and the construction costs in the same time period. Once you sell the building, you'll transfer the WIP totals from the WIP accounts to the Job Related Costs account. In our example Chart of Accounts, we use 1480 WIP Land Development and 1490 WIP Construction.

▌ *Loan Accounts* — The loan accounts should total the amount of funds you borrowed for land acquisition, land development, and building construction. These loan accounts appear on your balance sheet as liabilities. When you pay off a loan or sell a property, the loan balances for the property will return to 0. We'll explain this rather complicated process, step-by-step, later in this chapter in the section on Recording the Sale of a Property. In our example Chart of Accounts, we use 2400 Land Acquisition Loan, 2405 Land Development Loan, and 2410 Construction Loan.

Setting Up a Development Job

To track the costs and income for each individual building in a development, set up each one as a customer. For example, our Twice Right Construction Company is developing property on Ellis Street. Since we don't know who the customer is yet, we set up a customer called Ellis Street. If you have more than one job in a single development, you can make the development the customer and set up the properties as individual jobs. For example, if Twice Right purchased three lots on Ellis Street, the customer would be Ellis Street Development and each job would be its street address — 1120 Ellis Street, 1130 Ellis Street, and 1140 Ellis Street, as shown in Figure 19-1. However, in most cases you'll be using a lot and block number, i.e., Lot 1, Block 10 or L1B10.

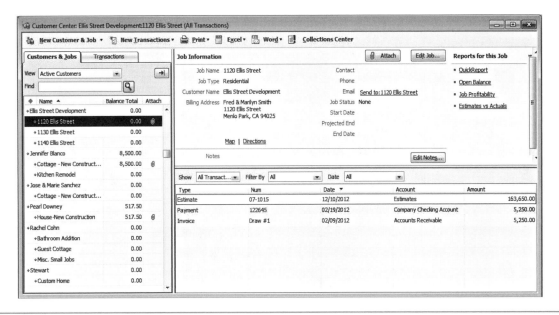

Figure 19-1
Notice that Ellis Street Development is the customer and the jobs are listed as the address of each piece of property. If you don't have an address for the property, you may have to list each job as Lot 1, Lot 2, etc.

Using Items to Track Construction Costs as WIP

The method shown here is only for a spec builder or developer who is setting up and linking items (job phases of construction). This is different from the way we showed you to link items in Chapter 4. In this section, we'll use WIP and Construction Loan accounts.

If you want to track the costs of development by phase, create items and subitems for each phase. Now let's see how to set up a new item for 34 Land Dev (short for Land Development Costs), and a subitem 34.1 Loan Fee (short for Land Development Loan Fees) as shown in Figures 19-2 and 19-3. To create the new item:

▌ Click **Home**, then click **Items & Services**, or from the **Lists** menu, choose **Item List**. In the **Item List** window, pull down the **Item** menu and choose **New**.

▌ In **Type**, select **Service**.

▌ In **Account**, enter a Land Purchase, Land Interest/Closing Costs, WIP — Land Development, or WIP — Construction account. In our example, we selected 1480 WIP — Land Development because all the costs related to this item get classified as land development costs.

▌ Fill in the other necessary fields and click **OK**.

Figure 19-2

When you set up an item, be sure to link it to the correct asset account.

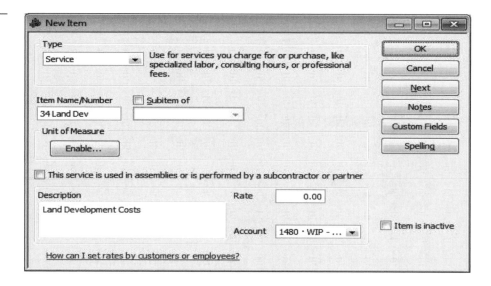

Figure 19-3

Here's an example of a new item that's a subitem. Notice that the "Subitem of" box is checked.

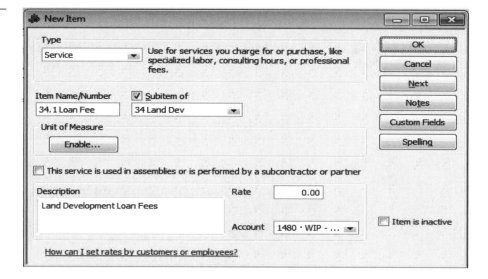

Keep in mind that each item needs to be linked to an asset account (in the Account box). Link land purchase items to a land purchase asset account such as 1470 Land Purchase. Link land development items to a WIP development asset account such as 1480 WIP Development. Construction cost items need to be set up similar to the items you created in Chapter 4. See Figure 4-3 for an example. The only difference is that in the **Expense Account** field you select a WIP construction asset account such as 1490 WIP Construction, and in the **Income Account** field you select a construction liability loan account, such as 2410 Construction Loan. Use the same procedure to create subitems, remembering to set up an item before setting up any subitems under it. Figure 19-3 shows how we created 34.1 Loan Fee as a subitem of the 34 Land Dev item. Later in this chapter, we'll add a few more items that will be used when the property is sold.

Figure 19-4

Here's an example of how to record earnest money you pay to a title company to start escrow.

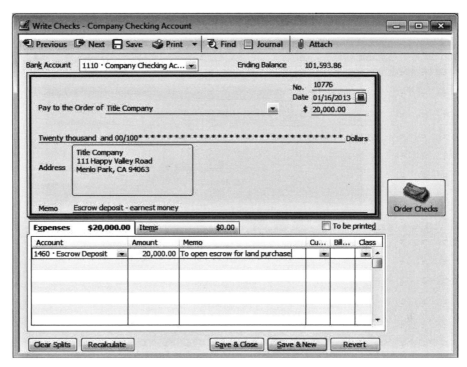

Land Purchase Transactions

Earnest Money

When a check is written to open escrow on a property purchase, the money is called earnest money. In effect, it's a good faith deposit. Here's how to record the transaction and write an earnest money check:

▌ Click **Home**, then click the **Write Checks** icon, or from the **Banking** menu, choose **Write Checks**. See our example in Figure 19-4.

▌ At the top of the Write Checks window, in **Bank Account**, make sure to select the correct checking account you write the check from.

▌ In **Pay to the Order of**, enter the name of the escrow company. Enter the check amount beside the company name.

▌ Make sure the check number is accurate, or leave it blank if you're going to print the check later.

▌ In **Memo**, enter a brief description stating that the check is for earnest money to open escrow.

▌ Click the **Expenses** tab.

Figure 19-5

Here's an example of an escrow closing statement for a land purchase.

YOUR TITLE COMPANY
111 HAPPY VALLEY RD.
MENLO PARK, CA 94063
Tel: (650) 555-1234
Fax: (650) 555-1235

Escrow No. 980723   **ESCROW STATEMENT**

Date: 1/24/2013

TWICE RIGHT CONSTRUCTION
2325 Alameda de Las Pulgas
Redwood City, CA 94063

Property Address:

		DEBITS	CREDITS
Vacant Land, Menlo Park, CA			
PURCHASE PRICE		517,500.00	
A	Original Earnest Money deposit		20,000.00
B	Note and Deed of Trust in favor of Seller, Henry Martin		300,000.00
C	Escrow Deposit in favor of Seller		199,013.00
D	Escrow Fee due Title Company	388.00	
E	Recording Fee to County	80.00	
F	Second Quarter Real Property Taxes	1,045.00	
TOTALS		$519,013.00	$519,013.00

▌ Click in the **Account** column and select your Escrow Deposit account from the account list. In our example, we used 1460 Escrow Deposit.

▌ In **Amount**, enter the full amount of the check.

▌ Leave **Customer:Job**, **Billable**, and **Class** blank.

▌ Click **Save & Close**.

Closing Escrow on a Land Purchase

Write another check to the escrow company when you complete the land purchase and the title to the land is switched into your company's name. When writing this check, you can also record that you paid closing costs. If you have a seller carryback loan or a loan from a bank, you can also record that on the check to the escrow company. Let's work through our example so you can see how to do this. In Figure 19-5, we show you an escrow closing sheet you can use to follow our example. Here are the steps:

▌ Click **Home**, then click **Write Checks**, or from the **Banking** menu, choose **Write Checks**. See our example in Figure 19-6.

Figure 19-6

Use the Items tab to record land purchase and closing costs. In this example, we used items 31.1 Land Purchase Price and 31.2 Land Closing Costs. Your items for land purchase and closing costs may be different.

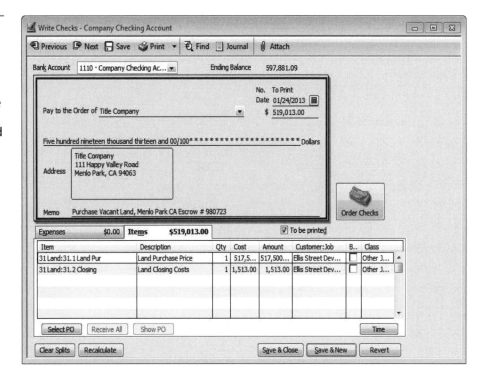

- In the Write Checks window, in **Bank Account**, select the account that you're issuing the funds from.
- In **Pay to the Order of**, enter the name of the escrow company.
- In the **$** field, enter the amount of the check you write to the escrow company when the escrow on the land closes.
- Click the **Items** tab.
- Click the **Item** column and select your land purchase item from the pull-down list.
- In **Amount**, enter the purchase price from the escrow settlement sheet. (In Figure 19-5, it's $517,500.)
- Click the **Customer:Job** column and select the customer for the transaction from the pull-down list.
- Click the next line in the **Item** column and select your land closing costs item from the pull-down list.
- In **Amount**, enter the sum of closing fees (lines D - F in Figure 19-5).
- Click the **Customer:Job** column and select the customer for the transaction from the pull-down list.

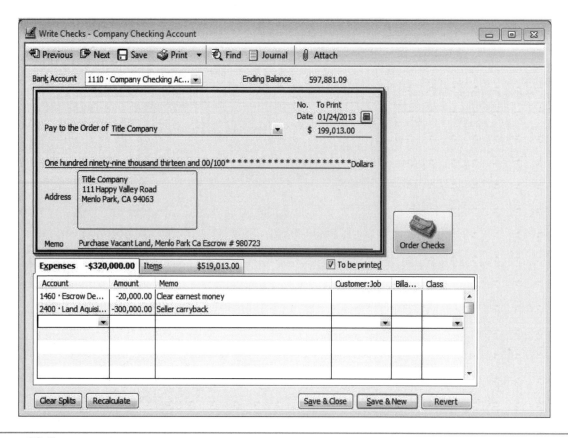

Figure 19-7

Here's how to enter a seller carryback loan on land and how to clear out the earnest money involved in the sale.

If the seller carries back a loan, record the loan amount on the Expenses tab:

▌ Click the **Expenses** tab. See Figure 19-7.

▌ Click in the **Account** column and select your Escrow Deposit account from the pull-down list. It's 1460 in our example.

▌ In **Amount**, enter the escrow earnest money as a negative number. In our example, it's −$20,000 (line A in Figure 19-5).

▌ Click the next line in the **Account** column and select the Land Acquisition Loan account from the pull-down list. It's 2400 in our example.

▌ In **Amount**, enter the total amount of the loan or seller carryback amount, as a negative number. In our example, it's −$300,000 (line B in Figure 19-5).

▌ Leave **Customer:Job**, **Billable** and **Class** blank.

▌ Click **Save & Close**.

Now you have recorded the close of escrow, a seller carryback loan (if needed), and closing costs.

Personal Loans

Most real estate developers or spec home builders need to borrow money to buy land or do some developing before they take out a construction or development loan. These are basically personal loans. Whenever you get a personal loan (not including a construction loan) from a new entity, add a new liability account to your Chart of Accounts. For example, let's say Twice Right Construction Company borrowed $25,000 from an investor. The investor is Paul Olsen, a long-time friend. We need to keep track of this money after we deposit it in our bank account. So we set up a new liability account for the loan.

If you don't have a loans payable header account in your Chart of Accounts, set that up first. In our example, we use 2300 Loans Payable as the loans payable header account.

Now, on to the subaccount for the lender. Keep in mind that this loan could be from an individual, another company, or a bank. In our example, the loan is from an individual, but the procedure is the same no matter what type of entity. However, don't set up a new account if the loan is a construction loan. Construction loans are handled differently and will be covered later in this chapter, under the heading Construction Loans.

▌ Click **Home**, then click the **Chart of Accounts** icon, or from the **Lists** menu, choose **Chart of Accounts**.

▌ In the Chart of Accounts window, pull down the **Account** menu and choose **New**.

▌ From the **Account Type** pull-down list, select **Other Current Liability**. Click **Continue**.

▌ In **Number**, enter the new account number. In our example it's 2320.

▌ In **Account Name**, enter Loan – name of entity (Paul Olsen in our example). See Figure 19-8.

▌ Click the **Subaccount of** box and select the loans payable header account number from the pull-down list. It's 2300 in our example.

▌ Click **Save & Close**.

Follow the same procedure for any other entities that loaned you money. Keep in mind that you only enter new accounts for loans that are not construction or development loans. Construction, development, and seller carryback loans on land purchases are handled differently from personal loans. Construction loans, for example, have draw schedules and have to be paid back during the close of escrow. Personal loans are typically more informal than construction loans.

Figure 19-8

Create a liability account for each personal loan from a new entity.

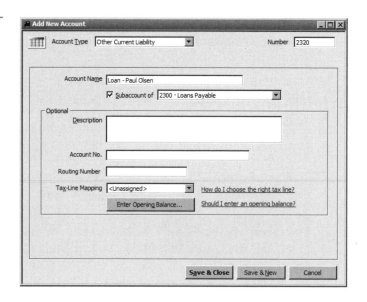

Depositing a Personal Loan

To record the deposit of money received from a personal loan, follow the instructions below. In our example, we deposit the $25,000 loan from Paul Olsen.

First, add the investor as a vendor. See Chapter 8 if you need help setting up a new vendor.

Second, make sure that this deposit is separate from your ordinary income deposits. For example, if you received three checks that need to be deposited, two checks from customers and one personal loan check, make sure you use a separate deposit slip for the personal loan check. The other two customer checks can be added together on the same deposit slip, but the personal loan has to be deposited separately. This is because it will be recorded individually in the QuickBooks checkbook reconciliation, and it would be best if the bank recorded it the same way.

❚ Click **Home**, then click the **Record Deposits** icon, or from the **Banking** menu, choose **Make Deposits**.

❚ In the Make Deposits window, from the pull-down **Deposit To** list, make sure you choose the checking account that you're going to deposit the money to. In our example shown in Figure 19-9, we use 1110 Company Checking.

❚ In **Date**, enter the date you'll be taking the deposit to the bank.

❚ In **Received From**, select the vendor you received the money from (not the job where you'll be using the money).

Figure 19-9

Here's how to record the deposit of a personal loan.

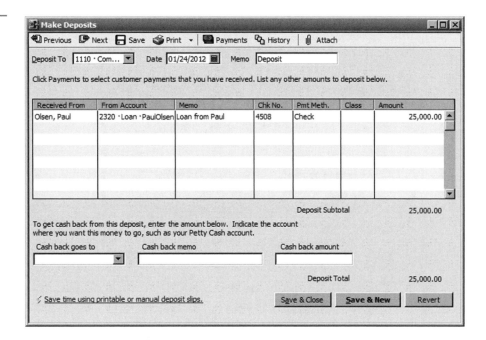

- In **From Account**, select the loan payable account from the pull-down list for the entity. In our example, it's 2320 Loan - Paul Olsen.

- In **Memo**, enter a description of the loan.

- In **Chk No.**, enter the check number from the entity.

- In **Pmt Meth.**, select from the pull-down list whether you received a check, cash, money order, or credit card payment.

- Leave **Class** blank.

- In **Amount**, enter the amount you're depositing.

- Click **Save & Close**.

Following these steps will record that you received and deposited the personal loan, and that you owe that entity for the personal loan. Whenever you print a Balance Sheet, the liability for this personal loan will appear, reminding you that you have to pay this personal loan back at some point.

Recording an Interest Payment on a Personal Loan

You may be required to pay interest on a personal loan on a periodic basis such as monthly, quarterly, or yearly. Or you may not have to pay both principal and interest until you pay back the personal loan. Regardless of when you pay the interest, the procedure is the same. Enter one transaction for the interest payment and one for the principal payment. However, the check you give to the entity may include just interest, or both interest and principal.

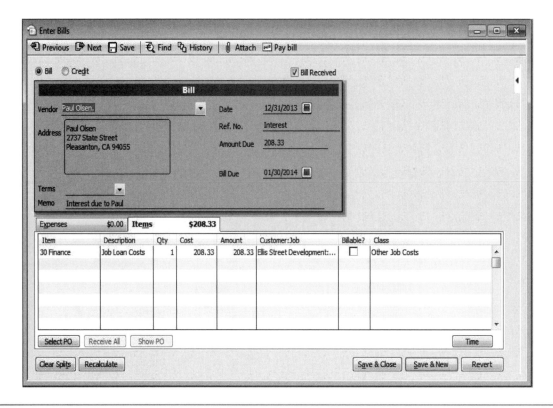

Figure 19-10
Here's how to record interest due on a loan.

To record an interest payment on a personal loan (even if you may not be writing the check for some time) enter a bill following the steps below. The bill will track the interest expense, a job expense on the job reports (if a job is associated with the expense), and a transaction in your Accounts Payable (for interest only) to the entity you borrowed the money from.

▌ Click **Home**, then click **Enter Bills**, or from the **Vendors** menu, choose **Enter Bills**.

▌ In the Enter Bills window, from the pull-down **Vendor** list, select the entity to pay. In our example shown in Figure 19-10, it's Paul Olsen.

▌ In **Date**, enter the date you owe the interest.

▌ If the entity has given you a bill or invoice for the interest, enter that number in the **Ref. No** field. In our example, we didn't have a bill from Paul Olsen, so we entered Interest.

▌ In **Amount Due**, enter the amount of the interest only.

▌ In **Memo**, enter a description for the bill.

▌ Click the **Items** tab.

Figure 19-11

Here's how to record paying back a personal loan.

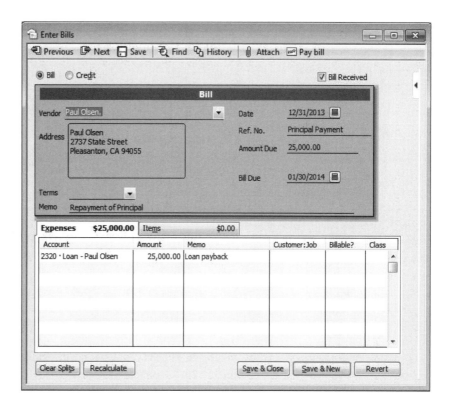

I Click in the **Item** column and from the pull-down **Item** list, select the appropriate item.

I Enter **Amount**, **Customer:Job**, and **Class**. This will capture the interest cost on job cost reports.

I Click **Save & Close**.

Entering this bill will record that you owe the entity for the interest. The bill will show up in the Pay Bills window when it's due.

Recording a Principal Payment on a Personal Loan

When it comes time to pay down (or pay off) the personal loan, follow these steps:

I Click **Home**, then click **Enter Bills**, or from the **Vendors** menu, choose **Enter Bills**.

I In the Enter Bills window, from the pull-down **Vendor** list, select the entity to pay. In our example shown in Figure 19-11, it's Paul Olsen.

I In **Date**, enter the date you decide to pay the principal.

- In **Ref. No**, enter the loan number or a description of the personal loan. In our example we didn't have a loan number, so we entered Principal Payment.

- In **Amount Due**, enter the amount of the principal only.

- In **Memo**, enter a description for the bill.

- Click the **Expenses** tab.

- Click in the **Account** column and select the appropriate loan account. In our example, the account is 2320 Loan — Paul Olsen.

- Click **Save & Close**.

Entering this bill will record that you owe that entity for a principal payment. The bill will show up in the Pay Bills window when it's due.

Development Loans

A development loan is a loan taken out specifically to develop the infrastructure of a land parcel, such as subdividing the land into lots, sidewalks, roads, common areas, bridges, parks, etc. Usually the lender of a development loan requires you to also pay off the land loan as part of the development loan. So include the balance of the land loan in the amount you borrow for a development loan.

Closing Escrow on a Development Loan

There are several transactions to record when closing escrow on a development loan. They are:

1. Record loan fees, including loan origination, document prep, processing, and underwriting fees.

2. Record escrow fees.

3. Record title insurance fees.

4. Record miscellaneous fees.

5. Record property tax payment.

6. Record payoff of the seller carryback loan on the land. Skip this step if there's no loan on the land.

7. Record interest on the land loan. Skip this step if you don't have an existing land loan.

Figure 19-12

Here's an escrow statement you can use to follow our example.

YOUR TITLE COMPANY
111 HAPPY VALLEY RD.
MENLO PARK, CA 94063
Tel: (650) 555-1234
Fax: (650) 555-1235

Escrow No. 123456-ABC   **ESCROW STATEMENT**

Date: 3/15/2012

TWICE RIGHT CONSTRUCTION
2325 Alameda de Las Pulgas
Redwood City, CA 94063

Property Address:

Vacant Land, Menlo Park, CA	**DEBITS**	**CREDITS**
YOUR ESCROW CO. Loan Proceeds		756,000.00
A Loan Origination Fee	22,680.00	
B Document Preparation Fee	650.00	
C Processing Fee at 0.5%	2,340.00	
D Fed Ex and Corp. Verif.	45.00	
E Processing & Underwriting Fee	800.00	
F Endorse (104.1) & Coll Set up	796.00	
G Escrow Fee to Your Escrow Co.	250.00	
H Title Insurance to Your Escrow Co.	1,266.50	
I Inspection Fee	100.00	
Record Documents	20.00	
Reconveyance Fee	110.00	
Recording Specific Guaranty	10.00	
J Property Taxes paid to the County	4,914.97	
K Seller carryback loan payoff		
Principal	248,863.06	
L Interest due at lot loan payoff date	5,178.20	
M Funds Available	467,976.27	
TOTALS	$756,000.00	$756,000.00

We'll take you through an example of these transactions. Use the Escrow Statement shown in Figure 19-12 to follow our example. To begin the process, we'll write the check shown in Figure 19-13.

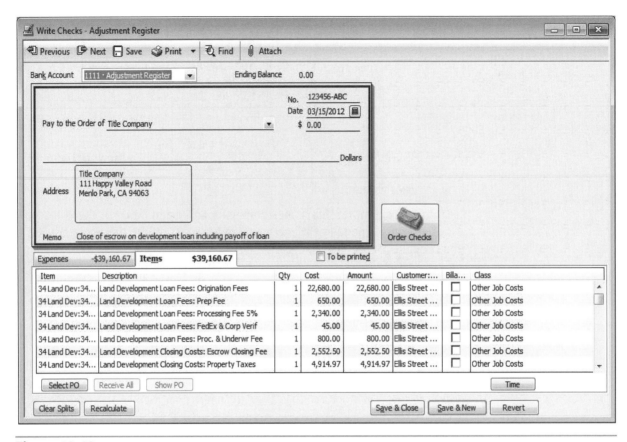

Figure 19-13
Use the Write Checks window to enter information from an escrow closing statement.

▌ Click **Home**, then click **Write Checks**, or from the **Banking** menu, choose **Write Checks**.

▌ In the Write Checks window, from the pull-down **Bank Account** list, select your Adjustment Register account if the development loan paid off the land loan. If you didn't pay off the land loan with the development loan and you wrote a check at the close of escrow, select the account you wrote that check from.

▌ In **$**, enter the amount of the check you wrote at the close of escrow. If you didn't have to write a check at the close of escrow because the new loan paid all of your costs, enter 0 as shown in the example. See Figure 19-13.

▌ In **No.**, enter the escrow number from the escrow statement.

▌ In **Date**, enter the date of the escrow statement.

▌ In **Pay to the Order of**, enter the name of your escrow company.

▌ In **Memo**, enter a description, such as close of escrow.

Recording Fees and Taxes on a Development Loan

Now let's enter the fees and taxes shown on the escrow closing statement. We'll go to the Items tab and enter lines in the Item column for these amounts. All the amounts entered here (except the land loan interest on line L) are charged to a subitem of 34 Land Dev Costs item. The amount on line L is the interest on the loan up to the escrow funding date. You charge it to item 30 Finance. The escrow closing costs include lines F through I, totaling $2,552.50. If you have a loan on the land, you'll be required to pay this interest. In our example, we paid the seller $5,178.20 for interest through escrow.

In our example, the property taxes hadn't been paid for the prior year, so there was a penalty tax payment due (line J). Also, the taxes needed to be prepaid for the current year.

▌ Click **Items** tab.

▌ Click in the **Item** column and enter necessary amounts in the **Amount** column. In our example shown in Figure 19-13, we enter the amounts shown in Figure 19-12.

Recording Paying off a Land Loan

Now we're ready to record the payoff of the loan on the land. We'll do that on the Expenses tab of the check shown in Figure 19-14. Since the full purchase price of the land was entered earlier (see the section titled Closing Escrow on a Land Purchase, which shows how we entered the full land value shown in Figures 19-5 and 19-6), all we want to do here is record the loan payoff. In our example in Figure 19-12, the seller carryback land loan balance was $248,863.06.

▌ Click the **Expenses** tab. See Figure 19-14.

▌ Click in the **Account** column and enter your land acquisition loan account. In our example, it's 2400 Land Acquisition Loan.

▌ In **Amount**, enter the total amount of the loan payoff. In our example shown in Figure 19-14, the amount is $248,863.06.

▌ If the development loan paid these costs, you need to select account 2405 Land Development Loan and enter as a negative number the total of the fees and the amount the bank paid on your behalf to pay off the land loan. This will increase the loan balance.

▌ Click **Save & Close**.

The total amount of the check should be zero *or* if you wrote a check at the close of escrow to cover some costs, the check should be made out for the amount paid at the close of escrow.

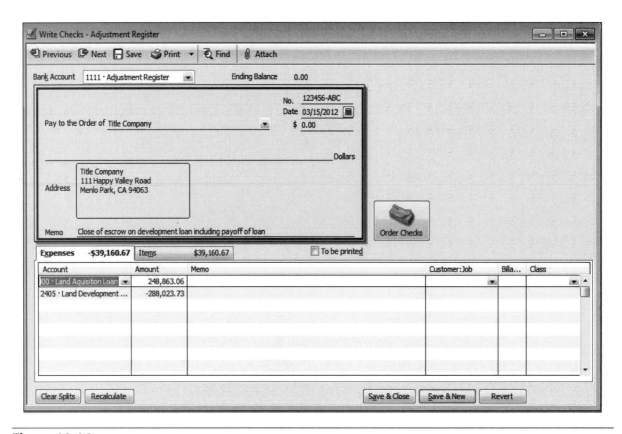

Figure 19-14

To enter an amount from an escrow closing statement use the Expenses tab of a Write Checks window.

Construction Loans

Entering a Construction Draw

When you draw funds for a development project, create an invoice before depositing the funds. And before creating the invoice, create an estimate for the project. Look back to Chapter 12 if you need help with estimates. Here's how to enter an invoice for a construction loan draw:

▮ Click **Home**, then click **Create Invoices**, or from the **Customers** menu, choose **Create Invoices**.

▮ In the Create Invoices window, select the **Customer:Job** you're requesting the funds for. In our example, we selected Ellis Street Development — 1120 Ellis Street.

▮ If you entered an estimate for this job, you'll see the Available Estimates dialog box. Select the estimate you would like to bill from.

▮ Click **OK**.

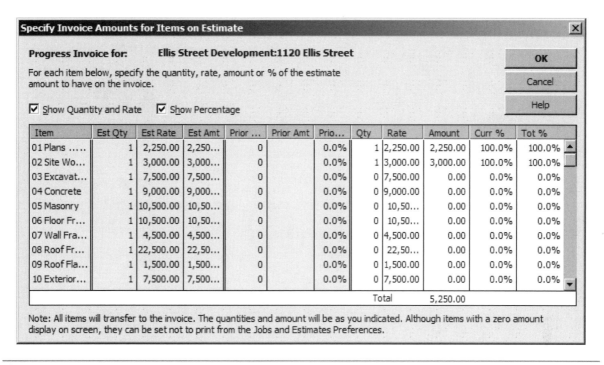

Figure 19-15
Use the Specify Invoice Amounts for Items on Estimate window to enter the amount or % for each line item of the draw.

▌ In the Create Progress Invoice Based on Estimate window, select **Create invoice for selected items or for different percentages of each item**.

▌ Click **OK**.

▌ In the Specify Invoice Amounts for Items on Estimate window, in **Amount**, enter the amount you're billing for. In our example, shown in Figure 19-15, the draw is for $5,250 for item 01 Plans and item 02 Site Work.

▌ Click **OK**.

Back in the Create Invoices window, make sure the correct amounts appear in the draw invoice. Since each job phase item was originally linked to the Construction Loan account, when this invoice gets generated the item will automatically track the draw as a liability.

▌ In **Bill To**, enter the bank or investor you're requesting the funds from. In our example, shown in Figure 19-16, we selected Fred and Marilyn Smith.

▌ Leave **Class** blank.

▌ Click **Save & Close** to create the invoice.

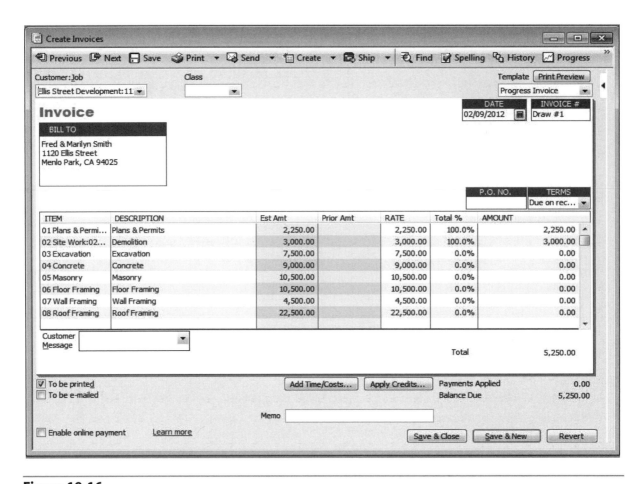

Figure 19-16
Use the Create Invoices window to record a construction draw.

Depositing the Draw Check into Your Account

When you receive the draw check:

▌ Click **Home**, then click **Receive Payments**, or from the **Customers** menu, choose **Receive Payments**.

▌ From the pull-down **Received From** list, select the same customer that's on the draw request. You should see the original draw request appear, as shown in Figure 19-17.

▌ Fill in the date you received the payment, the amount paid, the payment method, and the check number if paid by check.

▌ In **Memo**, enter the draw request number and the bank or investor you requested funds from.

▌ Click **Save & Close**.

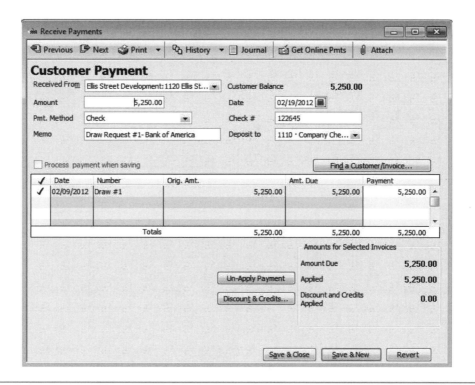

Figure 19-17
Use the Receive Payments window to record a draw request check.

Recording the Sale of a Property

When you sell the property:

1. Record the sale of the property.

2. Record paying off the construction loan.

3. Account for the closing costs.

4. Transfer the WIP accounts to the Cost of Goods Sold account.

This looks complicated, but we'll show you how to do it all in just one transaction. The transaction will be on the invoice you issue for the sale of the property. We'll walk you through the process of entering the invoice in QuickBooks. First, you need to set up these seven items that will be used in the process. Use the usual method to set up these items. Make sure you link the items to the proper accounts.

▌ *Building Sale* — link to your Construction Income account (4110 in our Chart of Accounts).

▌ *Building Costs* — link to your Job Related Costs account (5110 in our Chart of Accounts).

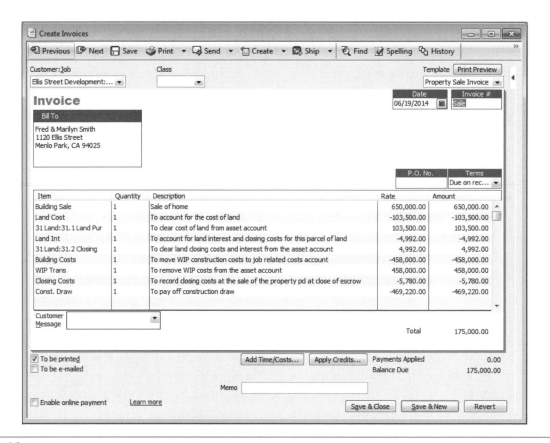

Figure 19-18
Use the Create Invoices window to record the sale of a property.

- *WIP Trans* — link to your WIP Construction account (1490 in our Chart of Accounts).

- *Closing Costs* — link to your Job Related Costs account (5110 in our Chart of Accounts).

- *Const. Draws* — link to your Construction Loan account (2410 in our Chart of Accounts).

- *Land Cost* — link to your Job Related Costs account (5110 in our Chart of Accounts).

- *Land Int* — link to your Job Related Costs account (5110 in our Chart of Accounts).

Recording an Invoice for the Sale of a Property

Now you're ready to create an invoice to record the sale and closing costs, and to clear the WIP assets and Construction Loan accounts. For our example, we created an invoice for 1120 Ellis Street when we received a check from the title company that closed the escrow on the new house. The invoice is shown in Figure 19-18. Let's take a close look at each item in the figure:

▌ *Building Sale* — This is the sale price of the property. Amount is the selling price of the home.

▌ *Land Cost* — Records the purchase price of the land in a Cost of Goods Sold (job related costs) account.

▌ *31.1 Land item* — This line clears the purchase price of the land out of the asset account. If you purchased several parcels in a subdivision, then the price is a portion of the original purchase price. For example, in Figures 19-5 and 19-6, we purchased land that was subdivided into five lots. Each lot was similar in size, so we divided the $517,500 by 5 to get an individual lot price of $103,500.

▌ *Land Int* — Records the land interest and closing costs in a Cost of Goods Sold (job related costs) account.

▌ *31.2 Land Int item* — This line clears out the land closing costs and interest through the end of the life of the land loan and divides the costs by the five lots. In our case, we paid $1,513 for closing costs plus $23,450 in interest. Divide that by the five lots and you have $4,992.00 per lot.

▌ *Building Costs* — This moves the WIP costs to the Cost of Goods Sold account. Amount is the same as the amount in the next line except it's a negative number.

▌ *WIP Trans* — This line clears the WIP Construction account total out of the asset account. Amount is the total WIP costs for the project. To figure out the total WIP costs for the job, print out a Profitability Detail Report. Chapter 17, Reports, has more information on this.

▌ *Closing Costs* — Amount is the total of the real estate commission fees, recording fees, title fees, and any other credits given to the buyer at the close of escrow for the sale of the property. This is also a negative number because the seller won't receive this money; it's been taken out of the funds to be disbursed to the seller (contractor).

▌ *Const Draw* — This is the amount the escrow company paid to the lender for the total amount of construction draws taken to date. This total will be listed on the closing papers as the loan payback. It's a negative number because it's being taken out of funds to be disbursed to the seller (contractor). This line pays back the construction loan.

The total amount of the cash sale needs to be exactly equal to the amount of money received at the close of escrow.

Recording a Title Company Payment for the Sale of a Property

To record the payment from the title company for the sale of a property:

▌ Click **Home**, then click **Receive Payments**, or from the **Customers** menu, choose **Receive Payments**.

▌ From the pull-down **Received From** list, select the same customer that's on the invoice for the sale of the property.

▌ In the list, select the invoice you received payment for.

▌ Fill in the date you received the payment, the amount paid, the payment method, and the check number if paid by check.

▌ Click **Save & Close**.

To record the payment after depositing it in the bank:

▌ From the **Banking** menu, choose **Make Deposits**.

In this chapter, you've learned how to set up QuickBooks to track each transaction using proper accounting methods for a spec builder. This chapter wasn't meant to be read just one time. In fact, this book wasn't meant to be read only one time. We hope you'll use this chapter and the whole book as a reference guide. For example, you can use this chapter to help set up and link items to track WIP and construction loans. When you sell a property, you'll need to refer back to this section and follow the instructions on how to record the sale of the property. When you receive the money, you can go through receiving the payment. Then when you deposit the money to the bank, you can follow our instructions again.

Conclusion

It's rare that we run across a contractor or builder who enjoys accounting, let alone job costing, payroll, workers' comp reports, or doing income taxes. If you enjoyed these things, you'd be an accountant, bookkeeper, or consultant. But if you've followed the instructions in this book, you're on your way to having an efficient and accurate accounting and job costing system. And the bottom line is the bottom line — with accurate reporting, you'll be more profitable.

By now you realize that setting up QuickBooks isn't an easy task. We've tried, however, to break up the tasks into manageable units that are simple to understand and duplicate. If you followed our directions in setting up QuickBooks, and were diligent in your efforts to enter transactions accurately, you'll be rewarded with clear and useful job cost reports — the Holy Grail of construction accounting. Of course, there are other important accounting reports you can get from QuickBooks. And we encourage you to continue to explore them as they apply to your business. Craftsman Book

Company (www.craftsman-book.com) publishes several "accounting for contractors" books, including *Markup & Profit* and *Builder's Guide to Accounting*, which will help you apply wisdom to your numbers. There are also several online sources you can use to increase your construction accounting knowledge. For nonspecific accounting problems, Intuit, the creator of QuickBooks, has its own website (www.intuit.com). For QuickBooks help specific to the construction business, take a look at www.onlineaccounting.com.

As you work with QuickBooks, you'll be amazed at its flexibility and power. We don't suggest that you turn a blind eye to new solutions. No one has all the answers, including us. We're constantly finding new solutions and "work-arounds" to make the process smoother. Also, everyone puts different emphasis on the value of individual reports, so one solution may not sit right with everyone. Remember, if the information is what you need, use it. Don't be misled by "pundits" that are selling the "right way."

In writing this book, we've tried to create a system or process that you can follow on a daily basis. We urge you to view accounting and job costing as a repeatable procedure that will get simpler as you do it over and over again. Repeatability works for you in several ways. It cuts down on mistakes and helps refine procedures for maximum productivity. It also makes it easier to train a new employee.

We also want to touch a little on the future of computerized construction accounting. There's no doubt in our minds that in the future, the Internet will play a major role in your business. You'll be estimating and purchasing online — it's not a question of if, but when. And Intuit is at the forefront of online accounting initiatives. This type of "e-commerce" will only get easier to do, cheaper to implement, and more popular. The paperless transaction is already here. For example, you no longer get a receipt when you charge something on your credit card over the phone. The construction trades are sometimes slow to catch on, but nevertheless, it won't be long before bills from your subs and suppliers will go directly into QuickBooks without you ever receiving a paper bill. And they'll even be earmarked with job costing codes so one day you'll turn on your computer and simply ask for a job cost. Without any input — the data will simply be there. Until then, we'll sit at our computer terminals, wishing we didn't have to code this invoice or break down that timecard.

Index

D

Practical References for Builders

Building Contractor's Exam Preparation Guide

Passing today's contractor's exams can be a major task. This book shows you how to study, how questions are likely to be worded, and the kinds of choices usually given for answers. Includes sample questions from actual state, county, and city examinations, plus a sample exam to practice on. This book isn't a substitute for the study material that your testing board recommends, but it will help prepare you for the types of questions — and their correct answers — that are likely to appear on the actual exam. Knowing how to answer these questions, as well as what to expect from the exam, can greatly increase your chances of passing.
320 pages, 8½ x 11, $35.00

National Home Improvement Estimator

Current labor and material prices for home improvement projects. Provides manhours for each job, recommended crew size, and the labor cost for removal and installation work. Material prices are current, with location adjustment factors and free monthly updates on the Web. Gives step-by-step instructions for the work, with helpful diagrams, and home improvement shortcuts and tips from experts. Includes a CD-ROM with an electronic version of the book, and *National Estimator*, a stand-alone *Windows*™ estimating program, plus an interactive multimedia tutorial that shows how to use the disk to compile home improvement cost estimates.
520 pages, 8½ x 11, $73.75. Revised annually

Construction Contract Writer

Write contracts that comply with law in your state and that fit each job exactly, anticipate the most likely disputes, as well as resolve key issues in your favor. You draft each contract by answering interview questions. No legal background needed. Favor either the contractor or the owner. Contracts can be as detailed, or as simple as the job requires. Includes legal updates for one year from purchase. If you get stuck, click the "Get Help from an Attorney" button. You'll have an answer in 24 hours. No charge. No limit. **$99.95**. www.constructioncontractwriter.com

Get FREE contracts created with the Construction Contract Writer program for your state at www.construction-contract.net

National Repair & Remodeling Estimator

The complete pricing guide for dwelling reconstruction costs. Reliable, specific data you can apply on every repair and remodeling job. Up-to-date material costs and labor figures based on thousands of jobs across the country. Provides recommended crew sizes; average production rates; exact material, equipment, and labor costs; a total unit cost and a total price including overhead and profit. Separate listings for high- and low-volume builders, so prices shown are specific for any size business. Estimating tips specific to repair and remodeling work to make your bids complete, realistic, and profitable. Includes a CD-ROM with an electronic version of the book with *National Estimator*, a stand-alone *Windows*™ estimating program, plus an interactive multimedia video that shows how to use the disk to compile construction cost estimates.
496 pages, 8½ x 11, $73.50. Revised annually

Estimating & Bidding for Builders & Remodelers

This 5th edition has all the information you need for estimating and bidding new construction and home improvement projects. It shows how to select jobs that will be profitable, do a labor and materials take-off from the plans, calculate overhead and figure your markup, and schedule the work. Includes a CD with an easy-to-use construction estimating program and a database of 50,000 current labor and material cost estimates for new construction and home improvement work, with area modifiers for every zip code. Price updates on the Web are free and automatic. **272 pages, 8½ x 11, $89.50**

Contractor's Plain-English Legal Guide

For today's contractors, legal problems are like snakes in the swamp — you might not see them, but you know they're there. This book tells you where the snakes are hiding and directs you to the safe path. With the directions in this easy-to-read handbook you're less likely to need a $200-an-hour lawyer. Includes simple directions for starting your business, writing contracts that cover just about any eventuality, collecting what's owed you, filing liens, protecting yourself from unethical subcontractors, and more. For about the price of 15 minutes in a lawyer's office, you'll have a guide that will make many of those visits unnecessary. Includes a CD-ROM with blank copies of all the forms and contracts in the book.
272 pages, 8½ x 11, $49.50

Paper Contracting: The How-To of Construction Management Contracting

Risk, and the headaches that go with it, have always been a major part of any construction project — risk of loss, negative cash flow, construction claims, regulations, excessive changes, disputes, slow pay — sometimes you'll make money, and often you won't. But many contractors today are avoiding almost all of that risk by working under a construction management contract, where they are simply a paid consultant to the owner, running the job, but leaving him the risk. This manual is the how-to of construction management contracting. You'll learn how the process works, how to get started as a CM contractor, what the job entails, how to deal with the issues that come up, when to step back, and how to get the job completed on time and on budget. Includes a link to free downloads of CM contracts legal in each state.
256 pages, 8½ x 11, $55.50

Getting Financing & Developing Land

Developing land is a major leap for most builders — yet that's where the big money is made. This book gives you the practical knowledge you need to make that leap. Learn how to prepare a market study, select a building site, obtain financing, guide your plans through approval, then control your building costs so you can ensure yourself a good profit. Includes a CD-ROM with forms, checklists, and a sample business plan you can customize and use to help you sell your idea to lenders and investors.
232 pages, 8½ x 11, $39.00

How to Succeed With Your Own Construction Business

Everything you need to start your own construction business: setting up the paperwork, finding the work, advertising, using contracts, dealing with lenders, estimating, scheduling, finding and keeping good employees, keeping the books, and coping with success. If you're considering starting your own construction business, all the knowledge, tips, and blank forms you need are here.
336 pages, 8½ x 11, $28.50

Construction Estimating

This unusually well-organized book shows the best and easiest way to estimate materials for room additions or residential structures. It gives estimating tables and procedures needed to make a fast, accurate, and complete material list of the structural members found in wood and steel-framed buildings. This book is divided into 72 units, each of them covering a separate element in the estimating procedure. Covers estimating foundations, floor framing, wall framing, ceiling framing, roof framing, roofing materials, exterior and interior finish materials, hardware, steel joist floor framing, steel stud framing, and steel ceiling joist and rafter framing. **496 pages, 8½ x 11, $49.50**

Building Code Compliance for Contractors & Inspectors

Have you ever failed a construction inspection? Have you ever dealt with an inspector who has his own interpretation of the Code and forces you to comply with it? This new book explains what it takes to pass inspections under the 2009 *International Residential Code*. It includes a Code checklist — with explanations and the Code section number — for every trade, covering some of the most common reasons why inspectors reject residential work. The author uses his 30 years' experience as a building code official to provide you with little-known information on what code officials look for during inspections. **232 pages, 8½ x 11, $32.50**

Contractor's Survival Manual Revised

The "real skinny" on the down-and-dirty survival skills that no one likes to talk about — unique, unconventional ways to get through a debt crisis: what to do when the bills can't be paid, finding money and buying time, conserving income, transferring debt, setting payment priorities, cash float techniques, dealing with judgments and liens, and laying the foundation for recovery. Here you'll find out how to survive a downturn and the key things you can do to pave the road to success. Have this book as your insurance policy; when hard times come to your business it will be your guide. **336 pages, 8½ x 11, $38.00**

Construction Forms for Contractors

This practical guide contains 78 practical forms, letters and checklists, guaranteed to help you streamline your office, organize your jobsites, gather and organize records and documents, keep a handle on your subs, reduce estimating errors, administer change orders and lien issues, monitor crew productivity, track your equipment use, and more. Includes accounting forms, change order forms, forms for customers, estimating forms, field work forms, HR forms, lien forms, office forms, bids and proposals, subcontracts, and more. All are also on the CD-ROM included, in *Excel* spreadsheets, as formatted Rich Text that you can fill out on your computer, and as PDFs. **360 pages, 8½ x 11, $48.50**

Builder's Guide to Accounting Revised

Step-by-step, easy-to-follow guidelines for setting up and maintaining records for your building business. This practical guide to all accounting methods shows how to meet state and federal accounting requirements, explains the new depreciation rules, and describes how the Tax Reform Act can affect the way you keep records. Full of charts, diagrams, simple directions and examples, to help you keep track of where your money is going. Recommended reading for many state contractor's exams. Each chapter ends with a set of test questions, and a CD-ROM included FREE has all the questions in interactive self-test software. Use the Study Mode to make studying for the exam much easier, and Exam Mode to practice your skills. **356 pages, 8½ x 11, $35.50**

Estimating With Microsoft *Excel*, 3rd Edition

Estimating With Microsoft *Excel* (3rd Edition)step-by-step instructions show you how to create your own customized automated spreadsheet estimating program for use with *Excel* 2007. You'll learn how to use the magic of *Excel* to create all the forms you need; detail sheets, cost breakdown summaries, and more. With *Excel* as your tool, you can easily estimate costs for all phases of the job, from pulling permits, to concrete, rebar, and roofing. You'll see how to create your own formulas and macros and apply them in your everyday projects. If you've wanted to use *Excel*, but were unsure of how to make use of all its features, let this new book show you how. Includes a CD-ROM that illustrates examples in the book and provides you with templates you can use to set up your own estimating system. **158 pages, 7 x 9½, $44.95**

Smart Business for Contractors

In this book, a construction attorney explains how you should charge for your work, how to figure your overhead expenses, and how to calculate a realistic hourly rate to apply on each estimate. Includes how to bill and collect on your invoices, what you should always include in your contracts, and creative new ways of dealing with contract disputes. Shows how to keep customers happy so they'll hand you referrals, how best to handle subcontractors, and how to find a good accountant. You'll learn the pros and cons of incorporating, how to handle tax issues such as what you can and can't deduct and what you're allowed to depreciate, and how to plan the future of your company. Reading this book is like getting good advice from a construction lawyer — at a fraction of the cost. **204 pages, 8½ x 11, $19.95.** Published by Taunton Press

CD Estimator

If your computer has *Windows*™ and a CD-ROM drive, CD Estimator puts at your fingertips over 150,000 construction costs for new construction, remodeling, renovation & insurance repair, home improvement, framing & finish carpentry, electrical, concrete & masonry, painting, earthwork & heavy equipment and plumbing & HVAC. Monthly cost updates are available at no charge on the Internet. You'll also have the *National Estimator program* — a stand-alone estimating program for *Windows*™ that Remodeling magazine called a "computer wiz," and *Job Cost Wizard*, a program that lets you export your estimates to *QuickBooks Pro* for actual job costing. A 60-minute interactive video teaches you how to use this CD-ROM to estimate construction costs. And to top it off, to help you create professional-looking estimates, the disk includes over 40 construction estimating and bidding forms in a format that's perfect for nearly any *Windows*™ word processing or spreadsheet program. **CD Estimator is $108.50**

Markup & Profit: A Contractor's Guide, Revisited

In order to succeed in a construction business, you have to be able to price your jobs to cover all labor, material and overhead expenses, and make a decent profit. But calculating markup is only part of the picture. If you're going to beat the odds and stay in business — profitably, you also need to know how to write good contracts, manage your crews, work with subcontractors and collect on your work. This book covers the business basics of running a construction company, whether you're a general or specialty contractor working in remodeling, new construction or commercial work. The principles outlined here apply to all construction-related businesses. You'll find tried and tested formulas to guarantee profits, with step-by-step instructions and easy-to-follow examples to help you learn how to operate your business successfully. Includes a link to free downloads of blank forms and checklists used in this book. **312 pages, 8½ x 11, $47.50**

Insurance Restoration Contracting: Startup to Success

Insurance restoration — the repair of buildings damaged by water, fire, smoke, storms, vandalism and other disasters — is an exciting field of construction that provides lucrative work that's immune to economic downturns. And, with insurance companies funding the repairs, your payment is virtually guaranteed. But this type of work requires special knowledge and equipment, and that's what you'll learn about in this book. It covers fire repairs and smoke damage, water losses and specialized drying methods, mold remediation, content restoration, even damage to mobile and manufactured homes. You'll also find information on equipment needs, training classes, estimating books and software, and how restoration leads to lucrative remodeling jobs. It covers all you need to know to start and succeed as the restoration contractor that both homeowners and insurance companies call on first for the best jobs. **640 pages, 8½ x 11, $69.00**

Handbook of Construction Contracting

Volume 1: Everything you need to know to start and run your construction business; the pros and cons of each type of contracting, the records you'll need to keep, and how to read and understand house plans and specs so you find any problems before the actual work begins. All aspects of construction are covered in detail, including all-weather wood foundations, practical math for the job site, and elementary surveying. **416 pages, 8½ x 11, $32.75**

Volume 2: Everything you need to know to keep your construction business profitable; different methods of estimating, keeping and controlling costs, estimating excavation, concrete, masonry, rough carpentry, roof covering, insulation, doors and windows, exterior finishes, specialty finishes, scheduling work flow, managing workers, advertising and sales, spec building and land development, and selecting the best legal structure for your business. **320 pages, 8½ x 11, $33.75**

Journeyman Electrician's Preparation & Study Guide

This is not only a great study guide filled with sample electrician's exam questions — it teaches you how to quickly turn to the code section that answers the questions. Most electrician's exams give you about 2 minutes per question — not enough time to browse through 800 pages of fine print looking for each answer. This manual, based on the 2008 and 2011 *NEC* editions, explains how the Code is organized, so you understand where the information you need is located. Then it shows how to rearrange and tab your copy of the Code to streamline your search efforts. Next, you learn a step-by-step search procedure, in which you're shown how to analyze the question to determine its subject, know where to look in the index, find the exact article, then turn right to the Code section that answers your question. **96 pages, 8½ x 11, $34.00**

Drafting House Plans

Here you'll find step-by-step instructions for drawing a complete set of home plans for a one-story house, an addition to an existing house, or a remodeling project. This book shows how to visualize spatial relationships, use architectural scales and symbols, sketch preliminary drawings, develop detailed floor plans and exterior elevations, and prepare a final plot plan. It even includes code-approved joist and rafter spans and how to make sure that drawings meet code requirements. **192 pages, 8½ x 11, $34.95**

2010 ADA Standards for Accessible Design

As of March 15, 2012, all public parks, hotels, country clubs, universities, restaurants, and even condominiums must comply with far-reaching 2010 ADA Standards. This volume presents the new 2010 Standards side-by-side with explanatory guidance and background information from the Department of Justice. In one complete volume, you get the 2010 ADA Standards as well as the requirements and background you need to meet those requirements. **362 pages, 8½ x 11, $74.95.** Published by BNI Building News.

Planning Drain, Waste & Vent Systems

How to design plumbing systems in residential, commercial, and industrial buildings. Covers designing systems that meet code requirements for homes, commercial buildings, private sewage disposal systems, and even mobile home parks. Includes relevant code sections and many illustrations to guide you through what the code requires in designing drainage, waste, and vent systems. **202 pages, 8½ x 11, $29.95**

Greenbook Standard Specifications for Public Works Construction 2012

The Greenbook gives approved standards for all types of public works construction — from the depth of paving on roads to the adhesive used on pavement markers. It standardizes public works plans and specs to provide guidelines for both cities and contractors so they can agree on construction practices used in public works. The book has been adopted by over 200 cities, counties, and agencies throughout the U.S. The 2012 edition is the 16th edition of this complete reference, providing uniform standards of quality and sound construction practice easily understood and used by engineers, public works officials, and contractors across the U.S. Includes hundreds of charts and tables. **450 pages, 8½ x 11, $84.50**

Electrician's Exam Preparation Guide to the 2011 *NEC*

Need help in passing the apprentice, journeyman, or master electrician's exam? This is a book of questions and answers based on actual electrician's exams over the last few years. Almost a thousand multiple-choice questions — exactly the type you'll find on the exam — cover every area of electrical installation: electrical drawings, services and systems, transformers, capacitors, distribution equipment, branch circuits, feeders, calculations, measuring and testing, and more. It gives you the correct answer, an explanation, and where to find it in the latest *NEC*. Also tells how to apply for the test, how best to study, and what to expect on examination day. Includes a FREE CD-ROM with all the questions in the book in interactive test-yourself software that makes studying for the exam almost fun! Updated to the 2011 *NEC*. **352 pages, 8½ x 11, $54.50**

Also available:
Electrician's Exam Preparation Guide 2008, $49.50
Electrician's Exam Preparation Guide 2005, $39.50
Electrician's Exam Preparation Guide 2002, $37.50

Code Check Building

Here is a condensed guide to commonly cited *IRC* code violations in the construction of one- and two-family dwellings. Designed to be used on-site for quick reference, this easy-to-read, completely illustrated flipchart will help you quickly find out if buildings meet recent code requirements for foundations, framing, exterior and interior walls, fireplaces and chimneys. **32 pages, 8½ x 11, $17.95.** Published by Taunton Press

Code Check Complete 2nd Edition

Every essential building, electrical and mechanical code requirement you're likely to encounter when building or remodeling residential and light commercial structures. Comes spiral-bound, with over 400 drawings that answer your code questions with up-to-date answers. Includes quick-glance summaries to alert you to important code changes. Compiled by code-certified building/home inspectors, this new book is like having four guides in one, big, easy-to-understand guide. **240 pages, 6½ x 8½, $45.00**

The Pocket Size Carpenter's Helper

This spiral-bound reference is small enough to fit in your shirt pocket! It contains most of the tables and formulas a carpenter needs on the job. Get immediate help calculating concrete mixes, estimating block and the depth of footings, safe loads for different types of lumber, and loading for steel and wood columns. You'll find span tables for rafters and joists, and even more data identifying various lumber grades. Explains most roofing and siding requirements. Gives formulas to calculate heat loss and determine R-values for most building materials. Also contains stair tread and wheelchair ramp formulas. You'll find illustrations, conversion charts, and all the other information you're likely to need on the job. **128 pages, 3½ x 5½, $14.95.** Published by Linden Publishing

Basic Construction Management:
The Superintendent's Job, 5th Edition

Today's construction projects are more complex than ever. Managing these projects has also become more complex. This perennial NAHB bestseller, now in its fifth edition, addresses the issues facing today's construction manager: maintaining impossible budgets, preparing and meeting exceptionally tight schedules, and ensuring quality control of the finished work. Also covers construction team building, working with owners and the importance of safety management. New managers can use this as a great training tool. Experienced superintendents can brush up on the latest techniques and technologies. **264 pages, 8½ x 11, $44.95**

Roof Framing

Shows how to frame any type of roof in common use today, even if you've never framed a roof before. Includes using a pocket calculator to figure any common, hip, valley, or jack rafter length in seconds. Over 400 illustrations cover every measurement and every cut on each type of roof: gable, hip, Dutch, Tudor, gambrel, shed, gazebo, and more. **480 pages, 5½ x 8½, $26.50**

Roof Framer's Bible

68 different pitch combinations of "bastard" hip roofs at your fingertips. Don't curse the architect — let this book make you an accomplished master of irregular pitched roof systems. You'll be the envy of your crew, and irregular or "bastard" roofs will be under your command. This rare pocket-sized book comes hardbound with a cloth marker like a true bible. **216 pages, 3¾ x 7½, $24.00**

Craftsman's Illustrated Dictionary of Construction Terms

Almost everything you could possibly want to know about any word or technique in construction. Hundreds of up-to-date construction terms, materials, drawings and pictures with detailed, illustrated articles describing equipment and methods. Terms and techniques are explained or illustrated in vivid detail. Use this valuable reference to check spelling, find clear, concise definitions of construction terms used on plans and construction documents, or learn about little-known tools, equipment, tests and methods used in the building industry. It's all here. **416 pages, 8½ x 11, $36.00**

JLC Field Guide to Residential Construction

Volume 1: Exteriors The ultimate visual quick-reference guide for construction professionals. Over 400 precisely-detailed drawings with clear concise notes and explanations that show you everything from estimating and selecting lumber to foundations, roofing, siding and exteriors. Explains code requirements for all U.S. building codes. Spiral bound. **386 pages, 11 x 8½, $69.95**

Volume 2: Interiors Over 300 detailed technical drawings, illustrations and tables giving key dimensions and critical details from accessible kitchens to zoned heating systems. This new version of JLC Field Guide has the field-proven principles, methods and materials on all facets of interior construction and remodeling. Spiral bound. **350 pages, 11 x 8½, $69.95**

Contractor's Guide to the Building Code, Revised

Explains in plain, simple English just what the 2006 *International Building Code* and *International Residential Code* require. Building codes are elaborate laws, designed for enforcement; they're not written to be helpful how-to instructions for builders. Here you'll find down-to-earth, easy-to-understand descriptions, helpful illustrations, and code tables that you can use to design and build residential and light commercial buildings that pass inspection the first time. Written by a former building inspector, it tells what works with the inspector to allow cost-saving methods, and warns what common building shortcuts are likely to get cited. Filled with the tables and illustrations from the *IBC* and *IRC* you're most likely to need, fully explained, with examples to guide you. Includes a CD-ROM with the entire book in PDF format, with an easy search feature. **408 pages, 8½ x 11, $66.75**

Residential Property Inspection Reports CD-ROM

This CD-ROM contains 50 pages of property inspection forms in both Rich Text and PDF formats. You can easily customize each form with your logo and address, and use them for your home inspections. Use the CD-ROM to write your inspections with your word processor, print them, and save copies for your records. Includes inspection forms for grounds and exterior, foundations, garages and carports, roofs and attics, pools and spas, electrical, plumbing and HVAC, living rooms, family rooms, dens, studies, kitchens, breakfast rooms, dining rooms, hallways, stairways, entries, and laundry rooms. **CD-ROM, $79.95**

Residential Wiring to the 2008 *NEC*

This completely revised manual explains in simple terms how to install rough and finish wiring in new construction, alterations, and additions. It takes you from basic electrical theory to current wiring methods that comply with the 2008 *National Electrical Code*. You'll find complete instructions on troubleshooting and repairs of existing wiring, and how to extend service into additions and remodels. Hundreds of drawings and photos show you the tools and gauges you need, and how to plan and install the wiring. Includes demand factors, circuit loads, the formulas you need, and over 20 pages of the most-needed 2008 *NEC* tables to help your wiring pass inspection the first time. Includes a CD-ROM with an Interactive Study Center that helps you retain what you've learned, and study for the electrician's exam. Also on the CD is the entire book in PDF format, with easy search features so you can quickly find answers to your residential wiring questions. **304 pages, 8½ x 11, $42.00**

Download all of Craftsman's most popular costbooks for one low price with the Craftsman Site License.
http://www.craftsmansitelicense.com
